A LONG WAY FROM HOME:

MY TIME IN IRAQ AND AFGHANISTAN 2002-2006

Christian Warren Freed (SFC, US Army Ret)

Cover design by BroseDesignz
Author Photograph by Anicie Freed

Warfighter Books
Holly Springs, North Carolina 27540
https://www.christianwfreed.com

Second Edition: November 2022

Library of Congress Cataloging-in-Publication Data
Name: Freed, Christian Warren, 1973- author.
Title: A Long Way From Home/ Christian Warren Freed
Description: Second Edition | Holly Springs, NC: Warfighter Books, 2021. Identifiers: LCCN 2022904790 | ISBN 9781957326122 (hardcover) | ISBN 9781957326139 (trade paperback) Subjects: Memoir | Autobiography |War | Military

Printed in the United States of America

10 9 8 7 6 5 4 3 2 1

Law of the Heretic
Immortality Shattered Book I

'If you're looking for a fun and exciting fantasy adventure, spend a few hours in the Free Lands with the Law of the Heretic.'

Where Have All the Elves Gone?

'Sometimes funny and other times a little dark, Where Have The Elves Gone? brings something fresh and new to fantasy mysteries. Whether you want to curl up with a mystery or read more about elves this book has something for everyone. Spend a few hours solving a mystery with a human and a couple of dwarves - you'll be glad you did.'

Other Books by Christian Warren Freed

The Northern Crusade
Hammers in the Wind
Tides of Blood and Steel
A Whisper After Midnight
Empire of Bones
The Madness of Gods and Kings
Even Gods Must Fall

The Histories of Malweir
Armies of the Silver Mage
The Dragon Hunters
Beyond the Edge of Dawn

Forgotten Gods
Dreams of Winter
The Madman on the Rocks
Anguish Once Possessed
Through Darkness Besieged
Under Tattered Banners
A Time for Tyrants*

Where Have All the Elves Gone?
One of Our Elves is Missing*
Tomorrow's Demise: The Extinction Campaign
Tomorrow's Demise: Salvation
Coward's Truth
The Lazarus Men
Repercussions: A Lazarus Men Agenda*
A Long Way From Home+

Immortality Shattered
Law of the Heretic
The Bitter War of Always
Land of Wicked Shadows
Storm Upon the Dawn

War Priests of Andrak Saga
The Children of Never

SO, You Want to Write a Book? +
SO, You Wrote a Book. Now What? +

*Forthcoming   + Nonfiction

CONTENTS

In Memory of:

MG Harold Greene
MAJ Tom Kennedy
CPT Mark Hayry
CPT Nate King
LT Tim Steele
CSM Scott Schade
SSG Jovandie Latorre
SSG Byron Brown
SGT Cornelius Hodges

Til Valhalla, Brothers.

FORWARD

So much has happened since I first wrote and published this book. Who could have imagined that over twenty years have passed since I first stepped off the plane in the middle of the night in Afghanistan or that the war would continue until 2021? Throughout the decades I have struggled with putting thoughts to paper, spent quiet hours alone thinking of old friends no longer with us, and continued to bear the burden of hearing about others fall.

Yet here we are. The wars are fading memories. Our enemies continue regrouping and rearming even as our society remains steadfast in forgetting the bad times. For my part, I proudly served among giants. The insanity of war seems ingrained in our chemical makeup. World peace is the great lie we tell ourselves to sleep easy at night, but history has proven others. To all the men and women who donned the uniform, sacrificed much throughout America's longest war, I raise my glass to you. We did what we did without question and came home to a world we no longer understood. Finding ways to fit back into society after enduring endless horrors is by far the more challenging of the two.

Perhaps one day we will evolve beyond the need for military violence. Until that day we must all remain vigilant, even while praying the next war never comes.

Christian Warren Freed, August 2022.

INTRODUCTION

"It is only those who have never fired a shot nor heard the shrieks and groans of the wounded who cry aloud for blood, more vengeance, more desolation. War is Hell." –General William Tecumseh Sherman

Sherman could not have said it better. War is Hell. Anyone who has ever put on a uniform and purposefully went to where the enemy was intent on killing him can attest to that. But instead of a singular definition of Hell that religion preaches, war is so much more. It is Hell on the families left behind. Hell on the mind and spirit. Hell on the nerves. Hell on coming home and trying to remember where you fit in. Yes, war is Hell.

Every man and woman serving in the modern U.S. military accepts these hazards freely and willingly. The draft is long gone, its effects a bad stain on our collective memory. Our military prides itself on being an all-volunteer force which encompasses all walks of life. Those of us in uniform train daily in the event that when the balloon goes up, we are ready for war. Sergeants grind their soldiers while officers come up with better and more effective training scenarios. The mind frame of the Cold War is dead. Today's soldier needs to be able to think small and act independently. Brand new lieutenants and staff sergeants are making decisions that were once made by company commanders. War has evolved and it is a nasty, ugly affair.

Recorded history suggests that war is a natural part of mankind. As a species we have excelled at violence. Men and women strive to develop new weapons, better munitions, all in the name of defense. But has it helped make us naturally violent? Our military is the best equipped, disciplined and trained in the world. It is also one of the most active in the world. The United States has been involved in military action on the average of every eighteen months since the War for Independence in 1776.[1]

---

[1] Statistics taken from www.PBS.org

National interests might change. Dictators and fanatic regimes rise to challenge the security of the free world from every direction. Occasionally we stick our noses where they don't belong, but regardless of the politics involved, every soldier does his/her part to ensure that their comrades are taken care of and the enemy never holds the battlefield at the end of the day.

Once every eighteen months. It was no small surprise that much of my career would be filled with near misses and combat deployments.

Warfare may have evolved over the course of time but there is always one constant: the soldier. Our uniforms change every few years. Our equipment improves. Weapons become deadlier, but the American soldier is the same person who stood up against the British government and said no more. Today's soldier is no different from my grandfather fighting in the Bocage country in 1944 France or my father in Hue City during the Tet Offensive in 1968. It doesn't matter what we call ourselves, soldier or marine, sailor or airman. We have all answered the call within our hearts to step forward, to become part of history. No one who has seen war should ever need to question if their lives have made a difference, if their contributions to society will go unnoticed. History is written through our deeds.

This book is not only a recollection of my own experiences but a testament to those I served with. Men and women with whom I have served contributed so that their voices can be heard as well. The United States Military represents the tiniest fraction of America but has the greatest responsibility. We stand the watch to keep the wolves at bay. We are the perpetual strength that is America. There are days when we bend, but we never break. Ten years of constant warfare has weeded out the weak and formed an impressive core of warriors who think little of themselves. Today's military is the proud continuation of those first militiamen who stood up to a far superior army and won a nation.

I would like to thank every man and woman who has served and continue to serve in our military and their families for their personal sacrifices in the defense of liberty. This book would not be possible without them because it is not only my story. I contend, always have and always will, that I have done nothing special. You are what makes America and our allies so special. My sincerest thanks also go out to the men and women who helped contribute their personal memoirs and pictures used within. Ladies and gentlemen, it was both an honor and a privilege to have served alongside you during such distressing times.

Sergeant First Class (Retired) Christian W. Freed

PART ONE:
Operation Enduring Freedom III

"We sleep safe in our beds because rough men stand ready in the night to visit violence on those who would do us harm." – George Orwell

Chapter One: Answering the Call

2001, Fort Bragg, North Carolina

September 11th 2001 was a special day for me. It was a day in which my life changed, just not the way I had intended. We had just brought my daughter home from the hospital. It was her first day in the real world and I couldn't have been more proud or happy. Little Ashlynne was born on the evening of the 8th and was finally where she belonged. I fell asleep on the floor next to the couch and her bassinet, happily listening to her mewling and cries. I'm not sure what woke me up or why, but I groggily looked up at the television in time to see the American Airlines flight 175 strike the south tower of the World Trade Centers.

Stunned and half asleep, I felt cold dread spread through me. The sheer impossibility of what I saw astounded me. Then I noticed the other tower already on fire and smoking. The ability to reason is slowed by a combination of sleep and confusion but one thing was plainly clear to me. We had just gone to war. But with whom?

I watched as Katie Couric theorized, "This is so shocking, of course to everyone watching". She went so far as to suggest this was a terrible coincidence, an accident of unprecedented proportions. Was she blind? The United States of America was under attack. While the cast of the NBC morning program dithered over the improbable events; everything from a terrible accident to wondering if air traffic control was having issues, I looked up and said one fateful sentence that would come to define the next five years of my life:

"We're going to war."

The war at home began about an hour later when I got a phone call from my battery commander telling me to report in full gear. The only redeeming factor was that I was on maternity leave for ten days and therefore not required to go in. That didn't stop the rest of the Army from going into reaction mode. Every military base in the nation went on full lockdown, eventually leading to permanent security checkpoints and fences being established. That first day it took over five hours for anyone to get on base.

I'd seen it once before, though from the inside. In late 1994 Fort Bragg went under full lockdown, complete with roving patrols through the streets. I vividly remember heading down to Pike Field to help push out the first two waves of assault troops from the 82nd Airborne Division as they began the invasion of Haiti. We knew we were on the list to deploy but political matters warmed and the operation transformed from combat invasion to peacekeeping. Those few days on base were surreal at the time and forgotten by 2001.

Daily life changed for good. It would take years for things to feel like they were back to normal, though in all actuality it was anything but. Getting on post was a mission in itself. Major buildings were marshaled off, everything from the post headquarters to the main Post Exchange. Anyone with business on Fort Bragg and every other base in the US military was forced to get up early just to make it to work and even then it was bare luck they managed to arrive on time. The one thing lacking was an air of fear. We were at war, and the sense of urgency was substantially heightened, but there was a decided lack of fear I found remarkable.

Revenge, on the other hand….

My unit was tasked with guarding XVIII Airborne Corps Headquarters and conducting roving patrols through the housing areas- with considerably more ammunition than the Haiti affair eight years ago. Contingencies were drawn up by not only the major planners but by every single soldier. Everyone had an opinion on who did what and what we were going to do in return. Soldiers excel at one thing where there isn't much to do. They come up with every possible scenario imaginable, most of them dire. The only constant thread was that we were suddenly shocked into a wartime footing. Peace evaporated the moment Al Qaeda highjacked those planes and declared war on the United States. Plans for deployment were theorized.

A few weeks later a good friend of mine, Staff Sergeant (SSG) Jimmie L. Harris, came over for lunch and we watched more of the continuing coverage of the 9/11 tragedy and clean up efforts. A native New Yorker, Jimmie was outright furious. CNN and FOX news entertained speculations about Al Qaeda in Afghanistan, suggesting the enemy attacks had been planned from there. Until now I don't think anyone in the western hemisphere actually cared about Afghanistan. All I knew was what I saw when the Soviets got their tails handed to them in 1980s. Of course, Rambo III didn't help any.

Over the course of a beer I looked at him and said, "You know we are going to go to Afghanistan right?"

He scoffed and told me, "We aren't going to Afghanistan. For what?"

For what? If what the major news channels were reporting was even remotely correct (I know…I know) a world of pain was about to erupt over there. Without a definitive answer, I shrugged, and we went back to watching the broadcast.

October 19, 2001

Sometimes I hate being right. Uncle Sam proved my earlier hunch about where we were going to go to war correct when elements of the 3rd Ranger Battalion jumped into Afghanistan and began combat operations. We were at war and with a target so large there would be no choice but to deploy. I figured it was a matter of being in the right place at the right time. Afghanistan is not suitable for massive armor deployments. The terrain is rocky, mountainous and too inhospitable to the bulky armored vehicles. Anyone who has ever had to fix a thrown track or pull the engine pack from a disabled sixty-ton vehicle understands the hardships involved with harsh terrain. The Soviets found this out 15 years earlier.[2]

The raid was inspiring. Men started requesting to transfer to units about to deploy. 1-377 was again denied, this time from the first combat deployment of the 101st Airborne Division since the Gulf War.[3] Rumor had it the Pentagon shot us down; citing the need for 155mm artillery support wasn't that great as we weren't facing a legitimate army. It seemed the long string of disappointment was never going to

---

[2] The Soviet War in Afghanistan lasted from 1979-1988. They lost more than 14,000 soldiers with another 50,000 wounded while the Afghans suffered up to an estimated 2,000,000 casualties.

[3] The battalion had been denied deployment orders for every major action since the 1990 Gulf War. (Haiti, Somalia, and Bosnia.)

end. Instead of being there to support the troops on the ground my unit got to sit at home during the Tora Bora campaign.

Desire, once to the point of overwhelming in many, slowly started to fade. Most of the northern half of the country fell rapidly under the combined strength of the Northern Alliance and limited U.S. ground forces. Warlords and tribal leaders set aside old hatreds long enough to drive Afghanistan's ruling body, the Taliban, out of office and into hiding, or so we assumed at the time. Hamid Karzai became the acting President in December, and the loose beginning of a central government was fleshed out by experts in Washington D.C. and NATO.[4] The global war on terror had officially begun and I got to sit at home and watch it.

Late Summer 2002

It was a Friday in late August. I had been transferred from my position in Alpha Battery to Headquarters Battery as the Assistant Operations Sergeant for my battalion. Not quite as glorious as being a Howitzer Section Chief and being down on the line with the soldiers, but a necessary evil almost every NCO must perform at some point. My job was relatively simple: I maintained the schools roster for roughly 500 personnel and helped develop operation schemes and planning large and small level training events. It was a far cry from standing in front of a ten man crew worrying whether or not the rounds we fired hit the target.

Nothing special happened on Fridays. Most of the senior staff had been called in to an impromptu meeting with the Old Man, giving the rest of the battalion the opportunity to go home a little early. I was about to head out the door for the weekend, my job complete for the week. I was passing through our battalion headquarters on my way to my car when our battalion executive officer, Maj. John Burdett, pulled me into his office. He looked me in the eye and said, "I have a job proposition for you."

Interesting, I thought, but I really wanted to go home. It had been a long week and I was ready to unwind and recharge. I told him ok and waited for it. Normally when a higher-ranking officer or NCO says something like that at the last minute it is not a good thing. He was

---

[4]   Karzai held the office as acting President from Dec. 2001-Dec. 2004. A decade later his office is mired in charges of corruption and he has long been considered a puppet of Western politics.

a good man, good leader, earning my respect months earlier when he was my supervisor. I appreciated his leadership and the leeway he afforded all of us in accomplishing our missions- to an extent. Any job offer from him had to be worth it.

"Yes, Sir," I said and stood at parade rest waiting.

"There is an operations sergeant job in Afghanistan open. We have one slot. Do you want it?" he asked with all seriousness.

Did I want it? Of course I did. My heart leapt as I realized what had just happened. I was just asked if I wanted to go to war. It was like a warped dream. I had been preparing for this for eleven years now and never thought the day was going to come. It felt like the clouds suddenly parted to bath me in glorious light, warm and promising. The logical side of my mind knew the offer was legitimate, but the practical side refused to believe it was happening.

The last year had been agonizing. I watched as Special Operations Forces conducted operations throughout Afghanistan in conjunction with the same Mujahedeen we had funded and armed against the Soviets. Mazar-E-Sharif fell in a public display of force both impressive and economical. The 101st Airborne Division deployed without us, even though 1-377 FAR was general support for the division. Our Charlie Battery had been stationed at Fort Campbell since the end of the Gulf War in 1991. We *expected* to deploy with the division. Being ignored was disappointing and puzzling.

Unfortunately for the enthusiastic side of me I had more to consider than just my own selfish desires. My daughter was about to turn one. My marriage, which had already suffered considerably during the last five years through various faults, was about to be placed in an even greater strain. Distance is a killer, but which distance is worse; being 9000 miles apart or an insurmountable gap between ends of the couch? I should have figured all wasn't right when I felt no conflict in my mind or heart. I knew where I needed to be. Looking back, I realize this sounds cold, but the situation left me with little choice. I had to go.

I looked Major Burdett in the eyes and reluctantly told him, "Sir, I need to call my wife and discuss it with her first."

The seriousness of the matter warranted me at least consulting the mother of my child before I took action on my own regardless of how little I wanted to stay married to her. It's not every day a man is asked if he wants to go to war. I was confused, if only slightly. This was everything I had trained for. Everything I had dreamed of since my days 'fighting' my brother in the woods behind our house with sticks for guns. Playing Army was a childhood favorite. Now I got to do it for real.

My best friend in first grade and I once made a pact that we would both join the Marine Corps. I moved at the beginning of third grade and never heard from him again, but my goals never changed. It made sense. Military life is in my blood. One of my mother's cousins traced our lineage back to around the year five hundred. I had relatives fight in England, with William the Conqueror and Jerusalem with Richard the Lionheart. My grandfather and his brother fought in Europe in WWII. His other brother was killed in action in the Philippines against the Japanese. My father spent the better part of three and a half years in Vietnam. This made sense. I was *supposed* to go to war.

He frowned and said, "I need to know by dinner."

My watch said it was already 16:30. "Dinner tonight, Sir?"

"Brigade needs and answer or they give the slot to another battalion."

Shit. That only made matters worse. "I'll be right back, Sir."

I went to the staff duty telephone and made the call.

"I got offered a job," I said nervously. I wasn't sure why I was nervous. The only thing keeping me at home was my daughter. "It's in Afghanistan."

Not surprisingly, she told me to go for it. I smiled. Done. I was going to war. I went back to Major Burdett's office and told him the good news. He proceeded to tell me that our Operations Sergeant had come in and taken the slot. Seriously? SFC Cofield was the kind of man who didn't have many friends at work. People avoided him. He was also my boss and outranked me. It was no secret that we didn't see eye to eye. I didn't like him and he couldn't stand me. And he had stolen my job.

I couldn't believe this turn of events. SFC Cofield couldn't even go to the field for a training exercise because of some mysterious medical skin condition and here he was volunteering to go to the asshole of the world? Two and two wasn't adding up. He wasn't the sort to jump up and volunteer for things. I decided not to back down. This was my hour!

"Sir, I really want this," I told him.

"Let me talk to the Old Man and see what he wants to do," he told me.

The next three nights stretched seemingly forever. It was one of the longest weekends I ever had. Nervous excitement struggled to break free. I couldn't concentrate. Realistically I went through the motions of being a husband. A father. My stomach rolled right up until Monday morning. Perhaps was the worst part. I was forced to endure an hour and a half of PT and then another hour before work call formation. All that time and still no word from the Old Man. Maybe they had changed their minds and went with someone else after all.

At some point the waiting got too much. Maybe it was the smug look I kept getting from SFC Cofield, or the strange mood I felt in the air. Things had definitely gotten more real since brigade called down. My slot wasn't the only one being offered. We were given a handful of slots for various ranks and positions. None of that mattered to me. Finally, after looking at the clock for the hundredth time, I said fuck it and went over to the XO's office.

"Good morning, Sir. Any word about that job?" I asked.

He looked up from his email and said, "You got it. Report to the Brigade conference room at 13:00."

Hell....yes. I grinned like a fool, told him thank you, and went back to my desk. I did it. I was finally going to war. But it wasn't as easy as that.

At some point I am sure I broke my mother's heart, despite the inevitability of the issue. No parent wants to hear that their child willingly wants to go to a combat zone. Sure, she'd known it was a very real possibility since the day I joined, all of those years ago during the summer of 1991. The actuality of what I had to tell her never sank in until I walked away from the Army for good on that last night. For now, this was my dream. Perhaps there was a large measure of selfishness, but I truly wanted to go, to do my part. The conflicts during the early part of my career were filled with youthful enthusiasm, but this was different. We had been attacked on our own soil.

Telling my parents what I was about to do was one of the hardest things I have ever done. The only other thing comparable was when I had to inform a family that their son had been killed in action years later. Calling home was sobering. The entire affair seemed more real. There wasn't much to say. The decision was made and I was locked in. I felt strange after hanging up. My mother was distraught. My father gave a quiet word of encouragement. Perhaps he thought back to the day he told his father he was shipping out to Vietnam for the first time.

I spent much of the weekend playing with my daughter and looking at her. I had asked to leave her for more than six months. (At the time a combat deployment for the Army was six months, three for the Air Force and seven for the Marines.) Did I really want to do that? I'll be the first to admit that I had absolutely no idea what to do with a brand-new infant. I mean she didn't do anything the first few months. I was in the kitchen the first time she decided to move for real. She rolled right off the coach and down the condo's hallway, giggling the whole way. She went from crawl to run without bothering to learn how to walk very well first. Leaving her was going to be much harder than I ever imagined.

So here I was, locked in for a deployment in support of Operation Enduring Freedom. I sat at my desk as little as possible for the rest of the morning. Too much nervous energy prevented me from keeping still. I wanted to throw it in SFC Cofield's face but deep down I wondered what his reasoning was for trying to sneak in and take the slot. Probably nothing, but my mind refused to believe that. He must have had an ulterior motive just to screw me over. It's funny what we come up with when we don't like people.

Lunch came and I pushed through a quick meal. My mind was still reeling despite my outward calm. I never had doubts about volunteering and still don't. I was in the Army and the Army goes to war. It is a natural progression, perfectly acceptable for anyone in uniform. Finally, it was time to head across the street to Brigade headquarters. I met up with the other guys from my unit deploying and we filed into the conference room. There were already a handful of soldiers waiting. I recognized a few and we made small talk until the Brigade Commander and the Command Sergeant Major entered. Thus began a seemingly unending series of briefings, pep talks, and countless hours spent sitting around waiting.

The time came to report to XVIII Airborne Corps Headquarters. That was our parent unit now and unlike any organization I had been a part of. You would think that being so high up there was no room for anything but strict discipline and rigidity lower units couldn't match. I came from an Army where it was shut up and do what you're told. Where every other word started with F and there was a natural air of aggression on constant display. Opinions were unnecessary and there was little room for anything but the best. I learned early on that I was supposed to be hard; to scream and berate people on a daily basis. Up until late October 2002 I was certain the entire Army was like this. I couldn't have been more wrong.

Corps HQ was a new animal. There was very little, if any, shouting or screaming. In fact, people here were downright nice. We were welcomed with open arms and quickly integrated into the existing system. My official title was to be the Joint Operations Center (JOC) Noncommissioned Officer in Charge. That sounded good, but I had no concept of what was supposed to happen. We were going to Bagram Air Base in the Parwan Province about an hour west of Kabul and I was supposed to maintain the joint operations center that ran the war. Not run it; that would be preposterous. The Army had Generals and Colonels for that sort of thing. My job was to ensure things went smoothly behind the scenes.

Not the glorious shoot and kill the bad guy I spent hours playing at when I was a kid running around the woods of northern Pennsylvania. Childhood dreams meant little when faced with an actual combat deployment. Still, I had a job to do and was filled with the excitement of going into hostile territory for the first time. We walked around Fort Bragg with chests out and an overinflated sense of self-importance after receiving our combat issue. There were few soldiers in desert fatigues those days and we felt special, though none of us would admit it. It felt good to have people look at your uniform and see the recognition that they knew you were deploying before them. Days went by, filled with briefings, equipment draws, rifle ranges, pre-deployment medical screenings and an array of inoculations. You would think that after a decade in the Army I had already gotten just about every shot I needed. Wrong.

The war was still young, and this was the first time the XVIII Airborne Corps was given the lead. Naturally they over prepared. They requisitioned at least two people for every position, a horrible waste of manpower that would cause placement issues once we got in country. My biggest eye opener came from our equipment draw. I wound up deploying with four duffel bags and an extra sized ruck sack. What in God's name was I going to do with so much crap? Turns out the answer was nothing. Most of those bags collected dust under my cot for eight months. I had an entire bag filled with chemical protection gear despite there being no credible chemical threat.

The two or three week period before we deployed went fast. We were given so much downtime it almost felt like vacation. We were released each day as soon as we had completed our task and given a time and a place for the next. PT was optional and wearing 'appropriate exercise clothing'. Some things weren't supposed to make sense I guess. It would be a cold day in Hell before we got the option of not doing PT back on the line. To say the least, I didn't go in that morning.

We had a few days off before the end and I took it and enjoyed what little time I had left with my daughter. Those days passed to fast. The last hours ticked away and I was dropped off behind Corps HQ where we lined up in formation and went through a series of last minute checks. Dog tags and identification cards. We loaded up the bags, drew our weapons and waited. Buses finally came rumbling in and then it was back to formation. One by one names were called out and we filed to the buses. It was time to go. The sun hadn't risen yet.

I did my best to get some sleep on the five-hour trip down to Charleston Air Force Base in South Carolina. It was early November and already cold. We got there and did some more waiting. By now we were masters at that task. The day was drab and overcast. The singular spark of good news came from going to the Air Force chow hall and everyone knew the Air Force had better food. Most of us were still strangers. I made friends with our supply sergeant, Jason Cooper, who we called Coop, and Lieutenant Riley Carson, one of our chemical officers.

There are few things from my career that I can admit being ashamed of. One of them was the misguided belief that women should not be in the Army. I wasn't raised that way and my mother would have been extremely disappointed to learn that, but it was the combat arms culture I spent so many years immersed in. Women simply didn't belong. Lt. Carson had a great hand in helping me realize the foolishness of my ways and helped open my eyes to what I had been missing. Somewhere along the way I realized I'd been duped from the start. We became friends and I think I am the better for it. (We would later serve together at the United States Military Academy at West Point, New York.)

The day wore on with agonizing slowness. Waiting in the personnel shed (PAX shed) I couldn't help but notice most of the people I was deploying with were lawyers and office workers. Some had been infantry officers early in their careers, but those days were lost in distant sunsets. Very few of my companions were combat troops. How disappointing. I wasn't left with any confidence inspiring feelings. Not that it would have prevented me from boarding the waiting C-17. Time was up. We had to leave.

Any thoughts, misgivings or doubts of what we had done and were about to do dissolved in the cold reality of what awaited. We took a short bus to the tarmac and then filed like ants into the waiting belly of the cargo plane. Air Force crew members busied strapping equipment down and guiding us to our seats. The one decent thing about traveling long distances on a C-17 is the comfort factor. C-130s are small and cramped. The C-141 I took to go fight forest fires in Montana back in 2000 was just as cramped. By comparison, the C-17 was a luxury jet. The back ramp closed, and the jet rocketed down the runway. We were finally wheels up.

Our first stop was Gander International Airport in Newfoundland. The name was slightly misleading considering just how small it was. A desolate place with an ocean of pine trees as far as you could see and it was damned cold. We stayed long enough for the jet to refuel and then it was on our way to Shannon, Ireland. Even in winter Ireland is the greenest place I have ever seen. Rain and light mist kept us from going outside but the people were friendly, and it was heated. We spent a few hours wandering the lobby area or trying to get some sleep. I'm not sure why but traveling so far for so long is very tiring.

By this time most people needed to shave again and deodorant had definitely worn off. Dark bags shadowed eyes, giving the appearance of men and women who were leaving a war zone, not going there. Our weary little group boarded the plane again. Next stop: Frankfurt, Germany.

It's no big secret that I have always wanted to visit the Fatherland. Many of my relatives came from Germany and I was finally getting to live a goal. Another five hours later the plane touched down and I was excited. And it was cold, miserably overcast and drizzling. Good old Germany in winter. One thing I noticed during my career was that the Army never sent me to nice places. Some of us joked about invading a warm Caribbean island rather than jungles and deserts. I'd gotten a mild case of frostbite in Korea, fought forest fires in the Rockies near the Canadian border, done training in the middle of nowhere Louisiana, gone to a lovely base in the middle of Arkansas and was now on the way to Afghanistan.

Fortunately, Germany would let us stay for a while. The beauty of flying airlift military command was that planes were not guaranteed. We wound up staying in Frankfurt for four days before finally securing a bird to Afghanistan. Those were some of the most fun and easily forgotten days I had had in a long time. I left Fort Bragg with about a hundred dollars in my pocket in case of emergencies and for personal hygiene supplies. That first night I bought one beer and it was the best beer I ever had. (Funny how those little things matter when you're not sure of tomorrow.) It was the only beer I bought during those four days but certainly not the only one I had.

A positive side effect of deploying with so many officers was that they had money to spend. I don't remember how many drinks random officers bought me and Coop, but it was a lot. Round after round came and went. One chemical officer (Chemo) started buying rounds of long island ice teas. Who were we to say no? It would be terribly offensive if we turned any of them down. Momma did raise me with manners after all.

By the fourth day we had settled into a pattern of stumble to formation, get told there was no plane, and then stumble back to sleep. Today was different. We saw the C-17 waiting behind the terminal. It was time to go. We said good-bye to Germany and boarded that last plane to uncertainty. Afghanistan was the Wild West. Rules were few and violence was an ingrained way of life. It is the kind of place where nations should go to fight their wars against their enemies.

And we were on an eight-hour direct flight there.

Chapter Two: Boots on the Ground

November, 2002

We left Germany on a dismal, rainy day. After a four-day layover I thought the men and women I was deploying with had grown complacent and unfocused. Staff officers spent most of their time drinking and worrying about death rather than staying focused. The time in Frankfurt was nice, but in only served as a distraction from the real thing. What I truly missed was the presence of combat arms people. The crew I was with lacked the rough sense of humor; the edgy anger that drives daily missions. I took comfort in the Long Range Surveillance Team that occupied some seats across from me. At least someone else on this bird was a combat soldier. I looked around at the various lawyers and adjutant general personnel taking their seats and wondered what I was in store for. Most of the men and women I deployed with probably hadn't fired their weapons but for one time in the last year. To say the least I was not feeling safe. The hangover I had certainly didn't help either.

We left Frankfurt on what was to become my first of many eight-hour trips to the Middle East. There wasn't much to see or do, and I really didn't feel well so I unbuckled my safety harness and found a comfortable spot on the floor of the C-17. I have to admit that it was probably the most comfortable ride I took on any of my deployments. The hours passed by uneventfully until we banked south through Uzbekistan and hit Afghan airspace.

Many of the Taliban fighters were former Mujahedeen that we had armed and supplied during their fight against the Soviets in the 1980s.[5] I remembered seeing the CBS footage of rebels firing stinger missiles at Soviet choppers during an anonymous battle. The Soviets made a mess of things and we were coming into what they had left behind. The enemy still had our old equipment, along with whatever the Soviets left behind during their panicked withdrawal. That made

---

[5]   *Operation Cyclone* was a CIA funded operation designed to train and arm the Afghan rebels so they could defeat the Soviets. This led to the Carter Doctrine of 1980: stating the U.S. would not let an outside force gain control of any area in the Persian Gulf. This doctrine helped get America more involved in Middle Eastern Affairs and would pave the way for America's eventual involvement in the Middle East in the 1990s.

their air defense threat very credible. We might have been in the largest Air Force cargo plane but that would only make a bigger explosion right? A red light bathed the interior of the plane in an eerie glow a moment before the pilot's voice came over the intercom.

The pilot's voice came over the intercom, "We have just entered Afghan airspace. Everyone put on your body armor and kevlars and strap in."

The plane came alive with activity and chatter. All the lawyers and administrative personnel onboard were overly excited, or perhaps it was the realization that they were going to war beginning to sink in. Who can tell at times like that? I sat next to Staff Sergeant (SSG) Wrilshxer Mendoza. (To this day I still can't say her first name right, no matter how many times she says it for me.) She and I really hadn't spoken before the red light went on but it was evident that she was far more excited than I.

I got it. This was the first time most of us were deploying, with exception of a few Special Forces guys. One who had already been to Afghanistan five times. There was natural excitement filling the plane. Like stepping up to the batter's box that first time, or desperately hoping the teacher didn't call on you when you failed to study. SSG Mendoza was filled with excitement. I could see it in her eyes. Hear it in her infliction. Little did I know that, months down the road, she would be the first woman in the 82nd Airborne to actually go on a foot patrol with the infantry. How cool is that?

Strapping on my helmet, I leaned back in my seat and tried to squeeze out that last little bit of sleep. Eighteen hours of flight time and numerous stops and layovers had taken a toll, not to mention the libations generously provided by the about-to-die officer corps I deployed with. Everyone handles stress differently. Some tapped their feet. Others talked. I tried to sleep.

The plane dropped low and banked, avoiding potential enemy anti-aircraft fire. It felt more like a 747 circling for landing than a plane full of troops dropping into a war zone. C-130 pilots, on the other hand, will pull your lunch up and I swear they enjoy it. The C-17 landed. We were here. Afghanistan. The armpit of the world. The graveyard of empires. It was late, pushing midnight and damned cold. Bagram, Afghanistan is a place of great history. Alexander the Great only conquered it around 320 BC by killing everyone he saw on his way to

India. It lies roughly 60 kilometers west of the capital, Kabul, at the junction of the Ghorband and Panjshir Valley.[6]

The airfield was a main Soviet command during the Afghan War. Wrecked MIGs lined the runway. Burned out tanks and BMPs (infantry carriers) rusted alongside the roads where the Mujahedeen killed them. The entire valley was filled with enough anti personnel mines to cover the Allied landings at Normandy in 1944. Supposedly the Soviets used it as a last stand while they were evacuating. A lone skeleton lay stretched out in the mine fields; the grizzly reminder of how villagers defeated a military giant.

Coalition Forces established command and control at Bagram with a secondary command south in Kandahar. Combined Joint Task Force 180 (CJTF-180) assumed command a month earlier and was still undergoing the initial disorientation of directing distinct combat units from a dozen nations across a large battle space. In late 2002 there were approximately 11,000 U.S. troops on the ground in Afghanistan. That was already double from fiscal year 2002 and a pale comparison for the massive levels of U.S. and Coalition soldiers by 2009.[7] By the summer of 2002 the Taliban was all but defeated, the remnants slipped away into Pakistan and the inhospitable mountain ranges along the border. Al-Qaeda was rumored to be less than five hundred and was in no mood to tackle Coalition Forces in a head on fire fight after the successive poundings they took in Tora Bora and the initial invasion campaigns. It was a matter of hide and seek: the perfect game for the U.S. Special Forces Command.

But someone had to direct the war and that fell on the XVIII Airborne Corps. The crew chief dropped the back ramp and a blast of frigid air assaulted us. Ground guides waved us off. My first glimpse of Afghanistan would have been impressive if I were there for the view. A full moon hung over the eastern mountains ringing the valley. Snow covered the tall peaks. It was almost serene. Then the deep explosion rumbled through the mountains. Serenity shattered. We were at war.

Incoming personnel shuffled into the reception building. It was more of a shack where you could get a warm cup of coffee and a place

---

[6]   Bagram's location is important for key reasons. It sits along the Silk Road, from India to the West and is close to the famed Khyber Pass, linking Pakistan and Afghanistan.

[7]   Troop levels are estimates compiled by the Congressional Research Service, July 2, 2009.

out of the cold for a while. I dropped my ruck and set my helmet down, my rifle never leaving my hands.

"What's up, Smoke?"

I looked up, glad to see one of my soldiers, Specialist (SPC) Bennett, smiling at me. He and a few others had been among the fortunate few to deploy on the first group or chalk the week prior. It was good to see a familiar face the first thing. SPC Bennett wound up working for the Bagram base operations office, a cell of a few officers and enlisted who oversaw daily life on the base. Not the sort of job I wanted but a necessary evil. His task was to help welcome newbies and provide orientation briefings.

"Not much man, how have you been?" I replied.

We made small talk for a few minutes before, you guessed it, some officer came in and proceeded to give us yet more briefings. I contend that no good NCO *wants* to sit through a meeting. Most often they are drawn out, pointless and a waste of time. All I need to know is what I am doing, when and where and what I will need/have to accomplish the task. Keep the rest of it and let me do my job. Unfortunately, one of the luxuries of rank puts us in unending meetings and briefings, stealing our time away from action and removing us from the soldiers. Thank God I never went to OCS!

The briefings ended and we were sent to reception tents to get some shut eye before being escorted to our new homes for the next six months. (I was one of the fortunate ones that got extended another two months- at the last minute and without asking for it. Hooah to that. Luckily I didn't mind being deployed or I would have gone nuts like those poor Air Force boys who got extended from three to six months when the Iraq build up began. Some of them actually whined to their Congressmen. The rest of us sucked it up.)

I was given the first of many disappointments the following morning. The JOC Sergeant Major (SGM)- not to be confused with a Command Sergeant Major, the regular SGM serves a staff function only- asked me what my position was supposed to be so I told him JOC NCOIC. He smirked and said, "Well, we'll put you somewhere."

What the fuck? This wasn't part of the deal. Say what you will of staff work, but these Corps guys were supposed to be squared away. And here this guy was telling me I can't do *my* job? Rank being what it is, I stood at parade rest and said, "Roger, Sergeant Major."

Discipline is what separates us from third world armies and ragtag bands of militias. Discipline wins wars. As an NCO I never tolerated disrespect or indiscipline and I damned sure wasn't about to do it to a senior NCO now. We have to have standards. Still, he and I never saw eye to eye. Technically I almost never saw him. He reminded me of a crooked old supply sergeant from one of those old war movies. I went to him one day asking for a pair of replacement boots for one of my soldiers and he had the nerve to ask, "What's in it for me?" Are you kidding? A senior NCO whose job it is to take care of his soldiers and he expected a favor in return? People like that should be force retired.

So I was thrown in to the JOC Operations NCO position. It wasn't a bad gig, but Corps already had four other guys for the job. Life was about to get really boring. For a while I worked one day on and two days off. If I didn't read or write my own books I would have gone crazy. We fell into a rhythm; I was lucky to get the day shifts. I don't care where you are, nights are always bad. Twelve hours is a long time to pay attention, especially for six straight months.

My job wasn't simple, but it wasn't very hard either. The worst part was putting up with the staff functionaries who didn't know anything but power point and theorizing. I never could stand sitting around and talking about things. I prefer to do (maybe that's why I never really got along with my peers as I progressed through the ranks. They stood and talked too much while I was quick to strip off my blouse, grab a shovel, and help my troops fill sandbags or dig foxholes). Someone up high had to have a sense of humor because I was placed in a position where there wasn't much doing going on.

I was plugged in to two computers and responsible for monitoring every minute aspect of the war. You name it and I had to know what was going on; everything from weather to troops in contact. I watched the big boards in the front of the JOC, occasionally updating them with pertinent information the senior commanders needed. It was an inglorious position best suited for people who wanted to be behind a computer. I didn't, but I was stuck.

I reported directly to the Corps G-3, the operations officer who reported directly to the Corps Commander. Every little aspect of what I did was under close scrutiny. The war was new to all of us, but at least the officers had been doing their jobs for a while already. The men who worked with me were making it up as we went along. One of the only upsides to this job stemmed from the sheer amount of information I processed. It was beyond anything I had experienced.

The moment a unit went in contact with the enemy it came directly to me. I knew we were engaged before the generals directing the war. The awesome responsibility with this knowledge was staggering. No comparison with actually being in contact, I was able to see how quickly and efficiently the command and control assets were at coordinating support. Air power, artillery, ground based reinforcements. All were spun into action based on the information I disseminated.

Aside from those harrowing moments when battles were being directed my job was routinely boring. Our signal people created a server with close to two hundred movies we could watch, on duty. Absolutely unheard of. A look around the tiered rows of staffers showed most of them with headphones on watching something. How many people didn't take immediate action because they weren't paying attention? Granted, most of the positions were pretty far down on the rolls and unimportant in the scheme of things, but they still had a job to do.

Right before dinner was the biggest event of the day: the battle update briefing (BUB). I set up the sharing system that linked dozens of computers, both in country and as far away as the Pentagon. Naturally anything that went wrong was my fault. People hit the wrong button on their computers and I took the blame. It was infuriating getting chewed out by the old man because some fool hit the wrong button, but it was one of those things I had to sit back and take, or it really would be my ass on the line. There was absolutely nothing glorious about the job, but it was mine for the better part of the next year.

Afghanistan was one of the most backwards, worst imaginable places in the world. How anyone called this desolate land home was beyond me. A few ragged trees grew but the valley was otherwise void of vegetation. No running water, no electricity. Afghanistan was locked in the Stone Age. No wonder no one had successfully conquered it. There was nothing here worth conquering. The weather only added to the misery of the land. High mountains and freezing winters combined to make a hard people. There was nothing friendly about Afghanistan. Nothing at all.

You could see the hardship echoed in the features of the locals. Their eyes had lost vibrancy, replaced by an unending struggle to remember hope. Decades of warfare tend to do that. I was reminded how fortunate I was to be from a country like America. Most of these people had nothing. For a while, we suffered alongside them. There were times when we had nothing but MREs to eat. Our resupply convoys were often attacked coming out of Pakistan. Most of the time we either had freezing water or no water. There were plenty of times I passed on a shower rather than freeze after waiting in line. Every once in a while the water was so hot it burned the skin off. There seemed no happy medium.

We had the option of turning our laundry in to be cleaned by the local KBR group. Most of the people I knew who did it always had complaints. I decided to take care of my own clothes. I would come to regret that decision in the middle of winter. There is nothing quite like sitting outside with your arms elbow deep in cold water hurriedly scrubbing and rinsing clothes. Then you took the chance of drying them on a makeshift line strung between two tents. Figuring out how long to keep your clothes outside was frustrating. Either you pulled them down still damp or they were as stiff as boards.

Winter was coming hard and Bagram (at least the coalition occupied portion) was unprepared. The city may have been ancient, but the base was just plain neglected. Many places along the wall still had only rusty strings of concertina wire for barriers. The local warlord wasn't inclined to make life easier. The Afghan warlords ruled with ruthlessness, much as they had for countless centuries. A legitimate central government was still an uneasy dream so the U.S. was forced to 'rent' the land we used from the warlords. I suppose we could have just set up our bases and went about persecuting the war, but the only way to drive the Taliban and Al Qaeda support out for good was to win over the opinions of the locals. So we paid the warlords. Ours decided he wasn't getting enough money.

The U.S. has a habit of employing local nationals for a fraction of the cost it would take to get American contractors. Not only does this cut costs from our end, but it helps boost local economies in the process. Local Afghan villagers came to our bases to help build structures, erect living tents, etc. They were paid a whole five dollars a day and there were a handful of the local warlord's goons waiting right outside of the gate at the end of the day. He got half. No questions asked. Military Police stood by and watched, powerless to get involved, as the warlord's men fleeced the workers.

The first week in country flew by. Surrounded by inhospitable mountains and the constant drone of small arms, rocket fire, and explosions, Afghanistan proved more than most of us were prepared for. I don't remember how many more briefings we were forced to sit through, but a few remain vivid to this day. The Base Ops NCO warned us about being captured with the proclamation that Afghans believed women were for babies and men for pleasure. Got it. Don't get captured. Next they brought out a dead camel spider and lunch unsettled. Looking like a cross between one of the props from John Carpenter's *The Thing* and a creature determined to kill you, it was massive and might as well been the nation's symbolic animal.

It was early November and our ragged little base was just now in the process of being 'winterized'. Growing up in western New York I had a pretty good idea about winter and how to stay warm. The Army had a different perspective. Our sleeping tents were huge eight-man monstrosities of yellow canvas with plywood flooring. Winterizing meant the Afghans came in and put plywood walls halfway up and then they moved on to the next one. The roofs were left canvassed, as well as the upper half of the walls. Realistically, one sheet of three-quarter inch plywood wasn't going to stop too much cold from getting in. I had a feeling it was going to be a cold winter.

I stayed in the tent on the day they came to do ours, to ensure they didn't steal anything more than any other reason. Turns out there had been a rash of petty thefts on the base lately. The Afghans worked quickly, too quick to be any good. Coming from different standards and quality of living, it was no surprise to see how filthy these people were. A shame really, and one based on circumstance rather than want. They may have been dealt a shitty hand from birth but they were proud. That didn't change the fact that they tried to nail up a board that was smeared with human shit to our tent.

A sudden commotion broke out from a few tent rows down. An Afghani went running by, followed closely by a pair of Military Police (MPs). The brand-new running shoes in his hand proved who was doing the stealing. One of my buddies worked the main gate leading into Bagram that day. They stopped the thief and recovered the stolen shoes before turning him over to the warlord's men. What happened next changed the thief's life. The warlord decided his image was stained because of the thief so he had his men break both of the thief's ankles *and* they took his pay. Afghanistan is not a friendly place. The weak perish young. The excitement done, people returned to whatever they were doing. Attention spans were understandably short here.

Bagram Airbase was divided into several main areas. Corps HQ occupied the rear down to the main runways, along with a South Korean hospital unit. Two real buildings housed the command group, supply office and various staff functionaries. The rest of us slept in neat rows of tents a stone throw from the wall. We had a shower trailer that had seen better days. Most of the time the water was either too hot or too cold. Sometimes they changed it up by running out of water. The one constant was the line. It was like being rushed through the mess hall.

About a dozen coalition nations had small camps to our west. The Italians had the largest compound, followed closely by the Thai engineers. For reasons beyond me no one really wanted to intermingle despite all being on the same side. There was a Spanish hospital unit in country when I first arrived. They left after the terrorist bombings in Madrid in 2004 when Spain officially pulled out of the War on Terror. Most nations only had a token force present, each unit specialized.

The mess hall would have been better off just serving MREs. Hot food is always welcome, despite how bad or little it is. Our mess hall was a Halliburton special. We had mechanics for cooks. Hanging out with the supply sergeants allows you to see how things really work. We would go and barter for extra food and supplies to take back to our tent. That's how I learned about the mechanics who were 'asked' to be cooks. Seems it's not just the Army that does that.

Disney Drive was the main road to anywhere. It led from the runway to the living area, but I'll be damned if I saw Mickey anywhere. There was a rundown looking gym at the main intersection, if a broken exercise bike and a handful of weights constitute a gym. The U.S. military presence was still a relatively new thing here and we were the lucky few who got to see the beginning of the transformation process.

Our wall was an amalgamation of crumbling stone and brick and newly arrived HESCO barriers still being filled with dirt. That was the one thing Afghanistan had in abundance. The surrounding landscape was desolate. I was reminded of a Charlton Heston bible movie. It was almost depressing. Most of the buildings were ruins. Even the trees were dying. I forgot the color green. Little Afghan boys would come up to the wall and throw bags of hashish at the guard towers in the hopes of getting paid for it. I'm sure more than one soldier took them up on the offer.

The Air Force side of the base, ever the connoisseurs of luxury living, had better tents with actual air conditioning and heating units. They slept in real beds and each tent had a refrigerator and a microwave. They had hot water for showers and guards at the gate to their little compound to keep the Army riff-raff out. Nothing is quite as demoralizing as seeing people in shorts and t shirts playing volleyball or laying out trying to get a tan when you are loaded with body armor, a helmet, and an eight pound rifle. The smell of grilled steak and chicken always seemed to come from their compound. I learned quickly that everyone *but* the Army intended to find a measure of fun while deployed. In fact, we guessed the Army went out of its way to make it just that little bit more miserable.

Directly across the street from the Air Force was the JOC compound. A huge tent complex comprised the brains of the war. Here every aspect of war fighting was managed, supervised, and relayed not only to the Pentagon and White House, but to various commands around the globe. Since a Corps is a three-star general command, he and his staff lived in the only other real building, secured safely in the middle of the compound. No one got into the compound without a reason. Identification badges were issued and we still had to go through a series of checkpoints just to get inside the tent. Security was paramount.

The tent itself was massive. Large generators (which I often took the blame for when they stopped working) powered hundreds of computers, printers, satellites and more twenty-four hours a day. Countless personnel manned stations everywhere you looked, to include numerous government civilian agencies. We had more than our share of people who officially 'didn't exist' working with us. The CIA being the least of them. Situational maps filled entire walls, riddled with symbols and codes. Every aircraft, every soldier operating outside of the bases was being tracked right down to the exact foot.

The 82nd Airborne Division supplied the bulk of the combat troops at the time. Division had its own operations center and practically remained isolated from the rest of the base. They had their own facilities, including a real chow hall with real cooks. SSG Mendoza went to the 82nd to do the same job as me and I didn't see her again for six months. An infantry battalion assigned to Bagram provided base security. Squads of grunts patrolled the walls and filled the guard towers. They reacted whenever we took incoming sniper fire or rockets. Artillery crews filled the nights with illumination rounds. The rest of the 82nd chose to stay in their area. Fine by me. There was a natural, and misunderstood, friendly animosity between the 82nd and every other unit stationed at Fort Bragg. Petty, to be sure, but it kept things lively.

The only reason for anyone to go anywhere besides their area was the rundown little Post Exchange (PX) building at the back of the base. If ever a building should be condemned it was that one. The roof was collapsed in several places. The back of the building wasn't even open due to structural collapse. Sandbag walls ringed the exterior. In all it was an unremarkable little building that should have been destroyed and rebuilt from the ground up. Still, that PX was averaging more than 100,000 dollars a month in sales. (Forget the fact the French came in from Kabul and bought all of the pillows in a particularly daring raid on civility.)

Special Forces command had their own private part of the base. From there they coordinated with the various teams across the country, both U.S. and foreign. We seldom saw them, though I distinctly remember taking 107mm rocket fire one day and, en route to the concrete bunker, I looked up and saw two German Special Forces guys tanning in Speedos. Only one bothered to look up before lying back down. I guess rocket attacks were no big deal for the Germans.

Of all of our allies, they were the most reckless. Halftrack vehicles, much like the WWII versions, were always seen tearing off on some mission or another. Each was armed to the teeth. Machine guns stuck out in every direction. One thing was clear: these guys had come to do business. I recall hearing about one of their helicopters breaking apart over Kabul because the pilots pushed it too hard. The German military is far from celebrated these days, the country going out of its way to keep their military secluded from the general population. (Sixty years isn't really that long in the grand scheme of time) The units deployed to Afghanistan were determined to change public opinion back home.

The rest of the coalition was placed at random away from the Americans. The Italians had a decent size contingent and their own chow hall. They served wine for lunch and generally had the best food. (American forces are the only ones that ban alcohol while deployed. Coalition nations seemed to encourage it, or at least they decided their soldiers were mature enough to be able to handle it.) I would later learn the Italian philosophy was *domani*, everything can wait for tomorrow. Maybe that's why they're not exactly renowned fighters.

Across the street was an Engineer battalion from Thailand and a scattering of various nations. I counted twenty-six different uniforms on Bagram. It was impressive seeing so many different peoples with different ideals coming together for the greater good of defending freedom against the horrors unleashed by Al Qaeda. Most of these soldiers didn't speak English and only knew that the United States had been attacked. Reasons didn't matter. They never do. Soldiers salute, pack up and get on the plane to whatever distant battleground their leaders want them to go. No one in Afghanistan was any different.

Twenty-seven different nations came to support us, if you included the mine clearing unit from Mozambique who wore every sort of civilian clothes. They weren't much for soldiers, but they were absolutely the nicest people I ever met. Each man took full advantage of the chow hall and was always filled with laughter and smiles. I suppose you had to keep a good sense of humor when your job was to go out into the middle of a mine field and try not to get killed as you cleared the decades old ordinance. Not the job I wanted. I was suddenly more comfortable sitting in the JOC. At least they didn't have any casualties during their deployment.

All in all it was a strange new world and it was home for the next eight months.

Chapter Three: Indoctrination

Afghanistan was unlike anything I had experienced. I saw things that I still have trouble relating to folks back home. War isn't a subject one can just sit down and explain to people who haven't been there. War is for warriors to remember. It is a quiet bond that separates us from the rest of the world. Just putting these words together has proven difficult as I stop from time to time and find myself lost in old memories.

Being in the artillery for so long I was accustomed to carrying my weapon for long periods of time and hearing explosions. Afghanistan had plenty of explosions. It felt like there was always something blowing up, sometimes buildings, sometimes people. And now I had to keep my weapon on me at all times. It became a friend, a boon companion to keep me company and my mind off things that were infinitely worse than what I had going on. Thankfully I didn't have to hump a heavy machine gun. I was content with my M-16 but could have done with a few hand grenades.

The sights and sounds of Bagram were alien. Despite that we did our best to keep grounded and to turn out little corner of Hell into home. We turned our tents into homes. Shelves were thrown up, heaters installed. (Air conditioning was a luxury we didn't think about since it was so cold- a mistake we'd regret in the spring) I snagged a bunch of free books from various places. Some of them were actually pretty good. I think I read more than 60 books during my time in country.

We'd listen to music at night, mostly jazz. Something quiet to help us forget the day. Plenty of bootleg movies were passed around. The biggest deal came when Coop brought back a full-sized refrigerator. Now we were living. Each of us took turns going to the mess hall to bring back as much Gatorade, water and fruit as we could. Soon enough the fridge was fully stocked and we were living the dream, so to speak. Joe Burke and I built a small kitchen area, complete with a table, shelves for food, coffee pot (always a necessity) and a toaster oven. What more could any of us have asked for?

Our life might have been made easier through our combined efforts, but life outside the walls remained miserable. Most of the Afghanis were decent people. I just didn't want anything to do with them. Our two cultures couldn't have been any more different. We had plenty of translators working for us, but the language barrier was where accurate translation ended. Most of what they knew of the West was fragmented, the Taliban rule so absolute. They were taught the West was corrupt and certainly not proper followers of Allah.

Coop brought one particular interpreter back to our tent one day. He called himself Fonzi because of the faded and worn leather jacket he wore. I don't care what he called himself, he was no Arthur Fonzerelli. He seemed like an ok kid, but you couldn't really tell. He also suffered from an aching perversion for Western porn. I was disgusted to find him and Coop sitting on a cot watching a dirty movie. This was definitely not what I volunteered for. I told both of them to get out; including Coop. Some lines just shouldn't be crossed.

Not that my opinion mattered much. I came back the next day to find three Afghans, Coop and SSG Elmer all watching another Pakistani porn. The title aptly summed the movie up: Two women and a dog. It was time to leave. I grabbed my shower kit and headed out. Halfway out the door I heard Elmer laugh and say, "yeah! That's the money shot." My stomach turned a little at the thought.

Every so often we got the chance to guard the walls. As an enlisted man I was more than accustomed to standing guard for hours on end. Blissfully, our shifts were only four hours each and I was paired up with an officer I actually liked talking to. Most of the shift was uneventful, just the way I liked it. A few stray rounds were fired from the village. An odd explosion here or there made us look over our shoulders, but nothing of great concern happened in our area.

In fact, we hardly saw a living soul. A handful of women dressed in burkhas marched through Bagram under the watchful stares of the males. I still don't understand the concept of concealing every part of their bodies except for the eyes. Then again, I don't really need to. Perhaps when my daughter is a teenager it might make a little more sense, but I didn't need to worry about it then. Two kids came snooping around the base of the wall armed with a wheelbarrow, digging through ruined buildings for who knew what. They went about their business with disturbing proficiency. Children shouldn't have to suffer so much.

I watched from the guard tower as an old man limped up to them and beat the two little boys pushing a wheelbarrow full of scrap metal. The boys ran and he took their hard-earned prize. He didn't bother looking up at us and there was nothing we could have done anyway. They posed no significant threat and, surprisingly, we mostly didn't care. Everyone has their problems and I learned through countless hours of counseling and leading soldiers not to get too deeply involved. Those things had a tendency of coming back on you.

The children seemed to suffer the most. Sure, they posed for pictures and had smiles bright enough to rival the sun, but there was an undeniable hurt lurking just behind. A pain from that glimpse of other cultures and the sudden knowledge that most people had better lives, more opportunities. The children suffered from tyrannical rule without fundamentally understanding what was happening.

I was walking with SFC Duwan Cratch to the Friday bazaar, a lively event closely monitored by the military. We were halfway down to the gate when another little boy, no older than eight, pointed a loaded AK-47 at me, smiled and said, "Hey mister, fuck you!"

Who was I to argue? I waved and kept walking. I didn't have qualms about shooting a kid with a weapon, but he was locked and loaded and pointing at me. U.S. policy at the time was to have a magazine in the rifle but no round in the chamber unless threatened. Chambering a round would have been a waste of time. I'd be dead before I knew what hit me. The worst part was he really smiled at me.

That served as my wake up call. I can't imagine my little boy pointing a real gun at anyone and telling them off, but it was the status quo for Afghan children. Playing army with friends is one thing, having real guns and no problems using them was another. I couldn't help but wonder what events led this young boy to the point where he was comfortable pointing a weapon at complete strangers. Worse, what did that say about the trio of old men sitting behind him in silent encouragement?

Decades of constant fighting and unfriendly conditions made hard people. Afghanistan has never been conquered despite its long history. Alexander the Great managed to do in a less than traditional sense by killing as many people as he could find and continuing on through into Pakistan and then India.[8] He never stopped to govern the newly subdued country, which remains the dividing line between his campaign and the rest of Afghanistan's would be rulers.

The British tried their hand at it and soon realized the errors of their ways. The Soviets followed suit and limped back to Mother Russia not long after. Modernity should have proven victorious, but when one nation lacks the fundamental understanding of its prey, bad

---

[8]   Alexander the Great spent 13 years and traveled some 22,000 miles during his campaigns to stretch the Macedonian Empire before his death in 323 B.C. at the age of 33.

things happen. Now it was our turn, only we weren't here to conquer. We were here for payback.

Warlords and tribalism kept what remained of the country fractionalized and it stayed that way until we arrived. This rivalry remains the single most relevant barrier to forming a nation. New Afghani soldiers came from almost every tribe and village. Trust doesn't come easily, for anyone. Try putting your trust in a man from a rival village or a former member of the Taliban regime. I can't imagine having to put my life in the hands of a man I have hated since childhood.

But that was life here in lovely Afghanistan. Life wasn't very valuable, or maybe it was the most precious commodity, lived by seconds instead of years. I wasn't sure. A Polish mine clearer was killed when he triggered the mine he was trying to defuse. An American would later die from wounds suffered while he tried the same. These events were tragic, partially horrifying but we had a way of drowning them out. Certain levels of numbness are associated with prolonged exposure to violent acts. We force the images from our minds, as much as possible, just so we can continue with our mission.

It didn't take long before events like this became routine. Day in-day out, we did mostly the same things. Random bits of excitement sprung up. One of my tentmates came back from dinner with a crazy look in his eyes. He told us he was walking to chow when a cobra popped up and hissed at him. Since it would be the next best thing to an actual crime to shoot his weapon, he backed away and let the snake be. We hadn't been briefed about any snakes in Afghanistan. Running across a cobra made everyone look under their cots each night. Stories like that make for good entertainment when boredom strikes.

One of the supply specialists went to the medics complaining about a knocking sound in her eardrum. The docs flushed her ears out and a baby camel spider came sliding out. Apparently it had crawled inside and started making a nest. And she got to sleep inside the real building. Ha! How do you go back to sleep after that? I would have worn ear plugs for the rest of the deployment.

I experienced something similar later in my deployment. I was sound asleep when I felt a pinch and a sting on my left thumb. Shaking my hand was a reaction before I even woke up, and I was rewarded by hearing a loud thump immediately after. Whatever bit me was gone. I went back to sleep and awoke the next morning with a severely swollen thumb. There were two little pinpricks of blood surrounded by a purple mass of flesh and it hurt like Hell.

Deciding not to be stubborn, I snatched my rifle and headed over to the hospital. Wrecks of old Soviet MIGs had been bulldozed against the barrier wall. They were a constant reminder that armies simply did not just *win* in Afghanistan. Inside, the nurses couldn't tell me definitively what had bitten me so they talked themselves into giving me the rabies vaccine just to be safe. I've had plenty of shots in my career, but rabies? Whatever. At least the vaccine had changed and I only got seven shots in the shoulder, spread out every other week, instead of twenty or so in the stomach. I suppose it was worth it. I read somewhere that very few people have survived rabies.[9] Not finished yet, the head nurse decided to give me an extra immunization booster in my ass, just because.

When did we start giving shots just because? I called her on it. She gave me a warm smile, as only a motherly figure could and said, "If you're shy we can raise the curtain so you'll have privacy."

Already mad, I undid my trousers and dropped them around my knees right there. "Just give me the damned shot, Ma'am."

Truthfully I think the sudden flush of rosy red on her face told me which one of us was more embarrassed.

One thing that took some getting used to was the massive influx of Inactive Ready Reserve (IRR) soldiers. These were men and women who didn't do Army stuff, well, pretty much at all. That's not to take away from their contributions and sacrifices. Most of them turned out to be pretty good soldiers, having done their time in the active duty but still owing the government time. Most people don't pay attention to their initial contracts but every single person owes the government a total of eight years before they are released from any obligation of service. The IRR soldiers are the Army's equivalent of an athlete who starts the season sitting at home and get called up three quarters of the way through when everyone else is too hurt to play.

They kept things interesting at least, more than can be said for a great number of active duty people.

My first experience came in the spring. We invited a guy named Ted to come live in our tent. He was an IRR guy and a Captain to boot (ours was a senior NCO tent, officers had their own) but he was also an MP. Since we already had two other MPS living with us one more

---

[9]   Reports vary, but less than ten humans have survived without the rabies vaccine. Prior to 1885 when the vaccine was create the virus had a mortality rate of 100%.

wouldn't hurt. He didn't seem to mind. Ted was an alright guy, even if he was still lost in the civilian mind frame. It can't be easy switching from suit and tie to rifle and helmet.

One day my buddy SFC Joe Burke and I went to get the mail and we saw old Ted had gotten a box from home. Customs protocols said any items needed to be declared on the exterior of the package. His father had made the mistake of listing *all* of the contents. Rule number one is that you don't list things you don't want your son/daughter to be embarrassed about. Seemed Ted's dad didn't think there was anything wrong with what he'd sent his son.

Joe read the customs slip first and broke out laughing. It was all he could do to show me the slip. Some things are just too good to be true. Sometimes you get lucky and good things fall in your lap. This had to be a good thing

We got back to the tent barely able to contain our laughter. Joe looked at Ted and said, "Mail call! We got a box from dad, Ted. You got a magazine, some candy, a book, oh and is little Teddy having trouble pooping? Looks like he sent you some stool softener to ease those bowels."

Ted's face burned crimson as he snatched the box away, but it was too late. He should have expected such treatment living with a handful of NCOs. "My dad is just playing a joke with me," he said in weak defense. No one bought it and it kept us in good humor for the next few days.

It was almost as good as when the Marine Captain we took to calling Biff (for all the obvious stereotypical reasons) went up to Cpt. Carson and asked her if she had any Midol for his headache. Priceless. Nothing in Afghanistan ever went according to plan however, as we found out later that night.

We went to sleep and woke up to a massive explosion and the ground shaking. I yawned and debated whether what I heard happened or not. I'd been around explosions in the field artillery for so long I seldom paid much attention to them anymore. A huge pillar of black smoke billowed up next to the wall, only about a hundred meters from our tent. It was the middle of the night and bone chilling cold. And we were under attack. One of my tentmates asked me what happened so I told him we got hit. He responded by burrowing deeper into his sleeping bag. Not hearing anything else, I decided to do the same.

Then the Army decided to play war. Infantry patrols were scrambled to ensure the perimeter was secure. The arty boys were popping illum rounds to light up the ruins and a pair of A-10 Warthogs dropped low and started circling. Base Ops people dressed in full battle gear went from tent to tent hustling people out of bed and into the bunkers. There was a pronounced sense of urgency- twenty minutes after the fact.

So far as we knew there had been only one explosion and the smoke from it was already gone. Still, there is no substitute for poor security measures. I didn't even bother grabbing a helmet or my body armor. It was enough that I took my rifle. I wasn't alone. Most of the others already there were in various states of dress and only the reservists came dressed for a fight. The item I'm glad I brought was my PT jacket, because it was damned cold.

Anyone who has ever been to Afghanistan will attest to that. It is also one of the most serene places at night. Most of the country didn't have running water so electricity was out of the question. That left the night sky so pure it was almost pitch black. I've never seen the stars shine so brightly before. It truly is beautiful, but we were high up in the mountains and the winds ripped through our little valley. I may have been from New York but I can't stand the cold.

We stood huddled around the makeshift bunker for what felt like hours though in truth probably wasn't more than twenty minutes. A quick look around was enough to show who the full time soldiers were. None of us were geared up. The reservists and IRR guys were in full battle rattle looking as uncomfortable as possible from the back of the heavy concrete. Me being me, I refused to get in the claustrophobic bunker and lit up a cigar. War's funny that way. Finally we got the all clear and were sent back to our tents, freezing and in a sour mood. No one ever did bother telling us the reasoning behind what happened.

Being so low on the list one tends to imagine a great deal of things the higher ups dream of and we almost always thought we knew better. A favorite rumor behind the reasoning for the attack revolved around the warlord wanting more 'rent' money. Dissatisfied, he sent some of his men to fire off a 107mm rocket at us on a 24 hour kitchen timer and then claimed it was the Taliban and he needed more money to protect us properly. How much protection did the man think we needed?

The subsequent investigation found the rocket launch site on the side of a nearby mountain. Our enemies learned early on that they simply could not stand up to us in a fight. They resorted to subversive tactics. An early favorite was to set the rockets up on a line of sight and attached a two dollar timer. Simple yet highly ineffective. It saves their lives and harasses us. Nine times out of ten they didn't hit anything but the assailants were long gone before the rocket went off.

Daily life in a combat zone is not the high octane burst of energy you see in the movies. War is ninety-nine percent boredom with the remaining one percent sheer terror. Afghanistan was nothing if not boring. Daily life took hold and we became trapped in an endless cycle. We tried our best to make our tent into a 'home'. Coop continued hooking us up with things that shouldn't have been possible but what we'd come to expect.

People back home liked to donate things. Most of it was disposable, everything from coffee to Girl Scout cookies. I swear those things are everywhere. Those cookies and cockroaches are the only things capable of surviving a nuclear war. The one thing I took comfort in was the amount of quality books, for free. Most of them I read and returned, satisfied for the moment. A few were worth keeping, but not many. It was here, that I decided to do the one thing that always made sense to me. With the help of a few others, I started writing what would become my first published fantasy novel. Over four hundred handwritten pages and vetted by friends from back home, New Zealand, and England. Quite the accomplishment, I like to think and the foundation for what eventually became a thriving authorship.

Days and nights blended together in an endless stream of monotony. I don't know how many cigars I smoked, how many pipes sitting on the front stoop waiting for the next task. War sucked, plain and simple but we endured. I made the mistake of letting one of the contractor barbers from Pakistan cut my hair once. He wore skinny jeans and had bright blue fingernails. The guy looked too young and started to caress my head while jabbering to his friends. That was too much for me. I paid and never returned. Fortunately, haircut and uniform standards were lessened. I stuck with one of my tentmates cutting my hair for the rest of my time. He wasn't very good at it and I swore I usually had more hair when he was finished than when he started but at least he didn't want to rub or caress my head. Different cultures I guess.

It didn't take long to feel like the entire deployment was a waste of time. Along the way I lost close to twenty-five pounds. That's what happens when there are no choices and not much food. We had too many people and most of them didn't contribute much. I made a few friends, people I'm still in touch with, but the vast majority became lost in passing memories. Most of the time I kept to myself. I read a lot, wrote a lot and used the unending periods of free time to reevaluate my life. Not everything was working as it should. Not that it mattered much. I was in the middle of Afghanistan doing my best to make it back in one piece.

Christmas Day found me sitting in the supply room with Coop when the building started to shake. I looked around, listening for the sound of incoming. It was strangely quiet. Maybe that's because the shaking was caused by a small earthquake. I'd been through tornados, hurricanes, killer monsoons in Korea, even went to Montana to fight wildfires in 2000. This was my first earthquake. I didn't like it.

New Year's Eve was interesting. My shift was over, and I returned to my tent, put my head on the pillow I had taken from the C-17 (a tiny thing hardly deserving of the name) and heard a clink. After pulling back my poncho liner I found a can of Fosters. Beer? How did a beer get in my tent? Not that it mattered, because it tasted damned good. Far better than the frozen cans of O'Doul's the MPS liked to drink. They'd freeze the cans and then cut the quarter inch sliver of alcohol from the top. Pretty sad, but the head MP on Bagram participated so I figured what harm could really come from me drinking a beer? It's not like I was the only one.

I'd like to think the higher ups weren't so naïve as to believe our soldiers didn't drink, but that might be wishful thinking. Every coalition nation could drink, except for the Muslim ones of course, and most of them weren't shy about sharing; the Brits especially. The quickest way to get someone to do something is tell them not to. Most of the Americans I knew had at least one beer during their time in Afghanistan. There was a New Year's Eve party down at the ADAG building filled with senior NCOs and officers and they all enjoyed a few libations to ring in the New Year. There's a difference between having a drink and getting drunk. Drunks get people killed.

Drug use was a rising problem as well. Home of the now infamous poppy fields, there was an abundance of illegal narcotics. Most of the active duty soldiers knew the severity of messing with drugs. It was a career killer and a fast trip to a military jail. The reservists however...

An undercover criminal investigation (CID) officer left through the back door of their building when he noticed a strange smoke smell. He turned and found three reservists leaning against the wall smoking hashish. How dumb can you get? All three were taken and booked within minutes. Due to some legal technicality from being in Afghanistan none of the three were allowed to be court martialed. That's what happens when there are too many regulations.

One of the best things about working in a joint environment is getting work with the other services and various coalition nations. Most of the Marines were pretty cool, but I came to learn they really loved their rank, to the point where they got aggressive if you didn't use the full title. I suppose that comes from not getting promoted very often. Either way it didn't make much difference to me. I did my best to stay in my lane.

I spent a great deal of time trying to decipher what Major David Hopkins told me through endless conversations about his country and himself. He was a New Zealand commando with a thick accent, a very thick accent. (Not quite as thick as the soldiers I met from the Scottish Highlands a few years ago.) One thing I learned was that New Zealand and England seem to be at some sort of unofficial odds with each other, at least in so far as the soldiers were concerned. Most of the information he gave me seemed absolutely petty in the grand scheme of things. I felt like a little kid on the playground listening to the cool kid talk about his summer.

I was informed that the Kiwi's declared war on Germany first in WWII. I didn't have the heart to go into the semantics of the international dateline or the relevancy of proximity to Nazi Germany. Besides, he outranked me. Maj. Hopkins was a good man and funny as Hell. He was the first to give me one of his nation's patches and a pin from his Special Forces unit engraved with the motto 'who dares wins'. Precisely.

My favorite person to mess with was LTC. Joe Grubich. He was an infantryman stuck in an unsatisfying position. I'm not sure who talked more smack to the other but he was a good man, and a better boss. Unlike certain others, he seldom grew angry or raised his voice. Capable and confident, I quickly learned not only to trust, but to like him. Truly good leaders are hard to come by. He was sitting behind his tent a few rows down from mine reading a book when I walked up behind him.

"Hey Sir, what are you reading?" I didn't have any malicious intent but it didn't matter.

He jumped like I just caught him stealing something. Ha, big bad infantry.

"Fucker," he snapped and punched me in the arm. "You scared the shit out of me."

For an old man he had a mean right hook. Little interactions like that kept me going when the doldrums struck. He claimed he hated racing so we would send him fake emails from different NASCAR drivers telling him how much they appreciated and missed him. Normally I never would have thought to do that to a LTC, but he made it clear from the beginning that if we were going to be successful we needed to keep the rank in the background. Anything I might have done that could be considered foolish was done when we were alone or in a small group of people I could trust not to take things the wrong way. Rank has a way of fouling things up.

On a random day he snatched up his cover to head out for the chow hall, mistakenly grabbing the wrong one. I looked at the subdued eagle and shook my head.

"You're not ready for that, Sir," I told him with as much seriousness as I could muster.

He looked down, saw the eagle and said, "Shit, this isn't ready for me."

Say what you will, but I found him one funny individual. I would run into him again in Baghdad a few years later. It is a comfortable feeling knowing you have full confidence in your superiors to do the right thing. LTC Grubich helped pass the time and ease the natural anxiety that comes from being deployed.

The terror aspect of the war took its time in coming. I was certainly no stranger to explosions or gunfire. Blowing things up was my job after all and I'd almost been killed more times than I like to remember. They were all controlled events. Afghanistan was not. You can't control an enemy intent on killing you for your beliefs. Like it or not, religion played a large part in our wars in the Middle East. Zealots fueled rage against infidels, influencing the weak minded and the downtrodden. Afghanistan offered a small taste of the true power in blind faith. Iraq showed us a deeper and more terrifying reality.

Hatred is a powerful weapon to the uneducated. Al-Qaeda used that hatred to build fervor among the disaffected youth and sent them to our gates, to mine the roads, and to give their lives so that they might be one with Allah. Not knowing who wanted to kill you awakened paranoia induced suspicions. Anyone could be the enemy and chances were that you'd be dead before you found out. Suspicions inspire rumors and much of a soldier's life revolves around rumors.

A longtime friend and acquaintance discovered the terrors of combat down along the Pakistani border. Michael Locklear, nicknamed Locktop, started as a fire direction center specialist in the artillery. His job was to plot coordinates for the fire missions the cannon crews executed. Locktop joined a few years before I did so he showed up at Fort Bragg with a shiny 1st Infantry Division combat patch from the Gulf War. Come to think of it, most of the men in that unit had combat patches.

He had it in his mind to try out for the Special Forces for the longest time and spent a good year or so training and trying to prepare. Three weeks of the selection process later (three weeks in which everyone says the training is harder than the actual course) he was invited to try out for the vaunted Green Beret. Six months later he made it. Conventional warfare went out the window once he donned the Green Beret. I had the opportunity to train with them during their last two weeks of the selection process and remain impressed to this day. He deployed to Afghanistan around the same time as I.

I didn't know it at the time, but he was in the middle of one of the most active areas in the country. Reports of ambushes and firefights coming from a pair of FOBS along the Pakistani border, Lwara (renamed FOB Tillman after fallen Army ranger and NFL player Pat Tillman) and Shkin (renamed FOB Lilley), filled the communications channels. That area was right where they sent Locktop. I don't care how well trained you are or what kind of equipment you have; it was a challenge just to survive down there. I respect the Hell out of Locktop, but I didn't envy him.

Action quieted down as winter deepened. No one seemed interested in fighting through the deep winter. Taliban and Al-Qaeda combatants retreated to their mountain holes while the Coalition continued to train and build the Afghan National Army. The stated goal was 70,000 men, but it was not a simple task. Afghanistan belonged to warlords and tribes. Making a consolidated army was harder than the public might believe. Put two men next to each other that have spent their lives hating each other and you have an ineffective unit. Early Afghan units were horribly underprepared to face the enemy, which amazed me all things considered. Why were the Taliban so successful when the regular Afghan man wasn't?

Corruption was the currency of the realm. Most of the nation's senior leaders came from negotiated dealings with the warlords. Hamid Karzi was emplaced as the Afghan national president but his circle of influence was reduced to Kabul, and even that was questionable. He was not the people's choice. Attack helicopters circled whenever he made a rare public appearance and he always had a contingent of U.S. security forces securing the perimeter. Many Afghans resented him, calling him a puppet of the United States. Matters became unnecessarily complicated because of their biases and anti-democracy sentiments the Taliban remnants fanned. Government corruption was rampant; another problem the Afghani people took issue with.

Life was hard. More for the Afghans than us, but they endured their hardships. I was over by the medical center when an ambulance rushed in. Orderlies unloaded a middle aged local with his guts hanging out. His wife took an AK-47 to him during a disagreement. The old man was screaming, clutching his stomach. Blood soaked the blankets and his face was already pale. I never did find out if he survived or not.

The days were full of quirky and disheartening moments. A medevac flew in from down south bringing in a 12 year old boy who had blown off both of his hands banging a shotgun shell with a rock. I wondered what people in the real world would think when they heard stories like this. I was there and found it unbelievable most of the time. Little kids were brought in after stepping on land mines. An American mine clearer was brought back to the hospital not long after, or rather what was left of him. The Soviet mine killed him instantly.

Not everything was doom and gloom. Our chaplain saw me smoking a pipe on the front stoop of our tent and ambled over. I told him I was smoking a Viking blend from the local shop in Fayetteville and we talked for a while. He told me he'd be right back and disappeared. A few minutes later he came back with a full pound of 'donated' tobacco from a company in Nashville. Now that was downright nice. He and I shared a few moments enjoying a good pipe before the war took back over.

Outback Steakhouse came over in November and cooked enough Victoria Filets for the hundreds of people on Bagram. The meal came complete with red and white checkered table clothes, bread and real live waitresses. How much better could life get? Paul Newman was a big fan as well. His company donated thousands of products for us to enjoy. It was a relief seeing so much support. Every little bit was a reminder of the love and support we had at home. Of the unity the 9/11 attacks produced. The tragedy of that day brought us all together, from every walk of life. How could we possibly fail with strength like that?

Unexpected support came when our brigade command team arrived to speak with all of the artillery people. The Colonel sat down for breakfast with everyone and apologized for the Sergeant Major not being able to make. It seemed he had more pressing affairs with an old friend from the 82nd Airborne than with the safety and quality of life of his own soldiers. I've said it for a long time and I'll keep on saying it. There are very few sergeant majors in the Army that are actually worth the money they're being paid. Instead of having the planned NCO meeting, we got to sit and listen to the old man speak at breakfast.

Life was what we made of it. While the support from home was nice, it wasn't something we could regularly count on. There were plenty of times when the mail didn't arrive; the supply convoys of jingle trucks never showed up, etc. The shipping company DHL lost their contract with us when it was discovered that certain employees were reading the customs declarations and stealing the electronic equipment loved ones were sending us. How's that for a kick in ass?

Coop came back from a run to Kabul and brought us a few things to take our minds off the war. He also brought in a slightly used twenty-five inch television he had proliferated from the sergeant majors' tent. It felt like we were living in an episode of MASH. The only thing missing was a still for homemade whiskey. SFC Duwan Cratch, another artilleryman from my brigade, hooked us up with a reservist who happened to be an electrician. (She was also a gynecologist in civilian life.) We soon had extra outlets and were working on getting internet run from the main building. That never happened but not for lack of want. SFC Cratch was also buddies with one of our mess hall mechanics. They'd worked together in the Army some years back and it paid off now. We always had fresh vegetables and fruits and even the occasional box of steaks.

NASCAR season was just getting spooled up and the Armed Forces Television Network says that enough soldiers like racing to put it on religiously. I didn't mind and it was a break from the lame shows no one wanted to watch. Coop was standing in the rear doorway smoking a cigarette and I was working on my book when a very loud whooshing sound went right over the tent. Coop dropped his cigarette and ducked.

"Oh shit, oh shit!" His eyes widened. "Did you hear that? We're under attack!"

"Relax man. I heard it. Just calm down," I told him.

You'd think by now the random explosion or rifle fire wouldn't bother anyone, especially someone who frequently made trips from Bagram to Kabul.

The muffled explosion was too far in the distance to be concerned with. I turned the TV up to drown him out. That only encouraged his hysteria. "Man shit! We're under attack!"

I sighed and looked up. "Coop, the fucking rocket already blew up in the village somewhere. We're fine."

"How can you be so calm about that?" he asked.

I shrugged and went back to watching the qualifiers for the Daytona 500. Anything was better than listening to his hysteria. Besides, the rocket had already exploded. There was nothing to worry about.

He didn't seem convinced but eventually bent down to finish his cigarette. Surprisingly there were no sirens or alarms for this. I heard later that night that one of the AH-64 Apache pilots fired off a Hellfire missile when he landed. The missile shot overhead and exploded somewhere around the village. Hot shot chopper jocks. They were more dangerous than the enemy sometimes. If negligent discharge for a rifle was a big deal I wondered what that meant for the poor guy who had just fired a missile.

The weather was getting better and combat activity started back up. We lost an Air Force Medevac in a bad storm, crashed into the side of a mountain while trying to rescue an Afghan gunshot victim down around Kandahar. All crewmembers were lost. The incident was terrible, many questioning whether it was worth it. We adults may be beyond salvation but any child's life should be considered precious. About a week later we lost another bird right in our back yard. Delta Force was out conducting a private training exercise (without informing Corps HQ) and one of their birds went down in the minefields. Recovery operations were complicated due to the mines, but they eventually got the bodies out and recovered the wreckage.

Two of the most memorable crashes during my time there happened when a C-130 Hercules came in too fast and blew its wheels out, stranding the plane in the middle of the runway. Thank you, Mr. Pilot. David Letterman was supposed to come up and film his talk show that night but seeing as how the runway was closed that didn't happen. At least the folks down in Kandahar got to enjoy the respite since he was forced to spend another day down south.

The second, and perhaps best, was on behalf of the Dutch. A Netherlands F-16 missed its landing and hit too far down the runway. Instead of stopping on the hardball it continued to roll straight into the minefield. The pilot punched out safely and the plane was stuck for a day or so until someone figured out that a CH-47 Chinook helicopter was strong enough to lift it out. They had to drain the fuel tanks and drop the unexpended ordinance first and the F-16 never got more than a few feet from the ground, but mechanics got it to safety. I wonder what kind of reprimand the pilot got for that? I've seen plenty of equipment sling loaded under helicopters, that was my military specialty after all, but that was by far the coolest.

Someone decided that we had become complacent so they switched up our shifts for a month. That meant I got to work the night shift. Nights suck. Period. There is a decided lack of life, vibrancy from the ghouls stuck on the night shift. I hated it. The worst part was going back to my tent and trying to sleep in the blistering heat. I was stripped down to a t shirt and underwear with a wet washcloth covering my face and it still wasn't enough.

One thing that kept me going during those long nights was what Joe Burke and I had taken to calling the Three Stooges or Curly, Curly and Curly. Two were Marine Corps Reservists and the third was one of the lead men in the Air Force's stealth fighter program that people called Woody. He was a down to earth guy that you could joke with despite the fact that he was a Lieutenant Colonel. The Air Force never did do much like the Army. Woody liked to show me top secret video clips of missiles and bombing runs. Nice guy and it passed the time.

The big boss was a full Colonel who I convinced to send me one of the new digital pattern camouflage hats the Marines had. I figured it would make a great gift to my dad; one of those 'continue the tradition' sort of things. He stormed through the JOC like *Al Bundy*. He'd even brought a Navy bell and had it fixed to the tent support frame. Every time the Corps Commander left the JOC the Colonel would ring the bell. I think he forgot we were on land and not the bridge of an aircraft carrier. He was also slightly forgetful. One night I was on duty and told Woody I had to use the latrine. He let me go since they were all sitting at their posts and nothing was going on. When I got back all three of them had disappeared. Al Bundy came ambling back from somewhere and immediately saw the Ops station unattended.

"Sergeant Freed! Why aren't you at your post?" he barked.

A few heads turned my way. I was just putting my weapon in the rack and setting my cover down. Talk about bad timing. A nasty retort came to mind but the man was one step away from being a general and I would have been crucified. I decided my career meant more than foolish pride and hustled back to the desk. "I'm on it, Sir."

That was the last time I worked nights.

The third man was also a Marine and an artilleryman. That made us family. He was by far my favorite target. I got a copy of a gag program that was perfect for him. The icon was a little yellow smiley face. When you clicked it a mock picture of the c drive popped up with an option box asking if you wanted to delete all files. You couldn't push no and before you knew it the list of files were erased before your eyes. Seeing as he had the main computer used in the day to day operation of the war I had to send it to him.

He opened his email and read it out loud, taking the time to look at Woody and ask, "Do I want to permanently delete the c drive files?"

Woody didn't miss a beat. "I wouldn't."

I struggled to keep from laughing when all I heard a few seconds later was, "oh shit!"

Woody leaned over and said, "Dude, someone sent you a virus."

I lost it. He really started to freak out. Woody raised an eyebrow and shot me a sidelong glance. Time to confess. Fortunately once the program ran a blank screen popped up with a running scroll that said aren't you glad this was just a game? He might have been pissed at first, but soon saw the humor in it. He even asked for a copy of it to send to his friends. The other two Curlys ribbed him for days.

Fortunately for them, the war was vast and much happened daily to keep us occupied. Half of the base at Kandahar burned down thanks to a small fire that quickly grew out of control. Afghanistan is a very dry country, so it doesn't take much. The country is also home a rare event lasting over 100 days. Heavy winds blow in and tear the country apart. Heavy is a relative term but we were told by our Air Force weather section that the winds were above 70 knots. Most of us scoffed when they brought this up in our daily briefing. 70 knots for a hundred days? That just didn't seem possible.

We found out the hard way. The winds roared across the Bagram valley. It was all I could do to walk without being blown down. I was carried a few meters several times but never fell, unlike a few others. We had to wear goggles and scarves over our mouths if we wanted to be outside. Staying inside wasn't much better. Sand and dust penetrated everything, covering our belongings in fine powder. There was no point in cleaning anything; it was only going to be filthy a few minutes later. Our tent was ripped from its moorings one day and nearly blew away before we could snatch the ropes and pull it back down. I was never happier than when the storms abated and life returned to normal.

We had our share of tragedies as well. A young soldier from the 82nd Airborne was accidentally shot in the head by one of his own men and killed. His partner had been cleaning his pistol and made the fundamental mistake of not clearing the weapon before fiddling with it. Declared brain dead the moment he was medevacked to Landstuhl Regional Medical Center in Germany.

I took some comfort in seeing the Army do the right thing. Doctors kept him on life support until the insurance paperwork was cleared so that his family could be taken care of. Once done, the family consented to let him pass. A brave man was dead and one of his close friends was responsible. That young man now spends the rest of his life knowing that he was responsible for the death of a friend. Sadly, he was not the only friendly casualty or accidental discharge incident.

Another unit was conducting dry fire practice with the standard anti-tank rocket, the AT-4, a bulkier, heavier upgrade from the Vietnam era LAW. The squad leader failed to notice he had a live round loaded when the private hefted it to his shoulder and depressed the trigger. Those types of booms were most unwelcome and almost always resulted in disciplinary action. Training or not, those types of accidents were potentially fatal.

Kandahar, main base for the 82nd combat units, was considered the Wild West. The previous two events showed us the harsh realities of war. Historically, most wartime casualties come from disease and accidents. It is a sad truth, but one the soldier has no choice but to accept. I remember a serious accident shortly before the Gulf War when the brakes locked up on one of our howitzers. Truck and gun flipped and three people were killed, almost everyone else was wounded. That was on the back stretch of Fort Bragg, not some distant battlefield where death was unwelcome but at least acceptable.

We had a Navy SEAL colonel that reminded me of John Astin, the original Gomez Addams. He had the moustache and a squeaky voice. Most of the SEALs I met were arrogant men who bore too much self importance (Granted they took the greatest risks with their lives and had earned the right to be arrogant, but not the right to be an asshole). This guy, at least, was funny. He was in the Corps Commander's building talking with the chief of staff when he decided to brandish his pistol. Another officer told him he should put it away in case of a discharge. He smiled and told them it wasn't loaded and proceeded to prove it to them by pulling the trigger. A small bang and cloud of descending dust drifting down from the ceiling later, he was banned from carrying a firearm on Bagram.

Stupidity also had its place. Someone decided to take a dump on the lid to one of the general's fancy toilet trailers. Very rude and of course no one admitted it. So, mass punishment being an Army favorite (one I generally enjoyed doing to achieve maximum results) the general blamed us all. Forget the fact that it could have been anyone from a dozen nations or even an Afghan national working on the base. We took the hit. That meant guard duty. Guard duty on a toilet trailer. How much lower could life get?

The senior leadership decided to step up and lead the way, rather than sitting back and letting the lower enlisted and junior officers to perform the task. All of the department colonels took the first shifts. I watched as an Air Force colonel used a broom handle as a rifle and marched back and forth in front of the door. The broom had two rolls of fresh toilet paper on it. Everyone admitted pulling guard on a toilet was a stupid thing. We used comedy to ease the pain of indignation. Our orders were to have one man stationed inside the trailer, another out. The man inside was responsible for checking the toilets after each use. Those were two hours of my life I will never get back.

The little things soon disappeared to memory once it got warm enough to fight again. Our combat troops geared up for the expected spring offensive. The Taliban wasn't about to give up control of their country without a good old fashioned guerrilla war.

Chapter Four: Now it's a War

February 2003

I woke up to the sounds of an all-out firefight going on right outside of our wire. Explosions rocked the compound and I saw red tracer rounds ricocheting up into the air. Familiar acrid smoke hovered just high enough to make me cover my mouth. A mounted MP patrol sped towards the battle. Gawkers and bystanders just stood there watching as the MPs blocked the road off and took up defensive positions along the wall.

The battle intensified. Mortars and rockets exploded from opposite sides of the valley. This was clearly not a U.S. action. It also wasn't enough to put us into combat gear. After being denied by the MPs from checking it out, I made my way into the JOC compound and conducted my changeover briefing with the night shift. Most of what happened inside that massive tent is still classified and, more than likely, unknown to most of us who worked there. I will say that the JOC reminded me of the war room in *Dr. Strangelove*. The only thing missing was George C. Scott ranting about the Commies. We did have the big board though; three massive screens constantly streaming tactical materials across the area of operations.

George C. Scott might not have been there, but I wound up working for the real life equivalent. Col. Yarbrough was the Corps G-3 and normally very calm. Very thorough and professional, he was the kind of man junior leaders should emulate. He naturally got amped up when I received the Troops in Contact (TIC) call from units in the field. Since I was the operations guy, all information passed through me before it got to the Corps commander. That kept life interesting.

The downside was Col. Yarbrough had unrealistic expectations of me, and the others in my position. If the main air conditioners went down he would bitch at me about it, wanting to know why I didn't fix it. Last time I checked the Army trained and paid me to blow things up, not repair machinery. We had mechanics and, oh yeah, a worthless SGM and his crew who were supposed to take care of that. My job here was to process the flow of information and coordinate efforts between the services, coalition, and internal departments of the task force.

The big boards showed what was happening in our happy little valley. Two units of rival militia were slugging it out in a death match. Fighters were dug in and engaging with heavy machine guns and mortars. We watched a middle aged man load what was left of his friend onto his back and carried him away from the battle. The man was missing both legs. Since this action didn't involve any American or Coalition troops we were ordered to stay out of it.

The battle continued for six straight days. Thankfully they took the nights off so we found some measure of peace. As with most things, their monumental waste of ammunition soon lost our interest. Aside from the occasional stray round we were safe and had no reason to worry. No one knew what sparked it or why, and we certainly never bothered to find out how many dead and wounded came from their 'disagreement'. Our war was against the remnants of the Taliban and al-Qaeda.

The Korean detachment got feisty one day in late February. A single gunshot rang out from their compound, about fifty meters behind my tent. MPs went to investigate and they discovered one dead Korean Captain and a very nervous Colonel trying to come up with a believable excuse. He had summoned the captain into his tent for counseling and the session got heated to the point where he shot the man point blank in the chest with his pistol. The MPs found him blocking the door with his foot while trying to stop the chest wound from bleeding. It was already too late. The captain was dead. The next day a combined effort between Army Engineers and Koreans started building a bigger barrier between our two compounds. The gate was patrolled by armed guards who did not look happy or friendly whenever someone passed by.

I already knew from my two years on spent on the Korean DMZ the ROKs were hardcore but coming from a hospital unit this was just ridiculous. They ran a clinic out of the back of the base. Locals would come down to their gate and get whatever medical treatment they needed. It not only freed up our medical staff to treat Coalition combat injuries but kept the locals from swamping us with a wide range of problems. The colonel was on the next bird out of Bagram just as fast the Korean commander could relieve him. Presumably he returned to Seoul for disciplinary actions. I've seen the inside of a South Korean military prison and it is not the place to go.

To help pass the time I went on convoy runs with some of the SF guys I deployed with. Apparently having an M-16 was something of an anomaly to them since they carried the smaller, lighter M-4s. It was the same weapon but had a collapsible stock and shorter barrel. That made me a commodity. I was constantly being asked if I wanted to go on a patrol or make a run to Kabul with them because they need a 'long rifle'. (OK, I did most of the asking but they were extremely generous.) Who was I to say no? Their use of the term long rifle made me feel like Davy Crockett about to go to the Alamo. Nothing ever happened on those runs but they did pick up some nice supplies and souvenirs from the capital.

One day I was lucky to ruck up with Joe Burke and a few Italian *carabinieri,* their version of Military Police, to go pick up a few prisoners from down south. A deuce and a half rolled up with four armed guards and a pair of orange jumpsuit prisoners in the back. They were waiting for a Blackhawk out. Both prisoners were cuffed and blindfolded. The guards also had a dog. Afghanis were terrified of dogs thanks to the Soviets. The Soviets were rumored to have used dogs to hunt the Afghanis and then pretend to release the prisoners after a ride into the middle of nowhere. Once the truck stopped the prisoners were executed and left to rot in the desert. We weren't sure if that ever happened or not, but our prisoners were scared shitless. Truth be told, these two were being released back to their village, and presumably watched to see if they went to some insurgent cell.

We waited on the tarmac most of the day before the Italians said the Hell with it and left. *Domani!* Different armies have different standards. Bored, Joe took me over to the prison complex we had on base. The first thing I did was sign a waiver saying I would not mention or disclose anything that happened inside the prison etc.... The last thing I needed was an angry intelligence operative after me (pick one, there were about a dozen different agencies operating on Bagram Air Base at the time.), so I signed and went inside. Nothing within felt wrong. There certainly weren't any water boarding stations set up. It was just a jail, not much different from what we had back home. (Not that I have ever been to prison, or jail for that matter) I left feeling very patriotic, I still didn't care for Madonna, and I was glad not to be a Taliban or al Qaeda prisoner of war.

Soldiers often found the oddest things laughable when under duress. Maybe it helps calm the nerves or takes off the edge from near death experiences. I laughed so hard when Coop turned pale and dropped his smoke the day the rocket slashed overhead. Now it was the higher up's turn to laugh. An infantry unit ran into a group of Taliban fighters. The enemy, seeing they were outgunned and outnumbered, fired off a few shots and headed towards the safety of Pakistan. Escape across the border was a favorite trick. They knew they couldn't match us militarily and needed any advantage they could find. Disappearing back into Pakistan was a big one. In 2003 the U.S. did not have an agreement with the Pakistani government so following the enemy across the border was akin to following the Viet Cong into Laos.

Political relations were solidifying though. A diplomatic effort was underway under the auspice of allowing U.S. combat troops into certain areas of Pakistan to engage and destroy the enemy. I received the request from Pegasus 6, the 82nd Airborne's aviation asset commander, to pursue and destroy across the border. My reaction was yes, but I was low man on the totem pole. I passed the request to Col. Yarbrough who took it to the Corps commander a few meters behind me. I looked back over my shoulder and saw this three star general with his legs propped up on his desk, hands clasped behind his head and leaning back in his chair.

He turned and looked at Col. Yarbrough with a wry grin and said, "Tell him to kill the mother fuckers."

Col. Yarbrough smiled and gave me a nod. "Send it."

God bless the simplicity of the infantry. I keyed the headset, "Pegasus 6, Dragon 6 says kill the mother fuckers."

Mission complete. Attack choppers dropped in and tore the enemy to shreds.

April 2003

The war intensified the warmer it got. A call came in from an Operational Detachment Team-Alpha (ODA) team west in the Helmund Province. They were caught in a village between two warlord militias and asking for air support. Normally it takes a very long time to get anything done in the Army, especially when the request has to go levels above you. It is amazing how fast the system can move when lives are on the line. The ODA team wasn't the target. They just had the misfortune of being caught in the wrong place at the wrong time.

Our air support section plotted the grid coordinates and dispatched a B-1 Bomber. Afghanistan air space was filled with rotating shifts of various aircraft; a healthy mix of fighters and bombers from a handful of nations. At this point the Afghan air force consisted of a few old men, an empty fuel truck and the little boy who told me to fuck off. They might have had a dog too, but no pilots and no planes.

The B-1 swooped in and dropped a pair of 1,000 pound bombs. The village was all but destroyed, as were the two militias. Fortunately the civilians who weren't part of the battle fled before the fighting became too intense. Early estimates were upwards of seventy dead and hundreds more wounded. Body parts littered the surrounding area, marking the blast radius. The ODA team got back in their vehicles and drove back to their base without suffering casualties.

A short while later word filtered back to us that a reserve SF Lieutenant Colonel had been shot in the thigh while traveling through a mountain pass and was being evaced back to Bagram for treatment. Little engagements like this happened daily. The Taliban discovered that if you shoot a rifle blindly into the air and in the general direction of a U.S. base that round was going to strike something. A colonel was standing in the chow line not far ahead of me when he yelled suddenly and reached behind him. Dark red blossomed across his uniform. He'd just been shot in the ass. Not life threatening, but it left him in a sour mood for the rest of the deployment. Making matters worse, it was from NATO ammunition so he wasn't eligible to receive the Purple Heart for being wounded in combat.[10]

I was preparing for the evening Battle Update Briefing (BUB) when a sharp whizzing brushed in front of me. Another stray round. One of the CIA operatives, a nice guy who talked cigars with me, did the forensics and announced it was from an AK-47 and fired indiscriminately from Bagram somewhere. There was no point in doing anything further since everyone had a gun. (Despite our efforts at trying to remove all unnecessary weapons from the population) Our favorite latrine duty one star general strolled in from lunch, asked what happened and gave a shrug with the immortal comment of, "huh, just missed it." No one commented that the round would have likely wounded the man had he been at his post. The end result was we had to walk around wearing body armor and helmets for about a week. We took a few more stray rounds, but nothing like I would experience a few years later in Iraq.

April quickly got busier. An 82nd Infantry patrol was ambushed coming up over a low rise. The Taliban had mined the road. They took out the lead vehicle and began firing down on the rest of the patrol from two sides. Standard procedure was to immediately call for air

---

[10] The Purple Heart was originally the Badge of Military Merit and was established by Gen. George Washington during the Revolutionary War to award those who were wounded or killed by enemy action.

support. Unfortunately for the 82nd, the first man killed was the Air Force Ground Forward Air Controller (GFAC). An enemy round took him right between the eyes. He also wasn't wearing a helmet. No matter what anyone from the 82nd patrol did, the pilots weren't going to respond. Pilots were trained not to respond to anyone on the ground that wasn't a trained GFAC. The 82nd were on their own until ground help arrived.

Col. Yarbrough, the Corps G-3 or Operations Officer, barked at me. "Freed, how long until the damned predator is on station?"

"A few minutes, Sir."

Drones were still new to our combat operations but provided invaluable real-time intel, when they were available.

A new message came in. A second man was dead, and then a third. Col. Yarbrough got pissed. "What the fuck is going on down there? I want to talk to someone in that command NOW!"

I wasn't really sure what he expected me to do. The ambush was taking place about a hundred miles south along the Pakistani border and the messages were time delayed from the unit engaged, to their command and then to us. I tried to patch through to that Brigade command but as you can imagine they were busy trying to solve the problem on their own. A fourth man was reported killed in action (KIA) before the quick reaction force was dispatched from Forward Operating Base Salerno (FOB) but it was going to take time to get there. In the meantime, a pair of 105mm howitzers was within firing range and began pumping HE rounds to suppress enemy fire.

Reinforcements arrived and were able to extract the battered patrol, recovering all of the bodies and ensuring there was no salvaging the wrecked vehicles. It was a black day for the Airborne. Those scars never heal.

Funny enough, death is the one thing soldiers don't talk about. It lurks like a shadow, familiar and dangerous, behind everything we do. No one thinks they are going to die when they raise their hand and step off that plane. Death is a constant companion left in shadow. Curiously watching us, waiting for that one terrible moment we hoped would never come.

The bitter taste of failure stung most of the senior staff. They didn't consider the ambush a defeat because the enemy quit the field first, but it marked a considerable failure in American tactics. The next battle erased any doubts and offered a modicum of revenge against a different enemy. It was just past dawn. A combined element of SF and

Afghan National Army (ANA) were patrolling the roads north from Kandahar to Bagram when they spotted a pair of Taliban fighters hiding in the ditch alongside the road. They tried to run but were captured and made to talk.

A large force of enemy fighters was using a nearby cave complex as an operating base. The SF acted quickly and moved towards the suspected mountain, leaving a platoon of ANA to block the nearby intersection in the event of enemy reinforcements. The Taliban may have been reduced to hiding in caves but they still had good enough technology to communicate with other cells. Driving in HMMWVs and Toyota pickups, the SF made their way to the base of the mountain before they started taking fire from the cave openings on the mountainside.

U.S. forces had become well versed with cave fighting earlier in the war. Operation Anaconda in March 2002 brought combined Special Forces teams and conventional infantry from the 10st Airborne Division and a substantial sized force of ANA forced the Taliban and al Qaeda to fight in the Shah-i-Kot Valley and the Arma Mountains near the Pakistan border. It marked the first major battle since the attempt to kill Osama bin Laden at Tora Bora in late 2001. It also provided enough experience in mountain warfare and the time necessary for lessons learned to be spread throughout the Army.

The SF and ANA took up defensive firing positions and returned fire, not so much in the hopes of hitting the enemy but to suppress them back into the caves. The volume of enemy fire increased rapidly as more fighters filled the cave mouths. Anaconda was a bitter defeat to the Taliban with casualty estimates as high as 500 KIA. This group was determined not to meet with similar results. They were in no hurry to expose themselves unnecessarily to superior weaponry and tactics of the U.S.

Clearly the intel given by the prisoners was actionable and the request for immediate reinforcements spread through the channels. The first to arrive was a pair of Apaches. Standard armament for an AH-64 is 1200 rounds of 30mm, 72 2.75 in rockets and a handful of Hellfire missiles. Both birds unloaded on the Taliban fighters and continued to do so until enemy fire finally drove them back. Initial reports came back with fifteen dead, but the Apaches ran too great of a risk of being shot down if they stayed longer. Ammunition expended, they returned to FOB Salerno to refit and refuel. A second team was already en route.

A full company of 82nd infantry was alerted and readied to deploy. Already on standby for pop up firefights, the first chalk was boarding Blackhawks in less than fifteen minutes. The SF was still battling hard, trying to conserve ammo and keep the enemy from escaping. This time the GFAC was alive and well and able to call in the air strike. Nearly a dozen Coalition craft broke their circling patterns and screamed towards the battlefield. F-16s and A-10s made strafing runs, dropping 500 pound bombs and raking the mountainside with heavy machinegun fire.

Live feed was run to the JOC through Predator drone imaging. Taliban reinforcements ran into the ANA blocking element. We watched men from both sides fell, their heat signatures cooling. For the moment, the ANA were holding their own. Anyone who has ever worked with either the initial Afghan military or police understands their severe deficiencies. These men held the intersection long enough to keep the reinforcements from getting to the mountain.

The battle intensified throughout the morning. What had started as an accidental spotting of Taliban scouts was now *the* major engagement in the country. The Afghan mountains are big, tall and just plain nasty to fight in. Apaches were not going to break the mountain open to get to the enemy. Ground observers called in the heavies. B-1 Bombers headed their way loaded with GBU-31s. The GBU-31, also known as the JDAM or Joint Direct Attack Munition, is a monster of bomb weighing 2000 pounds and a 'hard target' penetrator. It has a specific purpose of breaking open hard targets and obliterating everything inside.

The first B-1 released its first JDAM around 0800. Rock and debris were kicked up from the blast. Reverberations echoed down the entire valley. Nothing is quite so impressive as a massive piece of ordnance exploding nearby. Men were knocked to the ground. It is hard to imagine the nightmares the Taliban trapped in the caves were enduring. One thing mankind has excelled at is devising new ways to kill. The bunker busters hammered into the mountains, collapsing caves and tunnels. There is no accurate count of how many men died in cave-ins or collapses.

The Air Force dropped a total of seven JDAMs on the mountainside over the course of the morning. Clouds of smoke and dust choked the air as the first wave of Infantry touched down in a hasty landing zone about a klick away from the battle. Two platoons from the 82nd formed up and moved in. During all of this a team of

Navy SEALS was deployed to the rear of the mountain range with the hopes of intercepting escaping Taliban squirting out the back. Enemy casualties were mounting without any reported U.S. injuries. A few ANA were wounded but friendly casualties remained light.

Reports came in as fast as events happened. Another handful of enemy fighters were killed. Another two platoons of infantry ferried in, bringing their combat strength up to one hundred and twenty. The nearest artillery was too far out of range so 81mm mortars were brought in. They began bombarding the slopes by noon. By 1600 hours the combined force of U.S. and Afghan troops had the mountain complex surrounded.

The siege lasted for three days before what little remained of the enemy managed to flee. Victory belonged to the Coalition. It was just the spark we needed to turn the momentum around from the ambush along the Pakistani border a few weeks earlier. Enemy casualties were high; more than one hundred killed and an unconfirmed number of wounded. Coalition forces lost only a handful of ANA soldiers assigned to block the southern road. The mop up continued for some time, until command was convinced the Taliban had abandoned the field entirely and the area could be deemed secure.

May 2003

Few moments in life are powerful enough to bring emotional change at a core level. May 19th offered me one of those special moments. It became a unique introduction to the true cost of war and a moment I have never forgotten. A Special Forces NCO got killed around Kabul and his body was being flown home that night. HQ encouraged anyone not doing anything to line the road at midnight in tribute to the fallen. Joe Burke and I grabbed our rifles and took our places in the lines of soldiers along Disney Drive. We could see the HMMWV carrying the flag draped casket at the end of the road, waiting for the escort to get in place. Another hundred or so soldiers lined the road in solemn ranks.

Everything seemed to happen at once; almost a sensory overload. A C-17 just landed, bringing with it a fresh batch of soldiers from the 10th Mountain Division. None of the newbies were enthused. Many wore fearful looks, much the same as our merry group had upon entering enemy air space all those long months ago. Marching out from the opposite side of the road was a group of our guys heading home.

They were laughing and shouting in joy. Naturally there was some good-natured ribbing going on between the two groups. Combine them with our silent bunch and it was almost too much to understand.

Midnight chimed and the SF procession began. A color guard marched in front of the HMMWV, flags waving in a weak breeze. A C-17 waited. The back ramp was down and an ominous red glow filled the cavernous body. Directly behind the plane, almost as if Fate had a hand in this affair, the full moon hung low and bright, illuminating the distant snow-covered mountains.

Marching boots echoed in the silence. The honor guard was comprised of fellow SF men formed up on both sides of the vehicle. Many had tears in their eyes. Others that look of anger from being robbed of a friend. A pair of Apaches zipped overhead, followed by the heavy thump of Chinooks carrying a company from the 82nd. The soldiers lining the road snapped to attention and saluted as the funeral procession passed them. I could see the end of the casket now and it inspired strong emotions. Rage, sorrow, pride. I could clearly see the pain in those SF soldier's eyes as they escorted their friend and comrade down the flight line and up into the belly of the plane.

Joe and I went to attention and saluted with our rifles. It was much harder to keep a straight face than I imagined. I'd been to the occasional funeral back in the States, but those deaths were from training accidents, not combat. This man that none of us knew inspired me. He awakened raw emotions I forgot I had. Strange pride warmed me. I can't say where it came from but it was a moment I'll never forget. Seeing that casket roll by I suddenly realized why I was still in the Army and why I volunteered to go to Afghanistan.

Any lingering doubts were gone, replaced by a sense of satisfaction that came from knowing each and every one of the men and women standing beside me were ready to lay down their lives for people they hardly knew. That's it. That's all it is. Soldiers share a bond no newscaster or civilian will ever understand. We're here so you don't have to be. So you never need know the horrors of war. That's what makes us special. It's the undying devotion to each other that sets us apart regardless of race, creed or nationality.

I stayed in the Army all these years not for myself but for those next to me. We carry on despite seeing our comrades fall. We bury our heroes at the expense of our nation's freedom, whether they support us or not. But that is merely an afterthought. While deployed the only thing that matters is the people on our flanks. There's no way I can find to successfully convey the strength of emotions I felt after I dropped my salute. One thing I was sure of was that as long as men and women were willing to leave their lives behind to go fight in a country they never heard of, for people they've never met, I'll be right alongside wearing my nation's uniform and serving with pride.

The vehicle kept moving until it cleared the road and pulled up the waiting C17. That man's war was done. His sacrifices etched eternal in the memories of grieving family and friends. The war was still new for all of us but it was no a permanent fixture.

All these events helped make my deployment to Afghanistan an enduring memory that I can still see when I close my eyes on a quiet day. There are no words to describe the emotions that run through a deployed soldier's mind when he/she is exposed to such events. Even now as I write this, almost a decade later I can still see the wounded. Can still hear the machine guns and explosions. I can still feel the cold when I step outside and see mountains.

What I experienced in Afghanistan was exceptional when compared with the mundane lives back home in the States. It is difficult to describe war to those who have never been. My father offered fragments of what Vietnam was like, often when grumbling about the misrepresentations of a war movie. It wasn't until I came home that first time that he opened up and started telling me stories in detail. My grandfather was the same way. I remember hearing only one story about what France was like during the summer of the 1944.

Now I find I am the same. My children are always asking me to tell them about the war. I smile and immediately try to deflect and change the subject. My wife doesn't know half of what I've seen or done and I refuse to tell my mother. (If only for her only peace of mind. Of course that's out the window when she reads this.) How do you tell someone who has no conceptual basis for what you have done about being shot at or shooting back? At what point does morality draw the line and you decide to keep the horrors of war away from the ones you love?

Afghanistan tested the limits of my mental strength. Every soldier who was killed or wounded went through my station. Every firefight and troops in contact (TIC) came to me as soon as it started. The gut-wrenching feeling of having to report a friendly KIA. The feeling of gloom after a helicopter crashes into a mountainside or is downed from enemy fire. The joy of seeing an enemy vehicle lit up by attack helicopters as it tries to flee. Military training is intentionally difficult, but it cannot and does not prepare you for the mental aspect of combat. It was all coming to an end. I was scheduled to rotate home in early May with most of Corps.

That didn't happen.

The downside to doing your job well is that people want you to continue doing it. The time had come to redeploy and Col. Yarbrough pleasantly informed me that I was extended in order to train up the incoming Ops NCO properly. The 10th Mountain Division was coming in to take over for the XVIII Airborne Corps and we were treated to overactive greetings of 'Climb to Glory" or "To the Top" by new staff officers. I wasn't exactly enthused, especially not after six long months in a hostile environment without the comforts of home.

Col. Yarbrough rotated out and was replaced by a well known man in Special Forces community. My new boss was LTC Michael Steele, of the Black Hawk Down incident in Somalia. Some people are in awe of an actor or musician. That's all well and fine, but here was a man who had been deep in the shit, caught in an unimaginable experience. He was a legend. A man whose name was known by practically every soldier. And he was my boss.

He was a bull of a man that looked like the Hulk in uniform. He gave his men knives upon arrival and had no patience for slackers. I immediately noticed one key difference between him and outgoing staff officers. He wore only the U.S. flag, U.S. Army and his name tape whereas the others ironed their uniforms and had every little badge of self importance sown on. I liked him already. Steele was the sort who had no problem taking his blouse off and settling problems the old fashioned way instead of hiding behind rank. You stayed on his good side as long as you didn't bring up Somalia or the 'pussy British actor' who portrayed him in the movie. Check and check. The last thing I needed was to get body slammed by this man. (It's funny how life goes in circles. Years later when I was stationed at West Point, I met and worked with his son, who was a cadet, on occasion.)

The train up went well, but still took nearly a month to complete. CJTF-180 downsized from a three star general command to a two star. Stars didn't mean much, but Operation Iraqi Freedom was already underway and the Army didn't have many disposable assets to send to the mop-up operations in Afghanistan.

Finally, I was granted a pardon and told to go home. The only problem was I didn't want to go home. I wanted to go straight to Iraq.

Chapter Five: The Growing Shadow

Being forward deployed has many militaristic advantages. We were on the cutting edge of equipment, tactics and the cultural awareness of our new enemy. Unfortunately, we were also the guinea pigs. Our mistakes were already being used to train potential replacement units. Afghanistan, however, was not the only game in town. The U.S. military reacted with violent fury after the 9/11 attacks. We had forces engaged in missions in the Philippines and the Horn of Africa, all trying to disrupt al-Qaeda's ability to conduct terror operations against the democratic nations of the west.

It was an old hatred fueled by the rhetoric of a few firebrands. Osama bin Laden was the mouth and face of this iteration of the enemy. The war on terror, at least from the American soldier point of view, was never about Iraqi oil money or the longstanding rivalry between Christian and Muslim. It was sheer survival. We had been grievously attacked on our own soil, embarrassed and wounded. Retribution was severe. It had to be severe in order to keep the enemy off guard, from attacking again.[11]

We may have prevented them from attacking us on our soil again, but we weren't able to keep them from attacking other nations. The London subway bombings; the same in Madrid. The Bali night club bombing that killed hundreds. For every successful bombing, our intelligence assets stopped a hundred more. The enemy didn't play fair. The old rules of war were out. The Geneva Convention an outdated code of conduct only the West followed. This was a war of fundamentals. He with the strongest faith and conviction would become the winner.

Al-Qaeda had made the fundamental mistake of believing the United States was weak. The growing sentiment towards non-violence and inaction against previous terror attacks *abroad* helped form that opinion. Our limited response from the first World Trade Center

---

[11]   Keep in mind this information was 'at the time'. None of us on the ground were privy to why we invaded Iraq, nor did we care. Our perspectives stemmed from the need to avenge our losses. Nothing more. Let historians and politicians debate the morality of the Iraq War. The soldiers, marines, sailors, and airmen followed orders.

bombing in February 1993 emboldened the enemy. The August 1998 simultaneous bombings on U.S. embassies in Tanzania and Kenya received much attention immediately after but they were quickly passed up for other news. Not even the attack on the USS Cole in 2000, which left seventeen dead and thirty-nine others wounded, was enough to spark U.S. military intervention. Washington had grown complacent.

The Sunday Times of London reported in 2002 that President Clinton turned down three offers from foreign governments to apprehend bin Laden and turn him over to U.S. custody once it was determined that he was the mastermind behind the terror campaign.[12] The mistakes of the Oval Office now haunted the soldiers sworn to protect it. Not only that, but the rest of America held its breath, desperately hoping to be spared a repeat of the 9/11 horrors. The only thing missing was concrete evidence. Without it, our legal hands were tied.

The decision not to take bin Laden into custody didn't matter anymore. We were at war and doing our best to remove every one of his followers from this life. Wars are won in the will just as much as through the end of a rifle. Enraged, most of America stood united behind the military as we hunted al-Qaeda down. The early stages of this war proved most successful as enemy casualties rolled up under our heel. The price of our success was the enemy quickly realizing they were not the cohesive military force they thought they were and they fled into Pakistan, the mountains, Iran; wherever they could find refuge to regroup and attack in the manner they knew how. (Forget the videos the media insisted on showing of future terrorists training on monkey bars or bin Laden kneeling as he fired someone else's AK-47. It was all for show.) The coalition dominated the battlefield in every regard.

Washington already had its eye on another prize. Iraq had been a thorn in our side since the invasion of Kuwait in 1990. Saddam Hussein, the self professed student of Adolph Hitler, remained in power, openly defying the U.N. and mocking the United States. The time had come to finally do something about. Regardless for the reasoning behind going to war in Iraq, the men and women in our military began training intensively for invasion. I personally could not care less for the conspiracy theories, the uninformed public's various opinions or the rhetoric spun from the news. I was a soldier. It was my job to go where Uncle Sam said. (For obvious purposes the reasons for

---

[12]   Information taken from the Sunday Times of London, June 2002.

going to war in Iraq aren't important to this story and will not be covered. Moreover, I don't care why we went. What's done is done.)

The 2002 State of the Union address focused heavily on Iraq with the coining of the term 'axis of evil'. Attention quickly diverted from the ongoing war in Afghanistan as the White House began a campaign to enlist the aid and support of as many nations as it could for the coming invasion. I don't think there was ever any doubt in the President's mind that we were going to invade. That forgone conclusion propelled a frenzy of military action.

The groundwork had been laid during President Bush's speech on the evening of September 11, 2001. He vowed to punish those responsible for harboring terrorists. Iraq became the prize. Pentagon planners started drafting battle plans. October 2002 was not only the first time I deployed in support of the Global War on Terror, it also marked Congressional approval for the use of force against Iraq. Oplan 1003V was conceived, a vicious campaign attacking Iraq from the north and south.[13] Negotiations began with Turkey for the use of their land and airspace. All of our previous military bases in Turkey were closed and there was no U.S. military presence left. Turkey said no. Their denial left a kink in the plan, but military planners adjusted timelines and deployment schedules to ensure our greatest success.

The United Nations, ever loathe to allow matters to denigrate to open combat, passed Resolution 1441 in November 2002, citing Iraq was in 'material breach of its obligations' concerning nuclear, chemical and biological weapons programs. The White House continued to make pleas for Saddam Hussein to step down while flexing its muscle at the prospect of invading the desert nation. One thing I would come to learn is that the Iraqi people are very proud. How could we assume a man who had been in power for so long would just step aside and let us have our way? Optimists and fools may have thought otherwise, but war was a foregone conclusion.

I found it increasingly difficult to focus on my exposure to the war in Afghanistan. I knew that, being part of the XVIII Airborne Corps and a rapid response deployment unit, 1-377 FAR (AASLT) would be deploying to Iraq. Common sense said the Army was going to need as much firepower as possible to crush the Iraqi army as fast as

---

[13] Oplan 1003V was the U.S. military designation for the Iraq invasion or Operation Iraqi Freedom. Initially classified Top Secret, the information was leaked from undisclosed sources to various media outlets.

possible. The 100 hour campaign twelve years earlier was not forgotten by many, leastwise not the Iraqis. Everyone expected the coming war to be far worse. Initial estimates prepared for 10,000 Coalition casualties on the first day. I don't care how much training you've had, there is nothing to prepare you for that kind of bloodshed. The United States hadn't seen a battle of that magnitude since the D-Day invasion of 1944.

President Bush went before the U.N. to present the case for war against Iraq. Opposition from nations on the Security Council was stiff, most notably from France and Germany. Both nations were involved in operations in Afghanistan but once France openly voted against us all of the French soldiers-with their obscenely tight uniforms- seemed to disappear from view. Funny how some things don't change. In an impassioned plea, the president spoke of atrocities and the blatant disregard for U.N. jurisdiction by the Hussein Regime.

The speech did not fall entirely on deaf ears. Several nations stood beside us. Great Britain was our staunchest ally and would play a major role in the invasion. Others pledged monetary and logistic support. In the end the U.N. did not vote to approve the use of military force in Iraq, but it didn't matter. America and Iraq were on a collision course that stretched back twelve years. The conclusion was going to be reached soon enough. Combat forces began deploying to Kuwait.

March 2003

War was so close now. The world waited with tense anticipation, regardless of opinion or belief. A few Middle Eastern nations quietly urged Saddam to step aside, to avoid the ruination the coming war was going to leave his nation in. Iraq remained resolute. They intended to defy us until Baghdad fell. A lot of good men and boys were about to die for the vanity of a few.

Don't get me wrong, I fully supported the invasion of Iraq and continue to do so. Some things just can't be solved through empty words and well meaning gestures. The only way to deal with a dictator was through decisive violent action. You'd think the world would have remembered that after WWII, but no. Humanity's greatest failing is our inability to remember the relevance of the past.

Tensions continued to heighten. There was giddy excitement in Bagram. Many of us requested to be transferred, afraid we were going to miss everything. While not necessarily true, there is a certain level of disappointment to be taken from *not* deploying with your own unit and taking part in a major event like the invasion of a country. It was a great honor to be selected to go to Afghanistan at the beginning and help punish those forces responsible for the deaths of nearly 3000 innocent civilians. It also wasn't enough.

Back home, most of the Army was in some stage of pre-deployment preparation. My own unit was going through a cycle of hurry up and wait. Operational security is paramount to any successful mission. Soldiers weren't allowed to tell their families what was going on. I find it difficult to imagine the suffering a spouse must go through as her husband waits for that last minute phone telling him to report in full gear. Life was so much easier as the soldier. We could put our families and normal lives behind us once we got there. We don't have a choice. Men die otherwise. The spouses had nothing but their want and need to reunite with loved ones.

At last 1-377 deployed. I saw the original deployment orders and they were not on it, a good reason for the steady stream of false alarms. Ever since the first Gulf War in 1991 our Charlie Battery was stationed at Fort Campbell, KY with the 101st Airborne. They deployed, we were supposed to deploy with them. The plan called for Charlie Battery, but not the rest of the battalion. That wasn't good enough. I'm not sure how he managed it, but our battalion commander got the green light to go. He had just finished a tour at the University of Southern California as an ROTC instructor. This was his first assignment back in the rotation. He intended to make the most of it.

A buddy of mine told me the old man took the intercom from the stewardess once the plane landed in Kuwait and gave a rousing speech in which he cried. That's never a good sign. A leader shouldn't cry in front of his men BEFORE the war. Too many doubts surfaced and more rumors started. Making matters worse at the time our CSM was solely concerned about getting the 'fat tires' his unit used for their howitzers during Operation Desert Storm. Fat tires? Seriously? Your unit is about to go to war and the only thing you wanted was fat tires? I was glad to have been in Afghanistan when I found that out. He didn't last anyway. Scuttlebutt had him getting relieved after a hefty disagreement with the Old Man. He was sent home and transferred only a few months into the war.

At last, the time had come. There was no more waiting. No more empty rhetoric or hoping for a quick surrender to alleviate the coming bloodshed. President Bush's timeline expired. It was now time for action. On March 20, 2003, he sat down to address the nation:

> "My fellow citizens. At this hour, American and coalition forces are in the early stages of military operations to disarm Iraq, to free its people and to defend the world from grave danger. On my orders, coalition forces have begun striking selected targets of military importance to undermine Saddam Hussein's ability to wage war. These are opening stages of what will be a broad and concerted campaign."[14]

These words would haunt many of us for months. I was forced to watch them from the JOC as my friends, my soldiers, and the people I had spent most of my military career with back at Fort Bragg were suddenly thrown into a massive invasion involving nearly 35 nations in various capacities. It was disheartening, but inspiring. We sat in awe, much like most of you reading this, as Baghdad was bombed remorselessly. The 'shock and awe' campaign produced spectacular results with relatively few civilian casualties. (Any civilian life lost in a war is too much, but it could have been so much worse. Baghdad was under attack, but not in the terrible ways of WWII.)

I quickly grew dissatisfied with my job. I wanted to be in Iraq. I needed to be in Iraq. That damned desert country had been a thorn in my side since the day I joined the Army and here I was missing the whole fucking thing. God must have one sick sense of humor. Eventually the days blended together. I gave up hope of leaving Afghanistan early. Compounding my personal troubles, I had been involuntarily extended.

June 2003

Some things just don't turn out the way we want no matter how hard we try to make it happen. Going home was one of those things. Time finally came for my flight home. Like the song says, my bags were packed and I was ready to go. We formed up in the marshaling area and waited. A few Afghanis were cutting pipes and chain link fence towards the rear of the yard. The sun had only been up for a few hours and it was already miserably hot. Spirits were naturally high.

---

[14] President George W. Bush's speech at the beginning of combat operations in Iraq.

A sudden scream ripped the tranquility apart. I looked up in time to see a large chunk of something flying through the air. We moved as it crashed down beside the guy next to me. It was part of a shirt sleeve with a nice bloody chunk of flesh. I looked back to where the scream came from to see an Afghan worker clutching what remained of his right bicep. Somehow he managed to cut off most of his muscle with a circular saw. The man feinted. An MP walked over to see what was going on. He didn't have much urgency, but he eventually called for help.

SPC Walker, another of my soldiers from Fort Bragg who happened to be assigned as the G-3's driver, got his vehicle so they could load the wounded man up and take him to the hospital. I'm sure things weren't as severe as the lump of flesh suggested. The man's partner was already laughing even as he let the man fall to the ground. Conversely, I'm also sure that Col. Yarbrough was extremely pissed when he saw the back of his vehicle bloodstained and smelling.

Then the good news came. Our bird had not arrived. I was convinced this was all part of some cosmic scheme designed to pay me back for spending four days in Germany. Word filtered to us that the President was touring the Middle East to drum up support for the war in Iraq and needed every available C-17 for his hefty entourage of vehicles, press reporters, and military staff advisors. It's good to be king; not so good being the peasant. We stayed another seven days before the real C-17 showed and even then we didn't believe it until we were seated and preparing to taxi.

The big plane lumbered down the runway and lifted off, headed for Karshi-Khanabad or K2 Air Base in Uzbekistan. Finally it was over. Afghanistan was behind us but the war was far from over. My real unit had already deployed to Iraq in support of the 101st Airborne Division and there was no way I was going to sit home and wait for them to come home.

We arrived, after too many stops, at Fort Bragg and went through the very informal welcome home ceremony. Of the three I would come to have this was by far the least exciting. Plenty of family members were here, holding signs and waving flags. A motorcycle group was there, all vets, to support us. We got off the plane, having to step in a pan filled with some cleaning solution to kill any germs lingering on our boots, and then filed into the pax shed. The garrison commander greeted each of us as we de-boarded.

Another officer gave a less than rousing speech that still left us feeling good. We had gone to war, gone to serve our country and defend our way of life. Very few people get that privilege. It felt good knowing we had done our jobs and come back with all hands. No one will ever be able to take that away from me no matter what might happen. Lost in the euphoria of the moment, I started looking around for my wife. I didn't find her, and the crowd wasn't that big.

I had already made up my mind that I did not want to be married anymore. The only thing left was to figure out how to end it. I had tried staying together with her for my daughter's sake but that only made us more miserable. Almost as if adding insult to injury, I returned home after eight calendar months to no one. Captain Kim, our rear detachment commander and man I first met in Korea in 1998 as a newly commissioned lieutenant, met me at the reception but my wife was nowhere to be seen. I noticed how most wives were dressed extremely nice with their hair and makeup done.

Disappointment filled my heart. I dearly wanted and needed to see my daughter again. She was only a year old when I left, now she was almost two. Captain Kim offered to give me a ride back to battalion headquarters where I could turn my weapon in and drop off my bags. He even offered me a ride home after. I had no choice but to accept. We drove to the other side of the tarmac where the bags were being unloaded. I snatched mine up and threw them in the back of his pickup when I spied my wife heading my way.

She was dressed in a dirty tank top and sweat pants. I was insulted to say the least. She gave me some excuse about helping a friend move and she forgot…blah blah. I had stopped listening the moment she opened her mouth. Instead I reached for my daughter. Thoughts of her were the only thing that kept me going when times got bad. Her smile, the way she laughed and giggled when I played with her. Little Ashlynne cried and tried to stay away from me. She didn't recognize me. My heart shattered.

I was home but should have stayed in Afghanistan. At least things made sense there. Fortunately, I didn't need to wait long before I was getting back on a plane and heading to Iraq.

Soldiers from C Battery, 1-377 FAR (Air Assault) in position outside of Mosul, Iraq, 2003.

MSG Jeffrey Mays, April 2003

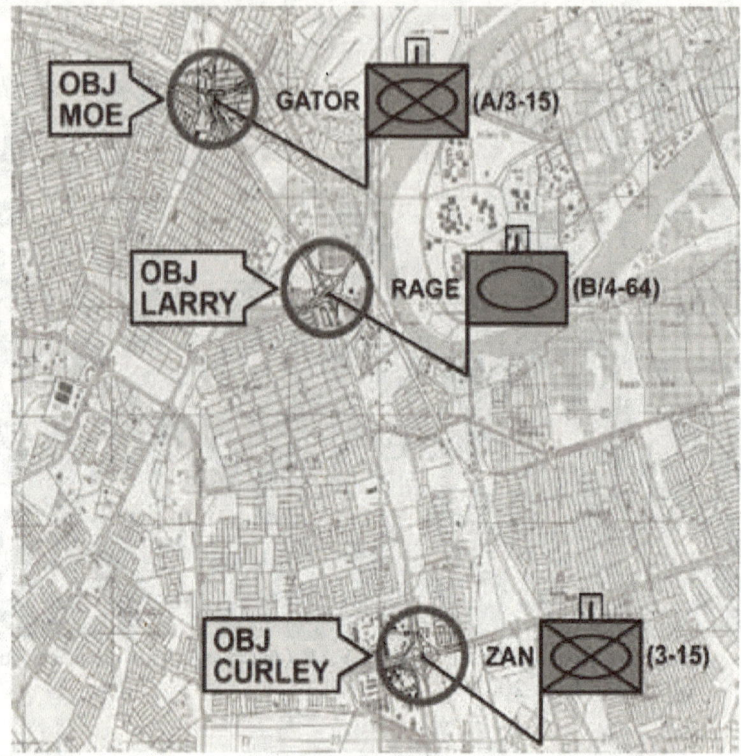

3rd Infantry Division Thunder Run II operation concept (unclassified)

TCP overwatch, Mosul, Iraq Nov 2003

Northern Iraq Dec 2003

Al-Faw Palace, Baghdad, Iraq Summer 2005

KBR escort detail, Zhako, Iraq Dec 2003

A BTRY 1-377 FAR Camp Doha, Kuwait Jan 2004

PART TWO:
Operation Iraqi Freedom I

"I can hear you, the rest of the world can hear you and the people who knocked these buildings down will hear all of us soon."- President George W. Bush

Chapter Six: Full Circle

Each of our lives is defined by significant events. Iraq certainly seemed to fit that description for the duration of my Army career. Ever since the day I went to the local recruiter in August of 1990 and told him I wanted to be a soldier I was haunted by the tyrannical reign of Saddam Hussein. I sat in class in 1989 and watched U.S. military operations in Panama, wishing I was there, doing my part. There was never any doubt that soon I would raise my right hand for the first time and speak the oath of enlistment.

Though I was still in high school, the Army eagerly accepted me as a future cannon crewmember. Of course I still had to graduate school before I could go play Army. Two weeks after I enlisted I was sitting in my bedroom watching the news. My world changed that night. The desert country of Iraq had just invaded neighboring Kuwait and President George H. W. Bush immediately sent a ghost force from the 82nd Airborne to secure Saudi Arabia from Iraqi aggression.

I don't remember whether I was more scared or excited. The buildup lasted months. My recruiter got tired of me constantly calling to ask if I could get out of school early and go to Kuwait. No means no so I was forced to watch the night vision images of Baghdad desperately trying to fight off Coalition bombers with the rest of the world. Now it was happening all over again. I was forced to watch a considerably more violent repeat of the January 1991 aerial campaign. Baghdad was in flames. Army divisions were rolling through Iraq with minimal resistance I got to watch it from the big boards in the JOC in the middle of an already forgotten war. I was ready to go home.

Finally being home, I felt alienated from most everything. The motor pool I had spent a decade working in was empty, reminiscent of a Wild West ghost town. I walked the empty halls of battalion headquarters seeing flashes of the men who should have been there. The men left behind weren't the cream of the crop. There were reasons

74

they were told not to go, and most of them were bad. Life quickly grew miserable and I felt lost in my own miseries.

Home life was less than stellar. Work was pointless. I didn't really have much reason to go to either one. Add to that an unquenchable desire to be with my guys in Mosul and I was downright unhappy. I had had enough and I was only home for a few weeks. I made the SFC promotion list back in August of 2002 and was still waiting to get pinned. Most of the school slots were cancelled so our men could deploy with as much combat strength as possible. I guess I slipped through the cracks.

SFC Cofield, my old buddy who tried to steal my Afghanistan slot from under me a year ago and now conveniently hadn't deployed to Iraq, seemed downright pissed that he hadn't been able to cancel my school date, but who cares? I was in my car heading off to Fort Sill, OK for the next five weeks. I sat through classes and learned a job that I already knew. I was the only one in my small group who had a combat patch from this war. Anyone who had been to Fort Sill can feel the pain of being stuck in the middle of nowhere. I felt like I was stranded in a warped form of Hell ever since I got home. I got promoted halfway through. Me and a couple other guys promoted ourselves in the hotel on the night our orders became official. It beat standing in a long drawn out ceremony. Thankfully the course passed quickly and I was soon on my way back to Fort Bragg.

The best news I got during those few months at home was SFC Cofield grinning as he told me that I was being sent to Iraq. About fucking time! This rear-d stuff was absolutely horrible. I was tired of hearing from whiny wives and cheating spouses about how their husbands weren't writing them. What made them think I cared and what was I supposed to do about it? Did they think that by crying to us we would magically make their husbands call home or write a long letter? Those men were at war and had more pressing concerns. Not to mention that a great many soldiers were in the same marital position as me. They didn't want to be married either.

I wouldn't stereotype soldiers any more than their spouses. People are people and there is nothing for it. Our CSM's wife came in one day demanding this and demanding that. She was only a Staff Sergeant and we all outranked her. She got tossed out the door on her ass and told to come back with some respect for her superiors. One thing I absolutely despise is when spouses wear their husband's rank.

Him I might have to listen to, but she needed to stand at parade rest and wait for me to address her.

Rear detachment is not a place for healthy soldiers to be. Good soldiers withered and died, much from their own stupidity as the inactivity and boredom. Family members got out of control; some for good, most for bad. Those are the events America doesn't see. The events the news fails to report. How many spouses go out and start living the 'party life' the moment their husbands are safely strapped into that big iron bird across the Atlantic.

One of my soldiers found out that his wife and his 20 yr old daughter were already out in the club picking up men the very night he deployed. Another came home to his wife's boyfriend living in his house. Is it any wonder (not that I would condone such) that soldiers go crazy and harm their spouses? Imagine coming home after twelve months of fighting, watching your men bleed and die, to find your wife pregnant by another man. How would you react?

Rear-D was a totally miserable experience; one that I believed couldn't get any worse. I would find out just how wrong I was after I returned home from my third deployment. Those were the times I almost wished I had a gun and the ability to take action accordingly. As it was now, we had the pleasant task of escorting one of our own down to the Marine Corps prison facility at Camp Lejuene. The kids got busted for doing drugs and was found guilty through a trial by court martial. A handful of us went through the MP training course on how to transport a prisoner. We took turns guarding him in the jail on Fort Bragg, a task I found redundant since it was located within the main MP building. Something about doing someone else's job just pisses me off but oh well.

Guilty, the time came to escort him down to a cozy prison stay for the next few years. I personally never understood the lure of drugs and sure didn't know why anyone was willing to throw their lives and careers away because of them. I found it amusing how he laughed and joked with us as we stopped at a McDonald's for dinner en route to Camp Lejuene. He was trying to be one of the guys and was putting on a pretty good show until he noticed how close we were starting to get.

The back of the van steadily grew quieter as the miles rolled by. We pulled into the base around 1900 or so. SFC Cofield and I went inside to do the handover paperwork while the others downloaded the prisoner's bag and had him wait. All of the fences and guards was very sobering, not to mention the chains and cuffs on his ankles, waist and wrists. Regardless, he was still trying to keep face and be tough for us. That changed as fast as a freak North Carolina summer thunderstorm.

The Marine Lance Corporal, the equivalent of an Army Private First Class, stepped outside and cleared his throat. He was a little guy with a big bark. He jumped off the deck and ripped our prisoner up one side and down the other, driving him to the point of tears. I had to turn around to keep him from seeing my laughter. It was hilarious for us; a nightmare for the prisoners. Drugs don't pay. Mission complete, we hoped back in the van and went home.

By now I couldn't wait to get back to the fight. I was slowly dying. Then a new mission came down. One I wasn't enthused to perform but needed to. From Bragg it was a 10 hour ride to Fort Campbell to go pick up a few guys who were coming home early: really early. They had only been deployed for three months and were coming home for good. I found that odd and disrespectful to the rest of the unit. You just don't leave your unit unless you're too shot up to continue. One of the guys was a battery commander.

We got to Campbell and spent most of the evening/night waiting for the bird to get in it. They showed up in the middle of the night and we hustled them into the van. Neither one would shut up. The others who went with me might have been impressed but an extended vacation in Afghanistan I didn't want to hear about their limited Iraq experience. That didn't stop them. They talked all 10 hours home, mostly repeating the same story when they thought no one was paying attention.

The only time it got concerning was when we stopped at some run-down gas station in eastern Tennessee. Most of the people didn't have teeth and they were all eyeing us like we were the Union coming to take their southern rights. I don't think I have felt that uncomfortable in a very long time. We convinced the one guy to stop telling stories, (there's nothing quite like hearing someone tell every single person he met "hi, I just got back from Iraq") and jumped in the van. To say the least none of the locals were impressed and I got the distinct impression one of them was ready to pull a knife. It was time to go.

We got back to Bragg and it was time to start the train up to deploy. There wasn't much actual train up. We watched a few videos and sat through a slew of incredibly boring lectures I was positive my grandfather endured before getting on the boat for Europe. It's funny how the Army tries to fight change and keep things the same. All we did was trade enemies and locations.

During this period the 101st managed to trap and kill Uday and Qusay Hussein in a vicious firefight that was rebroadcasted for a few days back home. My battery had the luxury of being at a palace swimming pool that day. It was a great success for us, but also marked a turning point in the war. The city of Mosul had been relatively peaceful until that day. We started getting attacked frequently once Saddam's kids were killed. The days of patrolling downtown Mosul with little fear of being attacked were over. The war had finally come back to Mosul.

None of that mattered to those of us trapped in the purgatory of rear-d. I went back to the rifle range, and then again. Aside from alleviating a lot of pent-up aggression, going to so many ranges allowed me to spend hours cleaning my rifle; a soldier's favorite pastime. One thing I was overly proficient at was cleaning weapons. The day came for us to load out. It was a day I had long anticipated, going all the way back to the build up phase while I was still in Afghanistan.

I grabbed my bags in the predawn hours and headed to work. Any doubts were gone this time around. I knew what I was getting into and where I was going. By now 377 and the rest of the Screaming Eagles had settled down in the northern city of Mosul. After saying goodbye to my wife, I jumped in the van and never looked back.

We took another 10 hour van ride, this time packed with men and gear and got to Fort Campbell on a Sunday evening. Everyone was starved and the only thing open on base was a KFC. There were only a handful of patrons. Most of the 101st was long gone. The place was a ghost town. Fortunately for us we were entertained by a few brand spanking new privates trying to talk themselves into being hyped for the deployment.

"Yeah, yeah, yeah. We going to Iraq baby!" one said in a pitiful attempt to impress his girlfriend.

I found it touching but she was a moron if she fell for his bullshit. He kept a good poker face but things like that change the minute the bird goes wheels up and it goes from being talked about to a real thing. They only looked at us once and quickly averted their eyes when they noticed my 10th Mountain combat patch. (I figured I might as wear that one since I had to work for them and the Corps patch was not something combat troops wanted to wear. 10th Mountain it was!) We finished dinner and headed to Campbell's airfield. The 101st had the most aviation assets out of any Army unit and their airfield was large enough for passenger planes to take off, making it the perfect place to stage and deploy.

One thing you learn quickly about the Army is the need for redundancy. I was fortunate enough to have gone through the pre-deployment medical screening before Afghanistan and again at Bragg before leaving. Now I got to do it again at Campbell in the main hangar. I never believed the saying you can have too much of a good thing until that night. Manifest call was at midnight so we had four hours to cycle through the last minute medical stations.

I think I have had every shot man conceived during my time in the Army. I was in Korea in 1998 when someone decided it was a great idea to inoculate us against anthrax. Those were quite possibly the most painful shots I ever received, all eight of them. The golf ball sized knots the virus left in our triceps hurt like a bitch for about a week. Soldiers being soldiers, we kept each other on our toes by sneaking up from behind and slugging each other over the shot area. Perhaps not the brightest idea, but what can you expect from a hundred early twenty something men?

The one shot I absolutely refused to get was the smallpox vaccine. No freaking way. I already had eczema and technically wasn't supposed to receive the shot anyway. That damned sure didn't stop the doc's from trying to stick me. The hangar was in total confusion so I just slipped by that station and threw some initials on my deployment papers. You can keep your smallpox. Anthrax was enough.

Finally finished, a little forgery not included, I turned my paperwork in and went to sit on my ruck. A baggage detail was raised and they took all of our gear except for the rifle, helmet, body armor and a small carryon bag. One thing of note I should mention is that when the Army first deployed to Iraq we were woefully under prepared for the enemy bombing campaign that followed the initial invasion. Roadside bombs or IEDs are a terrible, terrible thing. One of my friends in an engineer unit had gotten blown seventeen times in his armored vehicle during the first Iraq rotation. My unit had no armored HMMWVs and a limited amount of armor plates for our body armor. Most of the time we had to share our plates when we weren't on a mission and a buddy was. So I deployed to Iraq without any armor in my vest. It made a terrible fashion accessory and sure wasn't going to stop a bullet, much less shrapnel from an IED or rocket attack.

The route was pretty much the same as my first plane ride, minus the refueling stop in Newfoundland. We only spent a few hours in Germany this time. There was no four day layover to dull the stress of going to war. We were wheels up and cruising over the Mediterranean Sea in no time. The pilot was nice enough to inform us when we passed over the pyramids of Egypt. Even at the altitude we were flying they were an impressive sight. The next stop was Ali Al Salem Airbase in Kuwait.

Kuwait is by far the most miserable place I have been. You wouldn't think so judging by location and the amount of oil money the tiny country has. Kuwait City is beautiful and the country is overly clean with good roads and a strong infrastructure, but it is about twenty degrees hotter than any place I have ever been. Making matters worse, it was filled with people who would never hear a shot fired in anger. How was I supposed to relate to them?

The 101st Airborne Division had the distinction of sitting in Kuwait and watching the invasion, just like I did in Afghanistan. I wonder if they got to listen to a table full of contractors bet each other who wouldn't drink a full bottle of maple syrup at breakfast on the morning the 'shock and awe' air campaign began. Either way, my unit was disgruntled during the wait. All that waiting has a way of sapping your strength, draining the one thing you need to keep going in the heat of battle. That's when the bad things happen, things good men would normally be ashamed of. (Oh and the winner, if he could be called such, downed an entire bottle for the sum of 60$. Hopefully his bowels recovered in quick order.)

SPC Mark Lemere was a young soldier recently assigned to A Battery, 1-377 FAR. He deployed to Kuwait and got to sit and wait. I'd already heard the events he described to me so it wasn't just the ramblings of an angry soldier. This is his account of just how badly things can get out of control when you are forced to sit and wait without guidance and the kind of damage that happens to the cohesion and morale of a unit:

It was prior to us joining the 101st's push through Baghdad and up to Mosul. We were in these hot ass tents with no ac in Kuwait, sleeping on the floor or on our bags, loading ammo and prepping the trucks for the long ass convoy that awaited us. Our First Sergeant was hated in the battery and someone wrote in the portajohn outside our tent and I quote "If we go forward with 1SG Xxxx in charge, I swear on my mother's grave that I'm going to kill him." The First Sergeant found out and called the whole battery to formation on the hot sand with the battery commander and had us file through the portajohn one at a time to read it. You could tell that it was heavy on his mind. Knowing that your men had no confidence in your leadership ability must be terrible.

The battery commander actually drew a line in the sand and told us, "Anyone willing to follow First Sergeant Xxxx and me into Iraq needs to step across this line." No one moved. The Sergeant Major was standing in the back and finally convinced the NCOs to cross first. The rest of the battery followed but not because of the commander or First Sergeant.

We crossed the berm into Iraq and drove north where we caught up with the 101st in an improvised FOB in a random field in the middle of Baghdad. The city line almost completely surrounded the field and that night the Iraqis had hours and hours of celebratory fire with tracers making spirals in the air all around the field. The First Sergeant went out of his mind being scared and called everyone out of their sleeping bags (on top of trucks, on the hoods of trucks, on the ground) and to make a 360 perimeter in the prone around our formation of trucks. The sky was full of red tracers, an image I'll never forget and how our First Sergeant was scared out of his mind, at the Iraqis and at the battery. He got the nickname 'Scary Nine" after that.

Events concerning Alpha Battery's advance through Iraq were the farthest thing from my mind at the moment. I was deployed again and focused on the task ahead. Ground guides shuffled us to waiting buses and we were off, heading north for Camp Virginia. A series of U.S. bases had been established in northern and western Kuwait to prep for the invasion. Most of them were relatively inactive now, leaving a handful as hubs to push equipment and reinforcements into Iraq for the divisions taking part in the invasion. Camp Virginia was large enough to house a few brigades, though it only had a skeleton garrison and a few hundred replacements to push out.

We got to spend one night at Virginia before being divided into two chalks and told to wait for outgoing planes. A pair of C-130s came in later that day, ready to take us up to the far northern city of Mosul. I was on chalk two, along with SPC Walker and the others from my unit. We expected to wait a few more hours but Army logic took over. The first plane broke down on the runway, empty. Instead of taking the soldiers from chalk one and putting them on our plane, the people in charge decided to bypass them all together and load us up. It's not like the plane was specifically intended for us. First come first serve and all that.

We loaded the bird and took a short, choppy flight north. I stayed awake long enough to see Baghdad. The city was mostly dark. Getting electricity up and running was proving problematic for the Iraqis since the bombing campaign. Riding in any type of aircraft normally puts me to sleep so it was only fitting I dozed off en route to our final destination. It was a two hour flight from Kuwait to Mosul and one the pilots was determined to make it interesting. They performed maneuvers intended to confuse enemy antiaircraft fire, making more than one soldier queasy to the point of vomiting. I'd been on enough C-130s to know the heady fumes filling the interior and the bonkers flying of the pilots were a cocktail you never got used to.

The best part of the trip was flying with our young friends from the Fort Campbell KFC. SFC Allen and I noticed they got quieter the closer we got to the warzone. They reminded me of the prisoner I escorted down to Camp Lejuene. SFC Allen looked over at the two terrified kids and gave his huge smile. "Yeah, yeah, yeah, we in Iraq baby!'

We laughed all the way off the plane as both soldiers could only sit and gulp down their rising fear. As I said before, a soldier takes humor wherever he can find it. They should have known better than to try and impress girls when there were other soldiers around. It was a recipe for disaster. Perhaps now they realized going to war was no laughing matter. My old buddy Death was back, creeping along behind me. I wore the shackles of his specter far longer than I wanted.

Northern Iraq gets pretty damned cold in the winter. It was early November and freezing. Spots of snow were visible, surprising me greatly. We conducted a hasty inprocessing before being herded to overcrowded tents for what remained of the night. Thus far I was highly unimpressed with the entire process. Going to Afghanistan was much easier and proficient. Iraq was a waste of time. One of the first sights I witnessed was a row of port-a-potties so full the lids wouldn't close. There it was.

Dawn came and gave me my first images of the war in Iraq. Helicopters were buzzing all over the place. Hasty barriers and concertina wire was strung across the airfield. Guards patrolled the general area while countless others were filling sandbags and reinforcing the established perimeter. Even after months of occupation the Army was never satisfied with base security, and for good reason as we would tragically find out in early 2004 when a suicide bomber struck the mess hall on Mosul's main base.

All incoming personnel were loaded into the 101st database and sent out to the marshalling area to await our pickup. A convoy of my battalion's HMMWVs rolled up around lunch and loaded us up. It felt good to be back among familiar faces, even if they were reluctant to talk to us. One thing I quickly learned was how bad replacements felt. I'd seen war movies where guys who were absent from important events were ostracized when rejoining their units but never thought it would happen to me. I had been in Alpha Battery for my entire career minus two tours in Korea. And this was how they treated me? What the fuck? I went to war before all of them and they had the nerve to look down on me. I don't recall seeing any of them next to me during Christmas or Thanksgiving in Afghanistan.

We arrived in silence at the battalion logistics base or ALOC. First Sergeant Alexander greeted us. Finally, a man who actually talked to us! Nothing was worse than the feeling of being neglected by men you laughed and trained with only a few short months before. It is a feeling I never want to experience again. I'd known him for about the last six years but he was still above my pay grade so we weren't exactly friends.

The first friend I heard rather than saw. Big Vern Kinlaw was a monster of man who spent as much time in the gym as he did at work. He and I had worked together from my first day at Fort Bragg. I was greeted with a loud "Doooooou!" that instantly brought a smile to my face. Exhausted from days of travel and the let down of my arrival, I couldn't help but laugh.

"What's up rookie?" he asked as we clasped each other.

"I finally got here, man," I said.

"Where've you been?"

I smiled. "Afghanistan. I spent eight months over there."

"And they sent you over here?"

I shrugged. SGT Kinlaw was a veteran of the Gulf War and had been a friend for a long time. How could explain that I volunteered to leave home again so soon to be in Iraq? Fortunately I didn't need to. There was a lot to do and we still needed to get out to the main battalion compound.

We talked for a little more before First Sergeant (1SG or Top) Alexander came back out and told us our rides were here. 1-377 was positioned at a small electrical supply compound seven miles outside of Mosul proper. It was getting dark. Bravo Battery's 1SG was taking his men back out to the FOB and told us to hop in. I had worked for the

Silver Fox, affectionately named for his head of silver hair, once in the S-3 shop and he was a good man to be with.

Loaded up in the back of the 5 ton truck, he looked up and told us, "We need to get moving. It's getting dark and the 101st doesn't allow convoys at night."

SFC Allen didn't miss a beat when he looked back and said, "Then why the fuck are we leaving now?"

Those of us who had already been shot at enough broke out in laughter. Despite his apprehensions, we made it the seven miles to the FOB without incident. The scenery was remarkably similar to Afghanistan. Dumpy houses and buildings lined the roads. Trash was everywhere. The smell was awful. Stray dogs ran across the street and everywhere I looked where those little orange and white cars.

FOB Gunslinger was fairly large and made no sense. Our Charlie Battery decided that since they were alone at Fort Campbell they should be alone in Iraq. I'm not sure how or why, but they convinced the old man to let them take their own compound directly across the street. Tactically I suppose it was sound but their one hundred men occupied the same amount of real estate the rest of us did with four hundred.

We passed through a winding entrance, past the row of buildings the local Iraqis used as a cantina and barbershop. (After my first experience with a local national cutting hair I was disinclined to let them do it.) Old faces mixed with the new, fresh soldiers who had transferred in while I was off in the other war. Top dropped us off at battalion HQ where we were met by Maj. Jeff Toomer, another one of those guys I had known forever, at least since 97 when he was Bravo Battery's commander.

I got sent back to my old battery but any idea I had about being welcomed back quickly dissolved. The mood was dour at best. Everyone just wanted to go home and there was no end in sight. I dropped my gear next to an empty cot in the abandoned warehouse we'd claimed as home. The tin roof and sheet metal frame wasn't inspiring any confidence in our ability to defend against rocket or mortar attacks. I set it in my mind to get the 1SG to have some bunkers built. Afghanistan was sporadic, but the 101st was getting hit almost every night. I listened to our sister unit a few miles down the road taking a pounding like clockwork after the sun set.

Since they already had four other platoon sergeants, I was the fifth wheel. No one could figure out why they'd sent me back to Alpha, but here I was. I was home again. I settled in and prepared to tackle the new challenges Iraq presented. I might have been deployed, but (in my mind) I had already missed all of the good stuff.

Chapter Seven: To War!

The world bore witness to the frightening power of the Coalition forces in April 2003. Families sat glued to the television as bombs and rockets rained down on Baghdad. What those at home didn't see was the fury unleashed on the Kuwait-Iraq border. It has been estimated that nearly the first five miles of Iraqi lines were destroyed under a withering barrage of cannon, rocket and missile fire before the first tank from the 3rd Infantry Division growled forward.

Unknown to most of the world, the conventional U.S. ground forces included, Special Operations Forces had already been operating within Iraq. Navy SEALs were tasked with securing the offshore oil refinery before the Republican Guard had the opportunity to destroy it. Green Beret teams dropped into western Iraq and captured two airfields that would facilitate the quick movement and refueling of helicopters during the push up to Baghdad.

Artillery positions were a favorite target. The classic assault on German howitzer emplacements at Sainte-Marie-du-Mont on D-Day is still taught in the infantry school and in the hallowed halls of West Point, under the watchful gaze of the statues of George S. Patton and Dwight Eisenhower. Whether the Green Berets followed the textbook assault or not is moot. They executed their task with extreme proficiency. Each little task helped clear resistance before the first M-1 Abrams tank crossed the berm.

Conventional American and British forces attacked with ruthless efficiency. The Iraqi defense crumbled like a wave striking a child's sand castle. The blitzkrieg style offensive was more successful than anyone in the Pentagon could have hoped for. This was both a blessing and a boon. Armored columns pushed deep into Iraq, often outrunning their supply lines. Whole companies were forced onto flat bed trailers in order to conserve fuel. Everywhere the Iraqis fell back.

Iraq was supposed to be a two-pronged offensive. Turkey had already denied the use of airbases and staging areas so planners were forced to compromise. The 4th Infantry Division redeployed from the north to Kuwait. They were going to have to attack north along with everyone else. That left the only other viable asset capable of getting deep behind enemy lines; the 173rd Airborne Brigade. Special Forces teams were operating at will in northern Iraq thanks to the Kurdish army; the Peshmerga or *those who face death*. The 173rd jumped into northern Iraq and started attacking south with minimal resistance. (We'll forget that the airfield they jumped into was already secured by SF and Peshmerga elements.)

Only the vaunted Republican Guard stood and fought, but they were not enough. Most of their strength had been destroyed during the Gulf War in 1991. U.N. sanctions and the perpetual air presence in the no fly zones kept the Republican Guard in check. They were only a fraction of their pre-1991 strength when we hit them. It wasn't long before they fell back to defend Baghdad.

The blitzkrieg style advance moved much faster than anyone thought. Supply lines were stretched beyond capacity, struggling to keep up. Tanks were loaded up onto flat bed trailers and pushed forward in an effort to reduce fuel consumption. Tanks drink a lot of gas. The less time grinding through the southern Iraqi desert the better. A massive sandstorm halted the war, much to the defender's relief. Nothing they did was enough to even pause the Coalition.

Disasters happened. The now infamous Jessica Lynch incident could have been avoided but things happen in combat. What didn't make sense was how easily the Iraqis folded. Generals began to fear the area known as the Karbala Gap. Personally, I think they were reminded too much of the Fulda Gap in Germany; the supposed invasion route the Soviets were going to take when they went to war with the West. Regardless, our forces were drawing ever closer to Karbala.

The ancient city marked the beginning of the route into Baghdad. The Marines and British army were pushing up on the right. The 3rd Infantry Division was going to take Karbala head on. Saddam Hussein made a stand, a weak one. He sent hundreds of civilian vehicles towards the U.S; his Fedayeen. They were a paramilitary force whose name meant "Saddam's Men of Sacrifice".[15] Dressed in white and armed with AK-47s and RPGs, they attacked. And were destroyed. No fanatic can withstand a shot from the barrel of a main battle tank.

Our biggest concern was chemical weapons. The Karbala Gap was the red line, the last defense measure to slow or stop the Americans. We planned for thousands of casualties. Iraq was no stranger to chemical warfare. Tens of thousands of soldiers, Iraqi and Iranian, were killed by chemicals in the 1980s. Saddam then turned his

---

[15] It is estimated that the Fedayeen had between 30,000-40,000 fighters. They were all volunteers and reported directly to the Presidential palace, avoiding military channels entirely. Ironically, they were the ones who put up the most resistance to the Coalition by conducting a guerilla style war reminiscent of the Viet Cong.

chemicals on the Kurds to the north. It was no stretch of the imagination that he would do so against a militarily superior enemy deep in his nation.

The attack never came. The Fedayeen scattered after one failed attempt to attack the U.S. head on. Instead they began a guerilla campaign that had moderate success. Eventually Karbala fell. Baghdad was wide open. Coalition units took an operational pause once they got in position around the Iraqi capital. The first attack was against Baghdad International Airport (BIAP). The battle was long and furious, much more so than earlier fighting down south. Once that fell the 3rd ID prepared to enter the city proper.

Planners in Washington D.C. believed it was going to take five full divisions nearly five months to reach and then secure the Iraqi capital. American tanks and artillery were within range of Baghdad within weeks. The north was rolled up through the combined forces of the local Peshmerga and the 173rd Airborne Brigade with elements of the 10th Mountain Division and random Special Forces teams.

Contrary to popular civilian belief, not every soldier in the Army is a trigger puller. There is an average of four support soldiers for every one combat arms soldier. Most of those support personnel never expect to have to fire their weapon in combat nor do the overly dangerous missions. Staff Sergeant Jeffrey Mays was a communications specialist assigned to an artillery battalion in the 3rd Infantry Division. His job was to establish communication lines for advancing combat forces. Already a ten plus year veteran, he had no aspirations about getting into a serious firefight.

SSG Mays was the kind of man with a level head who normally knew better than to volunteer for craziness. He figured this mission wasn't going to be too much of deal and it was, after all, history in the making. American tanks rolling through one of the oldest cities in the world, the birthplace of modern civilization. Who wouldn't want to be a part of that? So, SSG Mays told his boss he wanted to go, figuring it would be relatively safe. He couldn't have been more wrong. This is his personal account of what is now infamously known as the Thunder Run II:

1745, 6 APRIL 2003

I stopped by brigade headquarters to talk to MSG Hunter. He asked if I would help him put together an M577 (tracked command vehicle) for the Thunder Run tomorrow. He outranked me so of course

I would. As I was helping him I asked about his plan. He told me that he was going to send a SPC and two PFCs on the mission tomorrow.

I asked him "MSG Hunter, do you really think that's a good idea?"

He told me no, but brigade wouldn't let him leave headquarters. He asked if I could spare an NCO to go with his guys to be in charge. I thought about my two NCOs. SGT Carpenter is a big ass kid, so no. SGT Davis will crack at the first sign of pressure so again, no. The only one left was me. I told MSG Hunter that I'd go with his guys on the mission. Little did I know that I would come close to dying that day!

7 APRIL 2003

0445. I'm a part of the second Thunder Run. We are what they call a "heavy metal" package, which means no soft skinned vehicles, or hummers. We were told it was supposed to take five divisions five months to take Baghdad. Where the hell were the other divisions? Third Infantry was the only division operating in or around the city. And it's a big ass city. The convoy is ready and we start driving.

We rolled by brigade headquarters and crept towards the city. I felt like superman! The group that I was with was supposed to secure Objective Curly. Curly was the main resupply route and vital to our operations in the area. There were 80 of us which comprised mostly of communications, maintenance, supply folks, medics and one Bradley with some infantry in it. We only had one tank. They called us Task Force Zan. Nobody was expecting us to find much resistance so we were support heavy. All of the enemy troops were supposed to have been wiped out when the infantry and armor went thru our objective a few days ago.

Everything was quiet for the first few miles. It wasn't until we passed through a mine field that the shit hit the fan! The tanks and Bradleys started shooting! They came over the radio and told everyone to button up, which means close up the hatches on the vehicles. Not me, I was gonna pop some caps in a few Iraqis! I saw an Iraqi standing under an overpass shooting. I squeezed off a couple rounds, he fell! Another one; popped his ass too! I heard bullets whizzing by my head! What the fuck! Guess I need to do like the man said and button up! As I was closing the hatch an RPG came within inches of my face! SHIT!

As I sat in the vehicle I heard the bullets hitting the side of it. It sounded like hail hitting a window. A LOT OF HAIL! I couldn't take it, I wanted to shoot! I opened the hatch and just as I did, I saw an Iraqi woman with a baby. She dropped the baby and pulled an AK-47 from under her dress! A Bradley's 20mm main gun cut her in half.[16]

The call came over the radio and told me that they couldn't put us in our primary RETRANS spot because there were Iraqis on top of the overpass. So we would have to setup beside the road. I opened the back door and was immediately greeted with bullets from everywhere! I closed it up quickly. Now as I said before, I ain't the smartest man in the world, but me and my guys were supposed to stand outside with no cover, bullets flying everywhere and setup an antenna? Not in this lifetime buddy! That dog just ain't gonna hunt! We closed up and setup what I called a "super whips" on top of the track. I jumped back in and checked the radios. It worked like a charm!

I opened the hatch and called one of the guys up with me. I told him we have to keep the site secure. Even though we have a Bradley with us, we have to fight. He just kept saying "Sergeant Mays we're gonna die, there's too many of them!" I told him 'shut up and keep shooting! If you stop shooting we WILL die!" After a few minutes of shooting, the Bradley just left us. They said they had to go 150 meters up the road to help 3-15 who was in a bad firefight. I remember thinking dude what the fuck! We need help here too!

As the Bradley was leaving I saw it shooting Iraqis. I saw one Iraqi get cut in half. His top portion fell back and his legs kept walking forward. WOW. Another Iraqi got blown into little chunks! There was a five or six story building on the far side of the road. It had Iraqi and Syrian fighters pouring out of it! What the fuck! Where are all these motherfuckers coming from?! I saw an Iraqi trying to surrender and as he stood up a technical (a white pickup with a gun mounted on it) slid into him and smashed him. It looked like the whole fucking Iraqi Army was trying to kill us!

I heard a screech; a technical pulled up in front of us and started shooting! I shouted at the guy that was in the hatch with me "close it, close it!" We closed the hatch and sat down. We were all alone on the side of the road. After a few minutes I heard voices at the back of the track. I could hear three distinct Iraqi voices trying to open

---

[16]   *I found out later that the baby was taken to our forward support unit. It stayed for a couple weeks before they found someone to take care of it. I wonder if that child will grow up hating Americans. J. Mays 2003.*

the back door of the vehicle. We were combat locked, but that didn't mean shit. They could just blow a hole in us. The technical was still shooting at us from the front. Right then I made a decision.

I grabbed a couple of hand grenades from the shelf in the vehicle and sat down. One of the guys looked at me and said "Sergeant Mays, what are you doing?"

I told him, "Dude, if by some chance they get in this track, they won't take us alive. I'm going to throw one grenade out at them and I'm dropping the other one in here with us. I will not let them take us alive!"

He looked at me with tears in his eyes and said 'as long as we're alive we got a chance."

I told him "Dude, do you really think they are gonna give us a chance if they take us?"

I heard a loud boom. The driver screamed "Sergeant Mays it's a tank, it's a tank!" SHIT, I thought it was an Iraqi tank. He said, "It popped yellow smoke!"

My mind raced. Yellow smoke? Iraqis don't use that shit, it's gotta be friendly! I heard a banging at the back door and some American voices. I opened the door and a sergeant asked "why the fuck are you guys on the side of the road by yourselves, you know there was a lot of Iraqis at the back trying to get in?" I told him that the Bradley we had for security just left us. He told us to follow him to a more secure area.

We rolled back a few hundred yards. I told the guys to get out and set up the antennas. The fighting wasn't as bad back there, yet. As the guys were on the ground setting up, I stood on top of the track. I heard something whiz by my head and turned to see three Iraqis squatting down on the side of a building taking shots at me! I told the guys, "Get in the track, get in the track!"

I grabbed my M16 and shot two of them, the other one ran. The next thing I saw was Iraqis and Syrians coming from everywhere around us! I shot and shot and kept shooting. They just seemed to keep fucking coming. You shoot one and three more take his place! What the fuck! We buttoned up again and five minutes later someone had called for "danger close artillery."[17]

---

[17] Standard U.S. Army field artillery doctrine defines 'danger close' as anything fired from 350 meters away and closer. The 155mm HE round has a kill radius of 50 meters and another 150 for wounding.

Artillery shells started falling everywhere around us! I could feel the vibrations inside the track. The driver started screaming "Sergeant Mays everyone is gone!" I asked him why he didn't follow them he told me "Because you didn't tell me to Sergeant!" What the fuck man!

We finally moved our vehicle over with everyone else. As soon as we did I heard on the radio that the brigade TOC had just been hit with a missile! They had four KIA and several wounded. The KIAs were two news reporters and two soldiers. I thought to myself the shit has REALLY hit the fucking fan now! The brigade TOC was in total chaos! I jumped out of the track to help out on the perimeter and as I did I saw one of our guys shooting a .50 cal on top of a vehicle. An RPG struck the top of the track and his body blew violently backwards. When they pulled him out he had no face or chest.

By now everyone was running dangerously low on ammunition, water and fuel. The mission was only supposed to last a couple hours, but so far it had gone on for nine long hours. This was literally the longest day of my life. I just knew that I was going to die, but I wanted to kill as many of them as I could so I could have some company in Hell! At one point even the chaplain picked up a weapon and started shooting. When asked why later he said "I was protecting my flock."

I got on the radio and called my Signal Officer (CPT Childers) and told him that we were running out of ammo and water, and if he could put together a crew and bring us some. As soon as I said that, the S-3 officer (MAJ Rice) got on the radio and said "Battleking 9 November (my call sign) we cannot bring you anything. You are a brigade asset and we can't risk sending anyone up there. There's a bad firefight at Objective Curly!"

No shit Sherlock! I'm at Objective Curly! I responded "Roger that, thanks for your support!"

Brigade eventually tried to send a resupply convoy up but it got hit hard. One of the platoon sergeants got caught in the chest with an RPG at close range. It blew him into bits (we never found all of him to send back home). One of the ammo trucks was hit with an RPG and caught on fire. A specialist ran up to the truck next to it jumped in and drove away. Later when asked why he did that, he said the driver of that truck had a family, if he died he would be missed. He had no family so if he died no one would miss him.

Division headquarters called out of nowhere and said there were too many American flags flying in Baghdad! In-fucking-credible. So everyone had to take them off of their vehicles. I guess the American public was having second thoughts about us taking Baghdad. Despite what we were going through at Curly, the Third Infantry had taken two palaces today. Up at another objective they are having problems with car bombers. It seems the bridge is filling up with blown up cars!

2-7 Infantry rolled up guns a blazing and saved our asses. I found out afterwards that there were over 300 Iraqi and Syrian fighters against us that day. After that I never volunteered for anything ever again. There was somewhat of a lull in the action for the next couple days and I really had time to think. I actually killed people. This was a lot different than the movies. When you sleep you see every face!

As I said before, they said it was going to take 5 divisions 5 months to take Baghdad. It only took one division 3 days!

Baghdad finally fell, despite Baghdad Bob's insistence that the Americans were nowhere near the ancient city. I guess he failed to look out his window at the armored columns marching through the streets. The last time I checked an M-1 doesn't look anything like a T-72. Not that he would know, considering most the Iraqi armor was destroyed in the first few days of the campaign. Whatever was left was already rusting in large fields of abandoned equipment. It wasn't long before Saddam went into hiding and Iraq officially surrendered.

Now came the hard part of the war, the part we hadn't been trained for. Regardless of what Washington or the media called it, we were involved in the complete occupation of Iraq. One of the first things the Coalition did upon the final surrender was to eliminate the army and police force. This would later prove to be one of the biggest and most consequential mistakes of the war. The American military is trained to fight, not occupy and rebuild a wounded nation. Valuable resources were drained to rebuild the infrastructure and to train and equip a new Iraqi army and police force. Both proved equally worthless in the early going of the new regime.

More terrorists flowed into Iraq, making the country the symbolic battleground between Muslim extremism and western belief. The media incorrectly continued to report about an insurgency when in truth ground forces were fighting foreign terrorists. Iranian suicide bombers funneled across the eastern border while Syrian dissidents tried the same in the west. Al-Qaeda decided to make Iraq their ultimate stand and the Coalition was caught unprepared. Throw in an emphasis on weapons of mass destruction and the uproar it caused back home and focus was scattered.

It would be irresponsible of me to theorize what went on behind closed doors in the White House or the Pentagon, or even the main palace in the now infamous Green Zone. My job, and that of the men and women who deployed to fight, was to win the war and pacify any uprising and terrorist presence. Two terror training camps were overrun en route to Baghdad. The presence of foreign fighters went largely unreported. Soldiers were dying daily, Coalition and Iraqi.

Civilian contractors flooded the California sized country. While a necessary part of the American led effort, they further muddled affairs. The first positive impact from having so many contractors in country was it freed soldiers to do the fighting instead of cooking food or washing laundry. That also meant more non-combat personnel were on the roads, producing potential liabilities. A reserve unit south of Logistics Support Area (LSA) Anaconda refused to perform their duty and run a convoy of much needed supplies north to Baghdad, claiming they were under armored and unprepared. 1-377 left Kuwait with no armor and didn't dare complain. There is something to be said for professionalism and selfless service.

Coalition forces settled in for the long haul. The uncertainty of when we would go home and put it behind us looming over each dawn. President Bush made history when he landed on the USS Abraham Lincoln in May and declared an end to major combat action in Iraq. The war instantly converted to stability and security operations, at least in the eyes of the powers that be. We were no longer invaders; we were occupiers.

Chapter Eight: FOB Gunslinger

The city of Mosul has Iraq's second highest population, totaling more than one million. It was once a jewel that dated back to the earliest days of biblical reference. Mosul was once known as Nineveh, legendary site of the tale of Jonah and the whale. Statues and mosques dotted the city of one million. The very church Jonah was reported to have prayed in still stands. Situated on the banks of the Tigris River, Mosul had once represented the potential Iraq might one day have. None of that mattered now. It didn't take long for the richness of history to be forgotten as the horrors of war returned.

The northern city lay in the middle of the Kurdish territory. The war spared most of Mosul thanks in large part to the UN no-fly zone and the heavy military presence of Peshmerga. The Kurds have long been hated and persecuted. Images of chemical attacks on Kurdish villages from the early 1990s can still be found. Fortunately, the Gulf War helped the Kurds extensively, which in turn helped the U.S. forces take down the Iraqi regime in the north quicker than the south. Mosul fell with relatively little violence when compared with most of the southern cities. The majority of Saddam's forces were either deployed on the Kuwaiti border in a wasted effort of repulsing the coalition advance or surrounding Baghdad in a last stand.

1-377 was sent to Mosul without specific purpose. Command from the 101st just didn't know what to do with the extra cannon battalion so they sent the firing batteries to secure the northern route in a pair of compounds seven miles north of the city and told them to put their howitzers up and grab their rifles.

The compound had few structures despite being relatively large. Concrete tresses to unfinished buildings lined the field to the rear like the skeletal remains of some great beast. Headquarters and Alpha batteries occupied a trio of tin sided warehouses close to the road. Battalion command took the small concrete building and Bravo battery was emplaced in a few buildings close to the gate.

There were no showers, no latrines, nothing to occupy a soldier's mind when he wasn't on a mission. Weights were brought in. Some of the more creative soldiers built showers from existing structures and a row of latrines. The water was usually cold and trickled on the best of days but the opportunity to bath was there.

May 2003

The 101st Airborne assumed control of a city of more than million from elements of the 10th Mountain and began stability and security operations. That meant a lot of trucks on the road and a lot of men and women constantly in harm's way. For us, life was on the road or being called in to pick up caches of unexploded ordinance (UXOs). Most of the heavy shooting was done so we got orders to park the guns in a motorpool and got a crash course in how to be an infantryman as well as military police. Nothing keeps a man on his toes like being thrown to the wolves and told 'good luck'.

Mounted patrols had the propensity to become quite terrifying. IEDs were still a relatively new concept for the insurgents and terrorists. Our battalion welder was able to find a ton of inch thick steel sheets and told to modify our soft skin HMMWVs. Layers of sandbags lined the floors and old style flak jackets were put on the door in the vain hope of stopping shrapnel from tearing through the cab. Triangular 'fins' were fixed to the back. Word was that a guy had been decapitated down in Baghdad by a tripwire strung across the road. The fins stood just high enough to cover the machine gunner in the back-hopefully. As a result our vehicles were bulky and grossly overweight.

SPC Lemere was one of the first ones to experience just how terrifying life on the Iraqi roads could be:

We were on our way back to the main camp in Mosul after picking up UXOs all morning and were looking forward to downloading the rounds and getting some good chow at the KBR tent. As we cut through the middle of the city just near the gate to the camp a dismounted infantry soldier walked up to the lead vehicle in our convoy and let us know that his squad was on patrol in the area and had found an IED about three to four hundred meters ahead.

We stopped in the middle of the city, locals staring at our 10 truck convoy; 3 of which were loaded up with African high explosive 155mm shells. I stayed in the driver seat of my M998 (with soft doors), as ordered, while the rest of the passengers and TC's got out to stand guard on the convoy. As we waited, you could sense a growing tension with us being there from the locals and sense of growing anxiety from the soldiers waiting in such an exposed area.

Suddenly, shots rang out from a roof top on the left side of the convoy and soldiers ducked behind the trucks parked in the middle of the road. Still I sat in my truck, about the 5th one back in the convoy, waiting for instructions. SGT Parker screamed at me to "make a second column and pull your truck up." I followed his order and broke the convoy in half and pulled my truck up to the left and pulled it alongside the lead vehicle in the convoy and all the trucks behind me followed.

As I executed I remember thinking, "I'm going to die, I'm going to die, I'm going to die." Because the driver side of the truck was exposed to the gunman and my door provided no protection from AK fire. A team took off after the gunman and the remaining soldiers took defensive positions between the vehicles. As the team returned empty handed, we all continued on to the camp and ate lunch laughing and pointing at each other claiming the other guy was more scared and wetting his pants.

His story was played out day after day, mostly without incident. It wasn't until SSG Ronald Savage's truck got hit with the first IED that things heated up. Sav was from Brooklyn and was a good friend, the kind you wanted to be with you when the shit hit the fan. He was also, I later discovered, the one guy you didn't want near you. He was a bullet magnet. Everywhere we went he came under fire. It seemed fitting he took the first IED.

The convoy was en route from AO Glory back to the FOB when the IED exploded. Shrapnel destroyed the windshield, blasting glass into the driver's eyes and face. More Iraqis got hurt than Americans. Sav checked the driver and jumped out to begin ground control. Crowds were gathering, some to cheer, and some to see what had happened. The combat lifesaver was a young kid from Nigeria. Sav found him on the back of the truck with a dazed look. He was in shock and unable to perform his duty.

Sav slapped him upside his head, hard. "Go up and fix Collins. He's got glass in his face."

Still dazed, the soldier ran forward to see what he could do. Wounded Iraqis were everywhere. An old man walked up to Sav with a piece of metal jutting out of his forearm. Sav ripped it out and wrapped a pressure dressing on the wound before sending him on his way. The crowd continued to get bigger. They were laughing now, taunting the wounded Americans and throwing rocks. The situation appeared desperate. One of Sav's soldiers, a deacon in the civilian world, waved his rifle up at the crowd lining the nearby wall.

"Please sergeant. Let me shoot one of them. If I shoot one they'll stop laughing and go away," he begged.

"Put the fucking gun down, Specialist," Sav ordered. "Don't pull that trigger."

Reluctantly he did so. The wounded convoy sat in place for a while before a passing infantry patrol swept the area. One of our gun truck convoys was en route from FOB Gunslinger but was too far out to get there in time. The infantry secured a wider perimeter and escorted our guys out of the kill zone.

Halfway through the deployment our sergeants major got swapped out. The real reason was well above my pay grade so I didn't worry too much about it. Bigger than all of us was the effect it had on morale and the lower enlisted's confidence in their leadership. I'd learned long ago that there were very few sergeant majors worth the money they were paid. These two were no different.

Our new battalion CSM must have watched *Platoon* before deploying. He pulled all of the NCOs available as well as junior officers into the chow hall for his inbriefing. Most of us had been through it too many times before and knew what to listen for. Anyone with radical ideas threatened the daily status and no one wanted things to change, especially not after getting into a solid routine.

The first thing he did was pop a cigarette in his mouth and light up. Exhaling a thick plume of smoke, he leveled his gaze around the room. We got the basics about where he came from, what he'd done in his career. Was he really smoking in our chow hall? Finally he got to the heart of the matter and told me everything I needed to know about the man.

"You all think you know about killing a man? You don't know shit," he told us sharply, adding a special hint of mean to his infliction. "I killed a fucking man back in Puerto Rico when I was young. I know what it's fucking like."

I didn't know whether to laugh or smack my head into the metal table. The Army promotion system is far from perfect and here was a perfect example. Good men and women get passed over for promotion so morons like John Wayne's Puerto Rican killing grandson can go through the ranks as high as possible. What an asshole! I rolled my eyes and looked around the room. No one was impressed.

At that point I stopped listening. He wasn't saying anything worth hearing and I had already gotten it into my mind that there was good chance he was going to get at least one of us killed. It was bad enough the Iraqis and various foreign fighters were already trying their damnedest to do that already, now we had this guy who thought he was Captain America. Maybe mom was right. Maybe I should have stayed home.

Dismissed, we ambled back to our barracks with the good sense not to say anything until we were sure he was not lurking around. The last thing we needed was a pissed of CSM breathing down our necks.

The threat of chemical warfare wasn't as large as what we expected in Afghanistan, though truthfully the threat was much higher here. Another day was mostly over when word came down from Division that there was a cloud of an unknown chemical substance blowing in our general direction. Panic ensured. The Army goes through great pains to conduct chemical warfare protection but despite the countless hours of donning protective masks and gear the overall confidence level is remarkably minimal.

Soldiers dug into their bags, desperately trying to at least find their masks. (I had taken an entire duffel bag of chemical gear to Afghanistan and wasn't even given a chemical protection suit for Iraq) I pulled mine, strapped it to my hip and went out to the guard towers to ensure the soldiers on guard duty were taken care of. Along the way I stopped at a pair of communication HMMWVs. Division had attached a signal element to us for nobody knew what reason.

Their senior SSG opened the back door and asked what was happening.

"There's a chemical cloud heading our way. You need to get your people into MOPP-1. There's no word on what the cloud is but be ready for a gas attack."[18]

Everything ceased. I saw a lot of eyes go wide. Whatever panic my men felt was doubled by this handful.

"SFC, we don't even have masks," the SSG told me. "What should we do?"

I looked around. There was no way any of them were getting my mask. Forget the bonds of fellowship. Anyone who has served will tell you there is no playing around with chemicals. We'd all seen the pictures of what Saddam did to the Kurds after the Gulf War. Training supported the selfishness of maintaining oneself before any other in this type of situation. Even the airlines insist you place your breather on

---

[18]   MOPP stands for Mission Oriented Protective Posture. It is an acronym the Army used to categorize different levels of chemical warfare preparedness. They ranged from gear readily accessible to being in full gear with mask.

before assisting the people near you. The Army was no different. Part of chemical training was that the proper way to test whether the air was clear or not was to have your most expendable soldier remove his mask under armed guard.

These kids in the commo truck probably weren't bad kids, but I had a greater responsibility to the fifty plus people under me. I clasped the sergeant on his shoulder and told him, "Button up this truck and hope it's sealed. With a little luck this cloud will either miss us or turn out to be nothing."

I felt like an ass without anything better to say. There was no secure area in our compound and no one had any extra gear, leastwise nothing that was readily accessible in time to prevent certain casualties. Fortunately nothing came of it. The cloud dissipated and life went back to normal.

Chapter Nine: Convoys and Firefights

December 2003

A bunch of us had been tasked with running convoy security from Mosul up to the town of Zakho, nestled along a pocket of the Turkish and Syrian border and moved over to the ALOC where we could reach the airfield quicker. From the moment I arrived in country I insisted on going outside the wire. Lead by example, right? When word came down for volunteers for this task I jumped. Nothing gets you back on track like a change of pace. For the next month we'd make the arduous trip north and then back again. It wasn't a bad gig and for 3 US dollars you could get enough fresh food to fill a table. We ate like kings at the border station.

It was another typical day in northern Iraq. We ran a convoy of KBR trucks back up to Zhako, up by the Turkish border and got a return convoy of about 75 fully loaded tractor trailers. The going was slow, really slow thanks to the dangerous roads and inexperienced drivers. The run usually took two and a half hours and stretched the limits of our fuel tanks. More than once one of our trucks ran out of fuel and had to be towed. Being stranded in a hostile environment is not a good feeling.

We were about halfway done with our run back, just south of the R-n-R city of Dohuk in what is now Kurdistan, when one of our trucks broke down. Lovely. Fortunately, we were in 'friendly' territory and under little chance for attack. The Kurds were a hated people for as long as history recorded. Good news for us was the terrorists and Baathists and were unwilling to get into a fight with the Kurds.

One of the first things I learned about Iraq was that there are children everywhere. We pulled to a stop at a light in Mosul and a teenager walked up with a cigarette in his mouth and about twenty additional cases in hand. The cigarette in his mouth was half smoked and he had an exceptionally hard look to him. It's a shame to see children mature this way. The joys of childhood were lost on most of Iraq's youth, certainly long before we got there.

"Hey mister!" he called. "What's your name?"

Everyone was Mister to the Iraqis. I looked back through my sunglasses, weapon pointed in the general direction and told him, "My name is Mister."

He smiled and said, "My name is Tony Montana."

Scarface? Fuck me. I waved my weapon at him and said, "Yeah, well he got killed. You need to go home before you are too."

He laughed and flipped me off. That's Iraq for you. This particular stop was in the middle of nowhere, about four hundred meters away from the nearest village. Not that it stopped the kids from rushing us. I stayed in the front along with SSG Marcus Roberts. Between our two trucks we had enough fire power to level the whole damned town and I was in no mood to deal with dozens of begging kids so I slumped down and tried to get some sleep, after I gave one of my soldiers a bag of butterscotch candies to pass out to the kids.

SFC Hawk and Lt. Holm went back to check on the busted truck. As luck would have it the vehicle was Sav's. Some guys just have no luck. The first hour crawled by. It was getting hot, even for winter. (Winter really happens in northern Iraq. It snows and gets so damned cold you think you're in Alaska.) Kids were laughing and playing with my soldiers, all under the apprehensive watch of parents and guardians. I was satisfied nothing was going to happen. We had a machine gunner covering the road ahead and another covering the left flank. We were safe.

Wrong. Enough AKs opened up I thought we just got ambushed. Kids ran screaming. The parents dropped to their knees with hands raised in surrender. SPC Edgar swung the M-249 squad automatic weapon (SAW) towards the village. "I see them on the roof, chief!"

The situation developed almost too quickly. I snatched up the hand mike to my radio and called the LT. "Sir, how much longer are you going to be with that vehicle?"

"Not sure. What's going on up there?"

Couldn't he hear it? "You might want to hurry. There's a lot of fire coming from the village."

SSG Roberts was probably the angriest man I have ever met, and both earned and deserved the nickname 'Angry Black'. He spit out the wad of chewing tobacco perpetually lodged in his cheek and stormed off to his HMMWV. By now my machine gunner had swung on the village and was asking to engage. "Cover the road. Edgar has the village," I ordered and jumped out of my truck.

Rob came back shaking his head. He took out a 40mm grenade and loaded it into his M203 grenade launched. "Fuck these motherfuckers, Freed."

While I reciprocated the sentiment, we weren't being shot at, yet. I took the fact the villagers were scared shitless as a sign they didn't have a clue as to what was happening. That changed when a beat up Mercedes came flying cross the sand. The driver was honking his horn like a madman. He slammed the brakes and jumped out. Thankfully he didn't have a weapon but was gibbering quickly in Arabic. What I would have given to have a translator. No one spoke English and none of us knew Arabic.

Fire from the village became sporadic, seemingly aimed into the sky. I'd already seen this trick in Afghanistan and was in no mood to get shot from a random bullet. The fifty pound steel plate I had in my chest armor wasn't going to be of much use with rounds coming straight down. It felt like an hour went by from the time we heard the first shot fired to now but in reality it was barely a few minutes.

The LT's truck pulled up and he jumped out. There wasn't much to report from my end. He told us Sav's truck was fixed and we were moving out. Good riddance. These Iraqis were just plain crazy. The convoy took off at best speed, which wasn't much given the amount of big trucks and the poorly kept winding road. Soon enough the village was well behind us. It took another hour before we reached Mosul's city limits. Then the rat race started. Iraqis have plenty of expensive cars, brand new Mercedes and BMWs, but they can't drive for nothing. They certainly didn't respect our bigger, meaner HMMWVs loaded with disgruntled soldiers and an abundance of ammo.

We always had six HMMWVs in our convoys. Once we got into Mosul, whether coming or going, we would leapfrog to the next intersection in pairs to block traffic. Otherwise we'd never get out of town. Iraqis weren't good drivers. Most of the streetlights were a waste of electricity. The barrel of a rifle worked much better. I had a tendency to jump out of my truck before PFC Dixon stopped most of the time. It helped having air support. Nothing was so reassuring as a pair of Apaches circling overhead.

A Mercedes tried to cut us off. Nine times out of ten it was just a reckless move. That tenth time was a car bomb. Call it paranoia, but don't try to judge us. Unless you've lived with the threat of being blown apart by some asshole in a car you should keep your mouth shut.

There is no time to rationalize or think in those situations. You react. Period. A soldier has to trust his instincts on whether to fire or not and I trusted my men to do the right thing. We might not have been trained for this before leaving Fort Bragg, but the road was a fast teacher. Every man in our convoy had been doing this same task for nearly a month.

This driver actually thought he could brush an armored vehicle aside. The result was one heavily damaged passenger side with a fuming Iraqi behind the wheel. We quickly learned not to take chances. Every situation was potentially life threatening. Another HMMWV jumped in front and cut the fool off. The driver's mood changed once he saw the machine gun barrel waggling at him. Our long convoy rolled by, forcing the driver to wait for the better part of a half hour.

We finally pulled into the marshalling yard at the KBR headquarters on the airfield. The older British manager came out with a huge grin. "Congratulations guys! You did it!"

We passed confused looks to each other, the obvious question in mind. What did we do? Certainly nothing special. We'd been doing this run for a few weeks now and it was getting old.

The LT shook his hand and asked the question. "What happened?"

The KBR guy looked taken aback. "You haven't heard? The 4th Infantry captured Saddam!"

We broke out into smiles, slapping backs and cracking jokes like we had something to do with it. I don't think any of us could say what part of the country the 4th ID was in charge of. None of that mattered. Saddam Hussein had been dug out of his little hole in the ground and shown to audiences around the world.[19] The self admitted student of Hitler was now a prisoner of war. The implications were twofold. Coalition forces were bolstered by the news and stepped up their campaign to eliminate enemy resistance in the major cities. On that same token, the enemy redoubled their efforts to knock us down. Attacks increased sharply throughout Iraq.

Mission complete, we trudged the last few miles to the refueling point. All of us were almost out of fuel but almost was good enough to get us where we needed to be. If you let your truck run out of fuel in peacetime training it was almost the death penalty, here it was part of

---

[19] Saddam Hussein was captured without a shot fired by the 4th Infantry Division in ad-Dawr, near his hometown of Tikrit on December 13, 2003.

the job. Our last run nearly proved disastrous, but that's what happens when people get involved when they don't need to.

We just reached Mosul's outer limits when word came down through the command net that there was a massive riot going on by the Saddam Bridge over the Tigris River. Orders were to find a place to hold up and stand fast. The bad part was we were less than a klick from the bridge and hadn't seen a soul on foot. Our two lead trucks drove the rest of the way to the bridge and came back reporting the way was clear. There was no riot. LT Holm was about to get on the horn and send the report back up when our battalion CSM decided to get involved.

He basically told us to shut up and do what we were told, the situation on the ground be damned. Orders are orders but this guy was an idiot. Too many times the commander on the ground was overridden by someone back in base camp with no actionable intel. One thing I learned long ago was to quickly ignore people like that. They were just bad news any way you looked at it. The bridge was clear. Any potential enemy presence had disbanded. There was absolutely nothing barring us from heading home. Nothing but the CSM and an outdated action report from division headquarters.

Forget division, the pencil pushers probably had never seen the Iraqi streets or met the enemy. Our real problem, if it could be called such, was the CSM. Granted the order was born out of the necessity to keep us from harm, but he had a habit of getting involved in business that didn't concern him. This was the same guy who told us, the men on the ground, that there was a riot and we didn't know what we were talking about. Absolutely ridiculous. But as I've said, orders are orders. We turned our hundred truck convoy around, all the while praying we didn't get hit by IEDs or snipers or a good old fashioned ambush. Turning around a hundred tractor trailer drivers who barely spoke English in the middle of a hostile city is no small feat but we did it.

Then Sav's truck blew out a tire. We rolled into a small parking lot and set up a perimeter while Sav and his guys started changing the tire. It didn't take long before Iraqis started coming by to see what was going on. About the same time a group of truck drivers decided they didn't want to wait any longer. No doesn't mean much if you plain don't care. Convoys were becoming a favorite target for terrorists and insurgents. Burned out hulls lined the roads in and out of town. There was even a burned out bus across the street from our main compound. The drivers were disinclined to stick around in a dangerous neighborhood and hope we didn't get hit. Not speaking English and us preoccupied with fixing our downed vehicle, there wasn't much we could do to stop any who wanted to leave.

We lost about a third of the trucks but had to focus on the other two thirds. Even those started to trickle out in small groups. I established a small perimeter, using the walls and buildings surrounding the area for natural cover. It didn't take long before Iraqis started poking their heads out their windows to see what we were doing. Small groups started to form just far enough back not to pose a threat. Trucks continued to trickle out in twos and threes. By the time we had the tire fixed and were ready to roll we were down to less than half of what we started with.

A normally two hour trip was now stretching into four. Combine that with the trip north and the slow pace of the truck drivers and the day was getting long. By now we'd been on the road from sun up to sun down and we were exhausted. That's when mistakes happen. Trucks missed their turns. Soldiers struggled to stay awake. Our first truck ran out of fuel five miles away from the KBR compound. The LT wanted me to give him a push but my tank was nearly dry so I couldn't do much. Fortunately Rob had confiscated a few fuel cans and always kept them filled. They proved the difference maker. He was the only one capable of towing the crippled truck back to the airbase. We dropped off the trucks and dragged our butts back to the base, every one of us cursing out the CSM the whole way.

The days continued to get longer while our patience waned. Everyone was tired and wanted to go home. Screw Iraq. Back in the motorpool we hooked up with the battalion maintenance NCO, SFC Tucker and his Iraqi liaison. This guy made no false pretenses of who he was. The Iraqi government capitulated easily. Most of the Baath Party members went into hiding but not this guy. He flaunted the fact he was a Baathist. So long as we were good to him, he was good to us. Tonight he brought bags of fresh vegetables and steaks; real, honest to god steaks.

The food was cooking (with a curious mix of fuel and charcoal) and we were standing around talking smack to each other, the Iraqi included, when a single rifle shot echoed from the guard tower atop the maintenance shed. SFC Hawk, Sav and I climbed up to the roof to investigate. One of the soldiers on duty saw us and turned back to watching the main avenue. That narrowed down who the culprit was.

Soldiers may not verbally rat on each other but even the dumbest knew when the shit was about to hit the fan.

SFC Hawk took the lead, "Who fired their weapon?"

I looked past the sandbag bunker. There was a main road less than twenty meters away and houses in the background. Hopefully this knucklehead didn't hit anything or anyone.

"I accidentally kicked over my weapon and it fired," the guilty solider told us hastily.

Wrong answer. Negligent discharge was a serious offense, punished under the uniform code of military justice, our version of the law. I'd already seen the ill effects of carelessness and prayed it didn't happen again.

Sav picked up the guy's rifle and slammed it down. "Bullshit. I just fucking threw your weapon and it didn't fire. What happened?"

He went on to explain and summarily got reamed out by each of us. Just imagine what might have happened if he had killed or wounded a civilian. We'd all seen or heard about civilian casualties and what happens to soldiers who commit the crimes. So close to going home, we weren't willing to accept foolish risks, not for us and not for our soldiers.

Now it was time to eat. The next day we got unexpected news. We had the day off. This was my first day off since I got in country and I literally had nothing to do. I got a huge care package from a group of nurses at my mom's hospital and passed most of it out to the men. After that we went over to the KBR mess tent, an enormous white tent in the middle of the base that happened to be a favorite target of the enemy. The enemy must have watched MASH because they were just like five o'clock Charlie. They never hit anything but kept on trying.

Sav was my bullet magnet friend and tended to get a little paranoid when things got hairy. He was talking away when I heard a pair of crumps in the background. Mortars. I looked over at him but he didn't seem to notice so I wasn't going to ruin lunch. I did let him know halfway back to the barracks.

"Yo, why the fuck didn't you say anything? We could have gotten killed."

Arguing was pointless, especially when a man knows he's being targeted. I let the subject drop but it wasn't the last time. Later that evening we did a stroll around the immediate compound. We hit the local bootleg DVD guy, the gym and then our little raggedy PX. The American military presence was still far from being built up so we found ourselves living hard, but getting by. The PX was a travesty. The shelves were always empty and it seldom carried more than beef jerky and Pringles. Forget personal hygiene items.

We had a place where we could use satellite phones to call home before AT&T put in a call center trailer. Seeing as how I wasn't in any rush to call home, I waited outside while Sav and Rob did their business. No sooner had they emerged than a mortar round blew up about a hundred meters away. I quickly decided that I wasn't going to hang out with Sav anymore, leastwise not until we got back home and it was safe. If he was going to get killed I didn't want to be nearby.

The detail of escorting KBR trucks lasted through most of December. While we were glad to be done with it, leaving AO Glory was bittersweet. The men there lived in captured Fedayeen buildings and had hot chow three times a day. Back at the FOB we were lucky to get an MRE for lunch. The seven mile trip back to Gunslinger at least proved uneventful.

Not all convoys were so fortunate. The CSM decided to do an NCO development class at the ALOC. His decision was dangerous, exposing men and equipment needlessly to enemy contact. A truck full of Charlie Battery's NCOs got hit by and IED on the way back to the FOB. No one was killed but they suffered a few wounded- all of which could have been prevented if we had done our class back at the FOB.

Mistakes, especially careless ones, happen all too often. I had fallen asleep early one evening and was awakened shortly afterward by the familiar sound of men gearing up and getting their rifles. I yawned and looked around, snatching up the nearest soldier. "Vivona, what's going on?"

He had a look that was half panicked- half complacent. "We're taking fire."

I decided to toss my PT jacket on and heading to see what the ruckus was. A quick pop of my head out the back door showed me about twenty men standing as close as possible to each other with most of their upper torsos exposed above the compound wall facing the main road. I'm not tactical genius, but that seemed plain dumb. I waved them off and went out the other door to the latrine.

It was over by the time I returned. Everyone was back inside and stripping out of their gear. Vivona looked at me and couldn't believe I hadn't bothered to get dressed. "I guess you must be used to it from being in Afghanistan."

I frowned. What a dumb ass. "Dude, if we were taking fire it was only a few rounds. That's no reason to get excited."

Turns out I was right. A quick investigation showed one of Charlie Battery's guards got anxious and cranked off a handful of rounds from his SAW. I was starting to get the feeling that I was in more danger from friendly fire than from the enemy. One thing that continued to stick in my mind was how lousy the enemy was at fighting. Were we just that good or was everyone else poorly trained? Naturally I thought the later. Iraq might have had the fourth largest army in the world before the Gulf War but the stuff we were dealing with was the bottom of the barrel.

The most exciting and boring time I had in Mosul was when the 101st called down for us to set up traffic control points (TCPs) on the roads leading into the city. Daily threat briefings provided us with who we were looking for. The package pushed out right after breakfast. Our position was at an intersection on a pair of secondary roads at the bottom of a small hill. A cemetery took up most the hill, a pair of apartment buildings a few hundred meters across the street.

I took a team halfway up the hill to an over watch position. A three man element went all the way up while the main body set up the wire and anti-vehicle obstacles. We had enough firepower to do serious damage to everything short of an armored vehicle. The day dragged on. The guys below searched the few random vehicles that actually used the roads. It was cold and drab. Things picked up when the report of an AK 47 rang out. My machine gun swiveled on the nearest building, the obvious point of origin. I moved around to the front of the HMMWV and watched.

A commotion on top of the hill drew my attention. The three man team came rushing down, bounding and rolling behind tombstones and looking like paid actors. The senior man popped up beside me covered in dirt and sweat and breathing hard. I just stood there.

"We're under attack," he told me.

I was hearing that a lot these days, but again, we had no positive identification so there was nothing to shoot back at. Forget the fact the firing had already stopped long before the three man team made from the top of the hill down to my truck. Most of the men operating the TCP even bothered to look in the direction the fire was coming from. This was Iraq. Gunfire was as common as stopping at a red light back home. I looked up at my machine gunner who had already trained his weapon on the only multistory building in the vicinity. It was a good five hundred meters away, which reduced the urgency or need for self-protection from enemy fire. Iraqis were generally poor shots and from that distance the danger was almost null. The rest of the operation went smoothly and we were able to return to the FOB for some hot chow.

Winter was settling in and it was getting more miserable daily. The most depressing sight I witnessed was a handful of NCOs standing or sitting around the pot belly stove with such worn down looks etched on their faces. You could feel the misery pulsing off of them. The holiday season was on us without the festive mood. Every day was drab. The fact that we did the same mundane tasks repeatedly didn't help. It almost felt like the 101st didn't know what to do with us. Or want us hanging around.

It wasn't just us. The rest of division artillery was being tasked with missions we technically weren't qualified to perform. Two Blackhawks crashed into each other after one took small arms fire in the middle of the night while on patrol. Standard operating procedure had them using night vision goggles instead of running lights. The lead pilot slashed right to avoid incoming and crashed into the second. Both went down in a fiery mess. The disaster was made worse by the loss of an entire cannon crew that was riding in the Blackhawks as a rapid quick reaction force. Seventeen men died in the crashes, nine of which were fellow artillerymen. Worsening things, the only soldier from the gun crew that wasn't involved in the collision had been killed only a few days before.

The funeral ceremony was gut wrenching. To see so many grown men sniffling back their tears or weeping openly tore at my heart. Keeping it together almost proved too hard a task. A long row of boots rested at the front, near the chaplain. Rifles pointed downward with helmets on top in an ageless tradition of respect for the fallen. Each pair of boots represented a life lost; a comrade gone to the great beyond. These men died doing what they were told, what they believed in. These particular men died without a fighting chance. And not a man attending the ceremony dared complain lest they dishonor the sacrifice of their peers.

Depression worsened as the days dragged by. I tried talking to one of my buddies, nothing serious just general small talk as we stood next to the pot belly stove at the rear of our warehouse home. He looked at me with this blank stare and said, "I want to go home."

What else needed saying? This man was one of the most squared away sergeants in the battery and he had thrown in the towel.

Moods like that are contagious and it spread quickly among the battery. I tried my best to keep spirits up. Anyone who knows me knows I would rather crack a joke than yell. Even that only managed to stem the tide for a little. More people saw what we were doing as pointless. Truthfully, it was. Our lone battalion occupied a nonessential compound seven miles outside of Mosul proper. Absolutely nothing happened this far out of the city. 1-377 was the sad recipient of a division not knowing what to do with us. And for it we suffered.

Morale dropped across the board. It became a struggle to keep the soldiers involved. That's not to suggest that everyone suffered from this lethargy, but enough did that it posed a potential problem. The leadership did what it could to address the problem. Schedules were adjusted. Soldiers were given both Thanksgiving and Christmas Day off from guard duty or patrols. The officers and NCOs took to the guard towers until midnight. I didn't mind. Part of me resented getting promoted to the platoon sergeant level. Rank may have its privileges but it comes at a price. I was removed from being among the men, an outsider they didn't want around lest I keep them from performing their tasks. I preferred to be doing things instead of watching others.

I took it upon myself to make my daily rounds around the Battery. I'd watch bits of pirated movies or watch them play a video game. Some of the more randy NCOs would sit around the small television we acquired and watch pirated porn from some channel in Europe. At least they were polite enough to keep the sound down. A group of guys figured out how to link a handful of laptops to a single game and would play it during all hours of the day and night. One of my nights checking the guard towers I was met with the sound of a computerized werewolf howling from the back of the warehouse. Damned Rob was still playing.

The First Sergeant helped liven things with his personal brand of madness. This was the same man who got the death threats in the portajohn back in Kuwait and he still hadn't adjusted his style. Soldiers called him Scary Nine when he wasn't around. Seems he had a reputation as the first guy to crack and run when things got tight. Platoon sergeants and above sat down at our evening meeting with the commander as usual. Not much new was mentioned. These are the sort of meetings you can't wait to get out of because you feel so unproductive in them.

We each had a turn to speak before it went to Top. He had this crazed look. "No one goes anywhere without full body armor and three vehicles. Period. One of the brigade sergeant major's got killed today because he was driving alone in a pickup truck. A fucking brigade sergeant major! And they just went into his truck and cut his throat."

Division policy stated that no vehicles were to be on the road at night or with less than a three truck convoy regardless of the time of day. We later found out that the CSM had made the run between his headquarters and division a hundred times and decided to slack on standards. Complacency killed him and his driver. The Iraqis couldn't fight us head to head but they were by no means a foolish enemy. They'd been waiting for him. One threw a rock at the windshield, causing the driver to swerve into a wall and crash. Dazed, neither American saw their killers. Both men were murdered, their gear was left undisturbed. This was an execution, a startling display of power and defiance.

Security amped up as a result but it also made us more anxious. The enemy had just killed one of the senior leaders in the 101st. A man who had no real place involved in actual combat operations. Immunity was a fleeting dream now for many. For us on the line it showed that complacency was as much of an enemy as the Iraqis. Every face we saw turned into a threat. Every curtain dropping back into place when we passed hid a sniper or worse.

One thing about death in a combat zone: it doesn't stop the mission. If anything it helps increase operations tempo and makes soldiers more cognizant, more aware of their surroundings. It also leads to personalized vengeance. The desire and need for each of us to find those responsible and punish them. Not that it was our place to become these exacting angels of vengeance, but the rage inside kept us going and helped us push past the cloud of funk miring us down.

The war went on.

We set up another TCP right outside of our compound. I was in the 'rundown' element. Three overweight HMMWVs waited just away from the TCP so as not to alarm potential insurgents. A BMW got close enough to see our control point before the drive turned around and hauled ass out of the area. Captain King, our battery commander, led my element and decided to give chase. It was a valiant effort but only succeeded in making us look like fools. We never got close. The BMW roared north, leaving us with nothing but a distant flash of taillights. Our trucks limped back to the staging area, filled with jokes and chides at the BC (Battery Commander)

"We tried," he laughed.

Yeah, we tried and got burned in the process. At least we got a good laugh out of it. I wonder what the driver thought when he saw three armored monstrosities lumber out of hiding in pursuit. Hopefully he at least needed to change his drawers when he got home. We reset and waited. There was bound to be another one. There always was.

Our next quarry wasn't so lucky. A crappy car came flying down the road. The driver had a panicked look, like he knew he was about to get shot. He plowed into our perimeter, waving his hands and shouting he didn't have brakes. It's funny how much English people know when their lives are on the line. The car swerved around the rows of concertina wire and pickets and drove up into the field on the side of the road where it stalled. Our trucks ran him down and quickly surrounded him. Soldiers jumped out. We dragged the driver from his car at gunpoint, putting him on the ground and cuffing his hands behind his back. Others methodically searched his car, dumping what he had on the ground. He was clean. No bombs, no bullets. Stupidity wasn't a good enough reason to detain him so we let the man go.

While this was happening an actual target crept into the holding pen. I truly believe luck is nothing more than a personal excuse. The Iraqi driver had none. He acted suspiciously from the moment he realized it was too late to turn around. We searched cars at random; stopping this one, letting that one go. Halfway up the hill I could hear SSG Vernon Forbes shouting to the holding area, "Let me get a hot one!"

A hot one he got. The selected car drove from the holding pen to the search area. Three men were made to get out so we could check the car. We popped the trunk and found American desert uniforms and a bunch of AK 47s. Jackpot! The driver and passengers were zip tied and blindfolded with torn sandbags placed over their heads and made ready for transport to the nearest Iraqi police station. Soldiers loaded the prisoners in the back of my HMMWV. They pushed and shoved the prisoners, angry and excited at once. One of my guys who was having a real bad day had it get worse when I caught his rifle barrel about an inch from the driver's face and shouting at him. The Iraqi didn't speak English and we didn't speak Arabic. Perfect.

"Put the fucking gun down," I growled. "I'm not filling out paperwork for a war crime. Sit your ass down or give me the gun."

He didn't like it but knew things would only end badly for all of us if he did anything stupid. Crisis averted, I reported we were ready to go. The Battery Commander got our vehicles together and we were about to roll out when unexpected complications halted us in place. What now? The day was mostly over. This capture was our final task and the TCP was being broken down and reset for tomorrow. It was time to get some chow, shower and unwind for the night. Well, the rest of the soldiers went to relax. The chosen few still had a bit to do.

Just then I spotted the battalion commander and the sergeant major walking out the side gate to our compound. They wanted in on our prize. We enjoyed the relative security of being set up right across the street from our compound for this one but there was a downside. Any positive report we sent up was immediately received and became actionable by the normally reclusive staff. Not that I can blame them. It doesn't sit right having combat soldiers sitting behind a desk while their friends are busy running in harm's way. So we were stuck.

You don't tell the Boss he can't do something. He wanted to ride shotgun so he did. The CSM decided he was going to drive the confiscated vehicle. (Ten years later I still laugh at the sight of him driving away in helmet and body armor, smoking a cigarette and pointing his 9mm pistol out the window, the little red laser light looking for targets in the gathering dusk.) I kept the prisoners on my truck and waited. Nothing ever goes right when command gets involved so there was no reason to believe it would this time either. The sun was starting to set by the time my element managed to untangle from the command hiccup.

It's remarkable how people tense up when the battalion command team goes with you. Not that there is any additional pressure to do your job better, but there is certainly more stress because they almost always want to offer 'suggested' ways to do things better. Those suggestions were often contradictory to our standard operating procedures. That's where the problems came from. Our KBR mission in November went so well because we had a lieutenant in charge.

The sun was already setting, throwing shadows everywhere. Bad guys tended to hide in shadows to launch RPGS or use snipers. We weren't breaking any land speed records trying to get to the police station. Our objective was in a rundown section of Mosul with limited friendly presence. Iraq in 2003 was the sort of place where the newly instated Iraqi Police were more scared than valuable. Anti-American sentiment was still high (though nowhere near as high as it would be a year later) and those who sided with us were deemed traitors or worse. Families were often taken hostage, sometimes outright murdered. Still, people needed to work in order to take care of those families. So they joined the new police force or the new army.

Our little convoy hooked a left off of the main highway and rolled up on a dark street. U.S. Army vehicles make a lot of noise. There's no hiding from the more curious, making us tempting targets for anyone with a gun. Crowds were already forming a few hundred meters away by the time we arrived. We may have been going to a police station but the immediate area was anything but secure. Most of the streetlights were out, broken or worse. The wreckage of a car bomb sat in the divider in the middle of the road like a painful warning. Making it worse, there were no police in sight.

My guard rose the closer we got to the station. AK-47 barrels stuck up from the back of the crowd. The few police in the station were hiding inside. Almost all of the station's windows were broken, either shot or smashed. Sheets of plywood covered the larger windows. There wasn't a single light on inside. It was clear there was no official presence in this part of town. The situation had the very real possibility of turning sour very quickly.

We were met by the highest-ranking policeman, or maybe the one who drew the shortest straw. Our battalion commander led the small group to see about handing the prisoners off. After a broken conversation it was decided they either couldn't or weren't going to take the prisoners. That meant another drive across town, at night, to the military holding facility on AO Glory. That bad feeling I had was getting worse.

The ride proved uneventful, and we were suddenly unencumbered. Fate smiled down on us. We got rid of the CSM and LTC after the police station debacle. They dropped off the captured vehicle to the Iraqi Police (Ips) and caught a ride back to the FOB. Go figure. We did the hard part and they went for the ride. The good thing was we were back down to battery command level and could operate freely. The convoy pulled into the holding facility and we unloaded the prisoners. None of them seemed particularly enthused about being drug off a truck and passed to American MPs and interrogators.

The prison building was a converted barracks. Wires, pickets and roving guards turned the outer compound into a heavily guarded enclosure. Bars had been thrown up in the windows. It had a very third world country feel to it, the kind of place you see in movies where someone is always dangling from the ceiling being cut with knives or electrocuted. I was glad to be on the outside.

CPT King, the battery commander, was senior man and even he wasn't allowed to go inside. So we waited around our vehicles for the MPs to finish. None of us expected what happened next. The prisoners were escorted out a short while later, free and scowling. Disappointment is an understatement. We did what we were supposed to, risked our lives to get these men into custody and now they were being released because some ex-Iraqi army official claimed they weren't insurgents. I felt like one of the storm troopers from Star Wars who had just been told these aren't the insurgents you are looking for. Mission complete, we loaded up and headed back home. The three ex-prisoners were released to go drum up anti-American sentiment.

The sad reality is that these types of events happened nearly daily in both wars. Suspects were round up and taken to holding facilities until interrogators were able to decide whether or not they were guilty or innocent. Nine out of ten times the prisoners were released. The mistake is easy enough to make. It doesn't help when almost every single military aged male has a long beard and everyone has a gun. Positive identification can be near impossible. A multitude of reasons offer us excuses for our actions: a wounded friend, bad news from home, a really bad day. If your convoy gets attacked, it is perfectly reasonable to want some measure of vengeance. So more 'suspected insurgents' are rounded up and hauled off to the nearest jail facility. Better safe than sorry. Anyone is capable of turning into a threat. The little boy pointing his rifle at me in Afghanistan was proof enough for me.

We climbed back into our trucks and drove away under a cloud of strained disappointment. Making our mood worse, we learned that our Bravo Battery TCP actually captured one of the main targets division intel was expecting: an Iraqi mortar team with their weapon and few rounds. It was still a victory, just not ours. The taste of defeat can be bitter sometimes. I didn't like it.

The war continued to drone on with unanticipated twists. Washington refused to call it an occupation but if one hundred thousand plus coalition combat soldiers sitting in Saddam's palaces or enforcing lockdowns in all of Saddam's major cities isn't an occupation I need to reread Webster's definition. The campaign planners at the Pentagon failed to mention to us that we were now responsible for rebuilding a wounded nation.

Inherent dangers come with any occupation. Riots of disaffected civilians, angry at how they are being treated. The change of mission from combat to support and stability operations forces soldiers to abandon their previous mindset (the one they spent months getting prepared for) and puts them in unexpected situations. We went from blowing up military targets to routine traffic stops, presence patrols and convoy escort.

One of our Bravo battery chow convoys got hit with an IED/ambush combo. The driver had a habit of running into Iraqi cars (I heard the tally was up around twenty or so) and the insurgents took offense. They were coming back from Mosul when a white pickup tried running our truck off the road. It wasn't a sound tactical plan considering this guy liked to hit cars and he was driving a rather large 5 ton truck, but it made the driver swerve. A 60mm mortar round half buried in a tire exploded close enough to pepper the tailgate with shrapnel. SFC Allen and his guys opened fire on the pickup before taking small arms fire from the concrete wall running along the right side of the road. The SAW gunner kept the fire from getting out of hand and the convoy sped back to the FOB without any casualties.

People do the damnedest things in combat. One of our mechanics, James King whom we called King James, took mortar shrapnel twice in the same shoulder. The doctors couldn't remove most of it so he walked around in constant misery. We were in the process of having our vehicles maintenanced for the impending long drive to Kuwait when a last-minute cache recovery mission came down. The NCOs decided to let the soldiers keep working and we went to division headquarters. I jumped in the nearest FMTV and started driving.

A team of Explosive Ordinance (EOD) was already sight by the time we arrived. I thought my guys took a lot of things lightly but these guys definitely had some screws loose. I watched as a pair of them started juggling RPG warheads. Did they want to die? What the Hell? The rest of the EOD guys crowded around to enjoy the show while I noticed most of our guys backed away. There are stupid chances not worth taking. This had to be one of them.

I jumped up on the back of the truck and started stacking boxes of blasting caps and IED making materials. There was a surprising amount found not far from the main division headquarters building. How it had remained undiscovered for months I'll never know. We made quick work loading the truck. There enough to fill the truck bed and more. An EOD guy tossed up a full sandbag.

"What's in this one?" I asked as I caught it.

He smiled. "Grenades. Some of them don't have pins though."

I opened the bag and found around fifty hand grenades. He was right. Some of them were only secured by a small piece of tape. I set the bag down and climbed off the truck. This was bullshit. I had crazies juggling rockets and people tossing armed grenades around like they were children's toys. Were we only weeks away from going home and, if you believed in superstition, this was the most dangerous time in the deployment. I recall our inbriefing to Korea. We were told the first and last thirty days in country was when most accidents happened. Right now we were definitely in that thirty day window.

EOD gave me a quizzical look. "What's wrong?"

What's wrong? Was I the only one who found issue with playing with explosives? I shook my head and walked away. He shrugged and went back to work.

SGT Harvey asked. "What's wrong Smoke?"

"Nothing. These people are fucking crazy. Come on, we're almost done."

I climbed back up and helped stacking the last few boxes of disintegrating blasting caps. Finished, we followed EOD to the demolition sight where the trucks were so big they naturally got stuck. I jumped out of the driver's seat and let Harvey get it. He was a good old boy from the Deep South and treated it like a four wheeler going through the mud. More power to him. After so many months of the same depression he deserved to have a little fun.

I've met plenty of people not quite right in the head, but not every person in a single job. These EOD boys weren't dealing with a full deck and it showed in everything they did. Tossing shape charges and blasting caps around. Recklessly endangering lives. It was all too much. They told us to drive back after we were finished downloading the truck. When asked how far their only answer was 'enough'. We pulled back and waited for the explosion. The noise was spectacular but the whole thing was unlike anything you'll find in movies. Most explosions are. No giant fireballs. No great gouts of flame. There was dust, whizzing shrapnel, and a billowing cloud of black smoke.

Time dragged painfully slow during this period. Days stretched endlessly. It felt like we were never going to leave. Every day we struggled to find out when division was going to cut us loose. Every day we went to bed disappointed. Waiting is every bit the enemy as any terrorist. Christmas came. The NCOs pulled guard duty again and let the soldiers enjoy their time off. We ate last, as a leader should. By the time the group I was with got to the serving line they had run out of food. I went back to the warehouse and found a turkey and mashed potatoes MRE. Not quite the meal I was looking forward to, but at least the soldiers got to eat.

SGT Hoy and I headed out for our guard shift at 2100. No one was expecting much to happen but that was the exact reason not to let your guard down. We'd been there only for a few minutes when a massive explosion came from somewhere around Mosul. The city was seven miles away and our guard tower shook from the impact.

Another guard tower got on the radio. "Did you hear that? Did you hear that?"

Hoy and I exchanged looks and shook our heads. There was no mistaking who's voice it was. The First Sergeant was at it again.

"I don't get it," Hoy said.

I shrugged. Neither did I. We turned the radio down and went back to staring out into the empty Iraqi countryside. A railroad ran behind us. The engine must have been one of the first prototypes because it was seriously old. Battalion staff had to get on the radio to calm down the other guard position, much to our amusement. Our shift might have taken forever without the comedy from the front of the compound.

The nightly firefight with our sister unit began shortly after the explosion. We could see the occasional tracer streaking across the field of fire. Those poor bastards got hit far too often. We counted ourselves fortunate to be placed in a forgotten compound with little tactical significance.

"They're at it again," Hoy told me.

I nodded. "Yep. They're taking a pounding. I hope they're actually killing some of them."

It was true. We wanted all of them dead. There was nothing personal involved. Most of the terrorists and insurgents were faceless enemies. An ideal more than an actual physical manifestation. People who have never faced an armed combatant won't understand. The enemy wants to kill every one of us, without hesitation. Soldiers have a way of dehumanizing the people in the country we go to war with. I didn't care about any of the Afghanis nor did I about the Iraqis. They were an obstacle keeping me from going home. Any casualties they suffered happened because they deserved it.

The ideal doesn't come home. I know most of the people I saw were decent, good-hearted people. I know they didn't want the daily violence any more than I did. I knew, and while I was there I didn't care. Every face was a potential enemy combatant. A potential threat needing to be eliminated. By reducing them to such basic terms I was able to cope with the amount of death and violence I saw.[20] Not much of an excuse, but I never promised one. War is ugly. Much of what we do can't be considered normal or natural. Nothing we did once we crossed the big puddle is comparable to what everyday people did back at home. Women and children die. Sad, but that's war.

Late December 2003

We'd been fairly lucky concerning attacks throughout the deployment. Our compound hadn't been hit at all and that was an accomplishment. One of our sister battalions from the 101st was located a few klicks away and was constantly being hit at night. Things didn't go south for us until we received official orders to redeploy. Someone from battalion staff (we later found it out it was our gung-ho sergeant major) went to the Iraqi cantina at the front of our compound and rudely kicked out the locals working there. Nothing screams poor operational security than displacing all the locals who supported us.

That night we got hit for the first time. A 107mm rocket slammed into the skeleton frame towards the compound's rear. There were no casualties and considerably little damage since the building was halted in mid-construction when we invaded. The aftereffects were what consumed us. The illusion of invincibility was shattered. Cold realization that we were just as vulnerable as every other unit (a ridiculous notion seeing as how the threat was always there).

Each battery received orders. Ours were to conduct night patrols from the vicinity we believed the attack was initiated. I took first patrol. If I'd have known we were would be heading out of the gates between 0100 and 0200 in the morning I might have changed my mind. The orderly on duty woke me and the LT up and went to get the rest of the soldiers. A natural chorus of groans and 'leave me alones' rippled through the warehouse, causing more complaints from soldiers not supposed to be awakened.

Geared up, we headed out to the trucks. The LT went first, I took middle and SSG Forbes took the tail. We didn't expect to find much of anything, most of us believing we were just going through the motions of a presence patrol to deter further enemy contact. We'd only

---

[20]   It is estimated that almost 120,000 Iraqi civilians have been killed or injured during the Iraq War from 2003-2011. www.iraqbodycount.org.

gone a few klicks when Forbes called over the net. "LT are we stopping anytime soon?"

"No, why?"

"Because I gotta take a massive shit."

I hadn't laughed so hard in a long time. Forget the fact we were in 'hostile' territory or that the enemy might still be lurking around to ambush us. That was funny! I'm sure the radio operators on duty at battalion headquarters were both shocked and amused. The LT graciously stopped so he could relieve himself. We pulled a loose over watch, taking every opportunity to shine our flashlights on him. It wouldn't do to have an accident in the middle of the night.

Forbes can jogging back with a roll of toilet paper and a forced glare. "Goddamn it, can't a man take a shit in peace?"

"We just wanted to make sure you were covered," I laughed.

The patrol pulled out, continuing to the spot where radar told us the launch site was. I never had much faith in our radar systems. There always seemed to be some sort of glitch or another but this time proved accurate. We found the blast marks and residue not far from the exact grid but nothing else. The patrol continued to the outskirts of a small and very dark village. The LT decided we didn't have enough firepower to go in there so we turned around and headed back to base.

The division commander, Major General David Petraeus, now the Director of the Central Intelligence Agency, and CSM Hill were making tours of every base and outpost under division command. They presented every single soldier with a combat coin commemorating the 101st's actions in Iraq. It was an honor to stand in front of him and accept this token. Even if we did have to scramble to find clean uniforms and boots.

Nothing else happened for a few nights, at least not until the night before we were scheduled to leave Mosul.

Chapter Ten: Redeployment

January 2004

I remember the night clearly. It was time. Our war was almost over. We were finally going home. It was the night before my battalion was scheduled to begin to pull out of Iraq. The 101st Airborne Division had done its job (or so we thought at the time) and were ordered home. We have the distinction of being the first unit from division to leave. All we had to do was make a three-day convoy from the northern city of Mosul down to Camp Doha, Kuwait. The plans called for a short ride down to Qayyarah Airfield or Q West, a captured Iraqi airbase just south of Mosul, and then the convoy to Kuwait. I had already volunteered to be the Noncommissioned Officer in Charge (NCOIC) of the reconnaissance team for the trip back. Our gear was packed, ammunition drawn, weapons cleaned and serviceable. All we had to do was get a good night's sleep and it was an early start for Kuwait. What could possibly go wrong?

Most of the senior NCOs were sitting around the platoon sergeant's cot going over the plan of action for tomorrow. There was finally an air of excitement in the tin roof warehouse we had lived in for the past ten months. Months of endless patrols, convoy security missions, random traffic stops and the occasional building clearance were coming to an end. We were about ten minutes into our meeting when the first loud BOOM was quickly followed with an equally loud WHOOSH. Goddamn it, we were under attack.

The first 107mm rocket exploded off in the desert beyond our compound but that didn't stop the insurgents (real ones, disgruntled ex-Republican Guardsmen, not the foreign fighters that entered Iraq in 04 that the media seemed to love to call insurgents. Which is slightly ridiculous considering insurgent is synonymous with rebellion and mutiny.) from firing more rockets. Our battery First Sergeant immediately yelled for everyone to sit on their cots and put their helmets on. I nearly got trampled by a pair of soldiers running back to their cots to get their kit. Panic took the Battery. Men scrambled in every direction as the insanity outside heightened.

Now I am not the smartest person in the world, but I would like to think that I am pretty far from the bottom of the list. Here we are, one hundred plus men sitting in a tin building hoping these huge 107mm rockets don't hit and wipe us out on our last night in country. Ha! Patton would have laughed. We had two very large, serviceable bunkers located within a pace of each main access door and the 1SG wanted us to sit on our bunks; a modern version of place your head between your legs and kiss your ass goodbye. Human nature is by far the most interesting aspect of combat. You never really know someone until they come under fire. And then, sit back and enjoy the show. Sit on the cots, my ass.

My own personal dilemma was slightly different. All my gear was outside. My helmet, my ammo and my body armor. All I had was my rifle. Huh. How was I supposed to get outside without getting chewed out for disobeying an order? Thankfully my soldiers bailed me out. Two men dashed out the front door to get in one of the huge bunkers I had built outside upon arriving in country. I know what you are thinking. Bunkers? Why were there knuckleheads sitting on cots in a tin building when there was adequate protection outside? Trust me, I thought the same thing. So I followed the soldiers outside yelling at them to get back here! Of course I closed the door behind me and continued on to my vehicle so I could gear up. I'd like to think they found their way into the back of the nearest bunker.

I made my way over to my vehicle and listened in on the traffic coming over the radios. A pair of Apaches was inbound. One of the guard towers spotted a white pickup truck with rocket launchers bolted in the bed firing on our position. The first flare whistled into the air, illuminating the scene. I started getting into my body armor, still hauling around that fifty-pound piece of steel for protection.

Geared up, I double checked my rifle. Another flare popped. Another rocket roared overhead, exploding somewhere in the distance. The Apache pilots weren't enthused with the use of flares.

"Tell whoever is firing the fucking flares to stop!" one of the pilots snarled over the radio, abandoning all communications protocol. "We can't see anything."

WHOOSH!

Of course they couldn't. Apaches flew lights out, using night vision. The flares were all but blinding them. Light machine gun fire erupted to my front. I looked around for the culprit and quickly found him. CSM Avila was on top of one of our trucks popping flares and cranking off a drum of M249 ammo. Unfortunately, he was firing in the wrong direction.

"Somebody help! The sergeant major's trying to kill us!" SGT Poole screamed over the radio.

I looked around and saw a cloud of dust billowing off of our rear guard tower. Tracers hit and missed the concrete tower. Thankfully our three-man guard team was able to take cover from the steady stream of rounds. By this point I had seen enough to know that something bad was probably going to happen and it was going to be self induced when it did.

I strapped on my helmet and went back inside the warehouse. Rob and Sav were waiting by the front door, listening to the commander talking with battalion and trying to get control of the soldiers.

Looking to my fellow NCOs I said, "We need to get these guys into the bunkers."

They were way ahead of me. A steady stream of soldiers started filing out the doors for the protection of the sandbagged lined bunkers. At the same time the call came down to send out the Quick Reaction Force (QRF) as fast as possible. It was my turn to be the senior NCO and I felt good with the possibility of taking out the insurgents firing on us. Unfortunately, I wasn't the only one. Three gun-trucks combined with about fifteen soldiers comprised the QRF. One lieutenant and a sergeant first class. I looked around and saw three sergeants and four LTs gearing up to go on the QRF.

Too much rank muddles things, raising the chances of friendly fire and accidents. Worse, with everyone virtually the same rank it would be near impossible for one person to assume command and the rest to fall back into a support role. I decided it was not in my best interest to go with the QRF this night. They didn't miss me. In fact, not a one of them, good men all, took the time to think about their actions. It was partially understandable. This was our last night in northern Iraq. Who wouldn't want to take part in the very last mission? I watched them head out to the trucks.

Satisfied, I turned back to what was happening inside. Most of the battery was outside and under cover. Sav had a fire team assembled just outside the door and was preparing to relieve the rear guard tower where SGT Poole was trying to avoid being killed by our CSM. That's when I noticed the battery commander gearing up to go with the QRF. Wrong answer.

Rob got to him first. "Sir, what the fuck do you think you're doing?"

"I'm going with the QRF," CPT King replied as casually as if it he was supposed to.

"Bullshit. You're staying in the BOC and commanding," Rob countered.[21]

I smirked, knowing this would have been disciplinary action if we were back at Fort Bragg. Here, in northern Iraq, it was the right thing to do. We need someone back to be in charge. The First Sergeant was nowhere in sight. Most of the other senior leaders were already boarding the trucks. I wasn't about to do it, so it had damned well better be the commander.

"SSG Rob, I'm going with them," he insisted. The look in his eyes suggested he knew he didn't stand a chance.

Rob and SGT Wade Hoy, our chemical sergeant, picked up CPT King and hauled him back inside the BOC with minimal protest.

"You're the commander now get your fucking ass back in here and command," Rob snarled. He wasn't called Angry for nothing. He was also one of the best people to have at your side when the shit hit the fan.

Calmed and mildly disappointed, CPT King went about the business of coordinating both defensive and offensive actions.[22]

I looked over at SGT Hoy. "I need two alpha rosters."

The Alpha roster is an alphabetical roster (hence the Alpha) with every person in the unit listed. We were under attack and had no accountability of our soldiers. I took one and gave the other to Sav. Rob came with me to the front bunker, where we started calling names. Halfway down the roster I got to the 1SG.

"I'm right here and you would be too if you were fucking smart," he called back.

I shined my flashlight and found him in the very back of the bunker. Not a fucking chance I thought. There was absolutely no way I was going to die in a bunker when I had people in danger. That and I wasn't about to be called a coward for hiding in a bunker with no visibility on what was happening around me. Finished with the names in my bunker I decided to make my rounds throughout the perimeter.

---

[21] BOC- Battery Operations Center.

[22] Captain Nathan King would go on to serve with me in Iraq in 2005. He died only a few months after returning home during a routine airborne operation. His death was a great loss to our battalion and he has been sorely missed.

125

Sav came back, handed me his roster and took off with his fire team. I tagged along while Rob went left to the auxiliary gate. Machine gun fire increased, somehow no one had been hit. Yet. Ducking low so as not to get taken out by the CSM, we arrived at the tower and went up. Dozens of bullet holes gouged the concrete. Thank God the Iraqis used cinder blocks for almost everything.

We snuck inside the main room and looked around. One soldier was smiling like a fool on the Fourth of July, another had a frightened look. SGT Poole was a mix between pissed and scared.

He looked back at us and asked, "What is he shooting at?"

Good question. The enemy was confirmed to be on the opposite side of the compound and was probably already running away before the Apaches arrived on station. Sav and I shrugged; no answer seeming good enough. The firing finally slacked off. I guess he had to reload. Taking advantage of the lull I decided to take a look down range to see what the CSM was shooting at. The only thing visible was that old tractor now riddled with bullet holes and a frightened Iraqi farmer hiding behind it.

Reloaded, the firing began again. Bullets zipped by the tower, some striking, some not. Dust puffed around the tractor. The sharp metallic ping of rounds hitting the poor tractor echoed above the machine gun's report. I couldn't help but think the whole thing was bordering the absurd. Clearly this farmer wasn't the threat. Confusion is a terrible thing, nearly as bad as boredom and anger. Years later, I contend that we were filled with a terrible tension that night and it threatened to consume us all.

The need for action, to take control of our situation, was driving everything that was happening. Unneeded, Sav took his fire team back to the warehouse while I circled around to the front guard towers. The Apaches were circling overhead by now. Enemy fire had ended. There was nothing left but the clean up.

While I was down at the guard tower, Rob was making his way to the front. White plumes of smoke billowed up from the back of an old pickup truck parked in the middle of a cemetery not more than a few hundred meters from our compound. Rob arrived at the nearest tower in time to catch SSG Andrews shoving the barrel of a loaded .50 cal aside before the gunner could fire on our own people. Like I said, accidents happen frequently. A single M2 round can, if striking just right, rip a human body to pieces. Imagine a string of 8-10 rounds hitting a group of unexpecting people.

Crisis averted, they turned their attention back to the fleeing enemy truck. Our QRF arrived too late to do any good. The Apaches left without firing a round. In all, the entire night proved nothing but a grand waste of time. There were no casualties, no confirmed enemy, nothing. The night wound down, allowing hundreds of tired, war weary soldiers the chance to go to bed. Tomorrow was going to be a long day.

The recon team left early. We linked up outside of battalion headquarters to get our inbriefing. The mission was simple. We were to ensure the route south was clear. In truth we were no better than target practice for potential enemies. That wasn't a problem. Moving ahead of the rest of the battalion with only a handful of soldiers suited me just fine. The ability to think and act independently from the main body has always appealed to me. I enjoy the freedom of being able to utilize my creativity to achieve maximum favorable results. The downside to being alone is that we would be alone.

Our first objective was to secure the notoriously poorly maintained traffic circle heading into Mosul. Iraqi police manned a small post in nearby but they were largely ineffective and completely useless. I suppose I might be too if I knew the enemy was specifically targeting 'traitors' who joined the American cause. A rash of attacks, murders and executions were occurring across most of Iraq. The victims were mostly the newly revamped Iraqi police.

We arrived early enough that traffic wasn't too much of a problem. That was bound to change quickly though. All four lanes were packed by the time the first gun convoy arrived. Our trucks blocked most of the incoming lanes while all personnel except the drivers and machine gunners dismounted and physically halted traffic. Most of the Iraqis were used to this sort of thing by now, but that didn't mean they liked having their day interrupted. The smaller percentage decided they had things to do and attempted to run our gauntlet. They didn't get far.

We stayed at the circle for over two hours. A squad of Iraqi police leaned back against their shack and watched. I now had doubts as to why the enemy was targeting the police when they were so worthless. It took a while before we caught up to battalion. My team jumped back in front and led the rest of the way to Q West, where we spent the first night. Maintenance was done on weapons and vehicles. Fuel tanks were topped off, to include additional cans. There was no way anyone wanted a repeat incident from the KBR convoys in November. It was the last good night of sleep we got before finally arriving in Kuwait three days later.

Dawn found us back on the road. We had to drive to a refueling station just south of Tikrit. Thankfully it was still cold enough to wear gloves and jackets. Most people tend to think of Iraq as an inhospitable desert with stifling heat. Not true. Northern Iraq was partially green and cold in the winter. It rained, snowed in the mountains, and left us feeling generally miserable. Right where a soldier needs to be.

Less than an hour south of Q West (we ranged ten to twenty miles ahead of the first convoy) a frantic call came over the net. Alpha Battery was engaged. One of the gun trucks opened fired on a passing pickup. They were forced to stop and secure the prisoners and wait for the MPs to arrive before continuing south. All that time my convoy was parked on the side of the road and exposed.

The rest of the day passed uneventfully and we led battalion into one of the larger resupply areas in the north. Tanks and Bradley fighting vehicles rumbled everywhere. The cold comfort of armored vehicles with unmatched destructive capabilities felt reassuring. Once nestled into our assigned area the battalion again went through refit and refuel operations. We were one step closer to home.

Our next objective was another major supply hub around the southern city of Nasiriyah. That meant going through Baghdad. My first glimpse of the fabled city was unimpressive. Rundown buildings and shacks lined the roads. A feeling of abject poverty projected from the faces of the people lining the streets. This was not the jewel described in so many movies and classic literature. Modern Baghdad was beaten down and ugly.

Anyone who has ever been to Baghdad can tell you that the roads are a hot mess. Our maps were relatively accurate but that didn't mean much when it came to the physical translation. At some point, where a handful of major roads intersected and crossed overhead, we took a left when we should have gone right. The road narrowed down to a single lane before we found a small, very small, traffic circle to turn around in. The LT passed the word back to our S3 so they wouldn't make the same mistake (they did anyway) and we were ordered to pull off to the side of the road and wait for the first convoy to catch up.

Nightfall spread over the war-ravaged city. This was ground zero for the shock and awe bombing campaign at the beginning of the war and my first look at the continued damage nine months later. Buildings were shredded with bullet holes. A burned out government Ministry building was a blackened ruin. Much of the city was still without power, leaving an impossibly dark hole in the middle of the largest city in Iraq. We pulled up below a series of confusing overpasses and waited. Then word came back that the first convoy had done the same thing we warned of. Damn. It felt like it took forever for that convoy to turn around. Remember there was barely room for us to maneuver much less the fifty-six foot long vehicle-howitzer combination.

Numerous Iraqis started opening windows and coming down the road to get a better look. My men were beginning to get nervous and so was I. There was a small measure of comfort from seeing a platoon of tanks emplaced nearby. At least if things went back we might be able to high tail it over there and take cover behind those armored monsters. It turns out our fears were unnecessary. The first HMMWV rolled into view a short time later and we were able to push on, this time on the correct road.

Half of the night was gone before we pulled into our rest stop. Riding in full body armor in an incredibly hot vehicle while watching for snipers, roadside bombs and potential ambushes was exhausting, throw in a few extra hours of driving and I felt like I could sleep for a few days. Unfortunately the night was short. The next day was more of the same thing. We took off and continued south. Kuwait was close now, so close that we were starting to lose focus. This far south the real danger wasn't insurgents or terrorists, but land based pirates. Bands of thieves scoured the roads, taking what they could and murdering who they wanted. I wonder if that lawlessness ever made it back to western media outlets. Probably not, knowing the nonsense I've seen on the television since.

We were less than an hour out from the Kuwaiti border when a loud snap came from my engine. Blue smoke poured into the cab. Shit! My driver, SPC Anthony Harms, who was also a certified mechanic in the civilian world, pulled us over and started doing his mechanic stuff. I'm more comfortable with blowing stuff up, not fixing it. Sure, I was a trained howitzer mechanic but that wasn't going to help here.

My assistant gunner, PFC Jeff Tankersley, or Tank, poked his head into the cab and asked with his hillbilly drawl, "What happened? Is it the transmission?"

Harms frowned, probably more from being disturbed than anything else. "No, it's not the tranny."

"It's got to be. Listen to it clunk," Tank insisted.

Harms had had enough. "You don't get blue smoke from a fucking blown tranny, Tank. That's coming from the oil. I think we threw a piston rod. Stop talking about it!"

"I still say it's the tranny, Smoke," he now addressed me.

"Pop the hood and take a look, Harms. Tank, help SGT Hoy keep watch," I ordered and then picked up the hand mike. "LT, I got something wrong with my engine. Not sure what but my driver is checking it out."

"Roger, I'm coming back to see."

What's he going to do? The LT and most of the other guys were from Charlie Battery so we weren't used to working with them closely. Still, after three long days we'd gotten along fine and had made it this far. Kuwait was less than an hour away and here I was broken down on the side of Highway 1. Not a very imaginative name. I think there has been a Highway 1 in every war in the last hundred years.

Harms wiped the oil from his hands. The dour look on his face told me all I needed to know. We were fucked. "We threw a rod."

"Can it get us back to Doha?" I asked optimistically.

He shrugged. "I don't know, Smoke. Maybe."

After a quick conversation with the LT, we decided to push on. The final objective was almost in sight. Speed reduced, we made it to the Kuwaiti border, where I gleefully snapped a few pictures of freedom. The destroyed Republican Guard tank guarding the berm was a testament to the awesome military might unleashed back in March. The battalion caught up at a customs checkpoint and I was notified that the recon element had done their job and we were to take up positions at the rear of the column.

I hadn't heard a more bullshit order in a long time. How dare the battalion commander have us at the sharp end for three days only to tell us thanks and then discard us so casually at the end? The LT and I protested and, to my surprise, we won. The recon team led the way into Kuwait and finally to Camp Doha. Along the way we stopped to turn in all of our ammunition, concertina wire and random bits of armor and gun mounts. All the while I remained worried that my truck wasn't going to make it.

Camp Doha finally came into view around 2300. At long last our war was over. There was no sense of accomplishment. No job well done. No cheering crowds to meet us. At the end of the day we were nothing but tired. Bone weary and ready to go home. Too bad we'd spend most of the next three weeks waiting for that final bus ride to Ali al Salem Air Base and the big, iron bird home.

Harms pulled the truck on line and killed the engine, in more ways than one. One of the local transportation soldiers wanted us to move forward some but the engine wouldn't start. The starter was frozen. Our truck was dead. Rest in peace. We downloaded our gear and left it for someone else's problem. Battalion was shown to our temporary living quarters, another set of warehouses. Weapons were turned in and we arrived in time for midnight chow. The concept was ridiculous considering I ate an MRE for Christmas dinner and we'd been lucky to have two hot meals a day throughout the deployment. Here we found the soldiers stationed hundreds of miles from the fight living the good life. I was disgusted.

Then it started raining. We were filthy, exhausted and in a generally foul mood just from seeing the clean, relatively happy soldiers in *civilian clothes*. A bunch of NCOs stood in the chow line, mostly silent. This was the end of my second deployment but the experience was unlike the first. In Afghanistan I got a plane and went home, nothing more. Here I got to go through the full process. It was laborious and boring. Definitely worse than my first tour. I wondered if my wife was going to be home waiting for me this time. Not that I cared anymore. The marriage was over; it just hadn't gone through the good graces of dying properly.

Through our silence we heard one of the pogues complain. "Man, there's never a line. Who are all these people? They're messing things up."

Way wrong answer.

SSG Andrews unleashed. "We're the ones who were fighting the fucking war so you motherfuckers didn't have to. So shut the fuck up and turn around before I beat the shit out of you and your friends."

The soldier and his two friends bowed their heads and snuck out of the chow hall without a peep. We didn't realize it but the entire chow hall had fallen silent during Andrew's tirade and, to be honest, it felt good. The food wasn't that good but there was plenty of it. I guess that's what comes from mouthing off.

The next sixteen days would be a continual trial not to let our emotions get the best of us. Actual danger may have passed but now we were faced with an equally challenging dilemma: what to do with 500 plus soldiers mixing with people who hadn't deployed forward and a lot of free time. The worst part of the equation was the abundance of women. I couldn't remember the last time I saw a woman, much less talked with one. I had a feeling this wasn't going to be a good time.

A group of us were walking to the chow hall for lunch one day when a tour bus pulled up in front of us. A bunch of soldiers got off; naturally all dressed in civilian clothes and were giving each other hive fives.

One of them was smiling as he said. "Man that was so cool! We went to the berm and I saw a blown up tank!"

My fist clenched reflexively and I took a step forward. A blown up tank? You have got to be kidding me. Part of me wanted to know what would happen if one of these kids actually took incoming fire, but the bigger part just wanted to punch a hole in his face. I made it three steps before my guys pulled me back. They laughed, I growled and we continued past the special tourists. Rear echelon people suck.

Kuwait offered simple luxuries many of us had long forgotten. There was a movie theater, fresh pizza and a Kentucky Fried Chicken. The chicken in Mosul was eat at your own risk. The chow hall's wasn't much better. Camp Doha was the first time I ever had Starbucks coffee. I still don't see what the big deal is and there is something disturbing about seeing a grown man in uniform ordering some foo-foo coffee with whipped cream. It did taste good though, much better than the motor oil we were used to up north.

By and large, most people were genuinely nice down here. The base was located on an inlet overlooking Kuwait City. We were the first combat troops to rotate home through here and it was evident. Still, having the freedom of walking around without a weapon or body was a blessed relief. We spent three days at the Doha wash rack pressure cleaning our vehicles so they could pass a very rigid inspection by U.S. Navy customs people. Too many vehicles failed to make the experience pleasurable.

Adjusting to semi-real life was a chore. A group of us was walking the mile or so back to our 'barracks' when a loud boom sounded behind us. We ducked for cover that wasn't there while a group of pogues smirked and struggled to keep from laughing at our foolishness. A golf cart had backfired when it drove by. To us, with months of combat conditioning, it was an IED or RPG exploding. To the rest, it was nothing but noise. I learned I don't like noise anymore.

The days blended together. When soldiers get bored they tend to border on the impractical, immature. I am no stranger to this, nor am I immune. I love a good practical joke. One day, with nothing in particular to do, I was relaxing on my cot reading. SGT Nate was across from me playing on his laptop. He then made the fatal error of going to the gym without locking it. I pulled two orderly room clerks over and we went to work. PFC Ithalangsly and PFC Bagnato set his screen saver to big, bouncing silver letters that simply said: I love the cock. Private I, as we called him, then looped the Boy George song 'Do you really want to hurt me' continuously. Our battery commander got in the act by putting a blank password so Nate couldn't log back on.

For over an hour all anyone could hear in that damned building was Boy George. The sad part of it was someone actually had that song on an MP3 player. I was starting to worry Nate's battery might die before he got back but sometimes God is good, really good. Nate entered the building, heard the music and asked loudly, "Who the fuck is listening to this gay ass shit?"

Snickers and stifled laughs rippled through the dozen or so soldiers around. Nate stalked up to his computer and just stood there reading the screen saver. His face twisted in a strange combination of anger and embarrassment. He knew he'd been had. I looked up from my book.

"It's about time you got back. Turn that shit off, Nate," I told him.

He tried. And failed. With no other recourse, Nate stood, faced the rest of us with his hands spread wide and admitted, "I love this song!"

Laughter continued for a good twenty minutes. The best part of it all was that we heard people humming, whistling or singing Boy George for a good two or three days. The unintended consequences made it all the funnier. Not to be outdone, I paid for it when my platoon got me a birthday card later that week, which I still have today. Some things just shouldn't be mentioned. Life was slow and boring, but enjoyable at last.

The battalion commander got a wild hair up his ass and decided to lead us on a full battalion run. Doha was only so big and the route was barely a mile and a half. We dug out PT gear out one early morning and formed up. The entire mile and half was loud and thunderous with cadences, mostly vulgar and officially 'banned' from everyday use because they had the potential to offend some soft skin or another. I think we managed to wake every single soul on base up and none of them were happy. Before our run we never saw any kind of organized PT. After, it seemed every commander and leader had been shamed into action. Here we were, a worn out, ready to go home combat unit that had spent too long in Iraq and we were out running. Those stationed at Doha had no excuse.

The final forty-eight hours arrived and we started the customs process. All bags and pockets were dumped and emptied. Soldiers were found outside of the main tent cutting up or destroying naked pictures of spouses and loved ones (occasionally someone else's loved ones). For some odd reason no one bothered to check it we received that stuff in country or left home with it, but it was against regulations to return home with it. Tell me how that makes sense. Most wartime memorabilia was contraband and I was about to lose the two Iraqi AK-47 bayonets I had until a ruling came down that we could keep them. I kept one and gave the other to my father, figuring it would go good with the two German officer pistols my grandfather had brought home from Europe.

Customs put us in a sealed off compound of holding tents until the buses arrived. I don't remember how many hours we sat and waited and waited but it was a lot. The Army excels at waiting and standing in lines. (Show me a line today and the temptation to go stand in it resurfaces.) We got to do both. Finally, the buses showed and were driven halfway around Kuwait City to the air base. The big, civilian airliner was one of the most welcome sights I had ever seen. We boarded and settled in for a nice, long eighteen-hour trip back to North Carolina with stops in Germany and Ireland. The unexpected happened en route from Shannon, Ireland to the U.S. A freak storm hit North Carolina. It was so bad we were diverted to Bangor, Maine. In the middle of January. If that's not bad luck I don't know what is. How could North Carolina be so cold we had to overnight in Maine?

Our plane landed in a frozen, snow-covered Bangor and we were escorted to a pair of hotels that graciously put us up for the night at no cost to the soldiers. They even went so far as to have the local veteran's organizations waiting for us when we arrived. It was very humbling to stroll down a corridor of WWII, Korea and Vietnam veterans all shaking our hands and thanking us for what we did. I was left with the feeling that we should thank them. Nothing in Iraq compared to what those brave men once did for us and their country.

I was greeted by a man who fought in Korea for nearly three years. We'd shared some of the same countryside but that's where the similarities ended. The Korean War was by far more destructive and damaging that anything the coalition did in Iraq or Afghanistan. And he thanked me! I have seldom felt as humbled as that moment. I graciously accepted his thanks and turned it around on him.

"I should be thanking you. You did far more than any of us," I told him and shook his hand.

Two soldiers fifty years apart and we stood shaking hands. There is nothing like the bonds of brotherhood being a combat veteran offers. No office job, no warehouse worker or bank teller can understand this bond. Nor should they. Men and women who willingly march into the enemy's teeth and come back out are irreversibly changed. There is a measure of comfort to be found just by meeting another, even if it was from half a century ago. WWII soldiers were hailed as heroes. Korean War soldiers were largely forgotten. Vietnam soldiers were reviled, hated by a misinformed population. We were being greeting with enthusiasm; a pride in our retribution for the 9/11 attacks. It didn't matter the reasons for the war in Iraq. All that mattered was that we delivered a tremendous blow to the enemies of the United States.

Soldiers streamed in to the USO office, using the dozens of prepaid calling cards to call home. Coffee and snacks were passed out by little old ladies with big smiles and the kindest hearts. It felt good. Damned good. We milled around the waiting area for about an hour before the senior leadership returned with billeting information. Guard shifts were established for the weapons. It wouldn't do to walk around parts of Bangor with rifles and machine guns.

The welcome home spirit was catching. Everyone we met was as excited to see us as we were to be back in America. Even the flight attendants showed their patriotism. One of our Bravo Battery soldiers convinced one of the flight attendants to go back to his room. They spent the night together and got married about a month later. Who can make up something like that? The marriage was rocky from the start but what could they expect from a spur of the moment night of passion. Which one was the bigger fool remains open for debate.

The final dawn came and we assembled back in the airport. Most everyone was jittery. Long months of hardship and painful memories were finally ending. The only thing standing between us and freedom was a four hour plane ride south. I can honestly say I don't remember anything about the previous night in Maine. I know people headed to the pool, but I didn't see the need to pack swim trunks for Iraq. I showered and went to sleep. Couldn't even tell you if I ate or not, though a buffet of deli meats and sandwich elements comes to mind. All I remember was that it was absolutely freezing.

The plane jumped into the sky to the chorus of cheers. Five hundred men roared like only victorious soldiers can. We had done it. We survived the invasion, the grueling long months of occupation (that the government vehemently denies), the countless ambushes and attacks, the numerous wounded, the bad news from home. It was over. No one thought they might go back to Iraq. This wasn't the time. For us, the war was over.

The most inspiring moment came when we touched down at Pope Air Force Base and the pilot came across the speakers, "Welcome home, gentlemen. Job well done."

Nothing else needs to be said. How can I convey the joy, the combination of sorrow from being gone for so long and the elation of seeing the task through, that surged through my heart? How can I tell a person who complains about leaving home for a week on business that they have no reason to complain? I watch a show like Survivor and get disgusted. One month away from their families and the contestants break down in tears and heartfelt emotions. Weaklings, every one of them. Try going away, without the promise of returning, for a year or more. Try worrying whether or not your men were going to get killed or if you were going to be able to feed them. Try walking a mile in our boots and then look back at your petty complaints. Just try.

We got off the plane much the same as when we boarded, only this time there was no general sending us off. Command formed us up into ranks and we marched into the PAX shed while the band played and families cheered. All the deployment fatigue fell from our shoulders. We marched taller, prouder. Pride can be a wonderful thing. I think every man in formation that had family found a greater reason to march. Wives and parents lined the way with signs and flags. Children were so excited they were unable to stand still. Several broke away from their mothers to run out and give their daddy's a hug around the legs.

The Army doesn't like to do anything without a ceremony, no matter how small. We filed into the PAX shed and waited while our brigade commander gave what was meant to be an inspiring speech. Honestly I believe it had to be for the family members because I didn't hear a word he said. I, like almost everyone else, was busy trying to shift through the crowds and see if my wife and daughter were present. Unlike Afghanistan, they were.

We were finally dismissed for fifteen minutes (there were still weapons to turn in, equipment to download, and a schedule of events to be published before we could go home. Families swarmed into us like a clash of ancient armies. I wormed through the crowds to come before my wife. Mixed emotions clouded my decisions, all except one. I smiled and reached for my daughter. My daughter who I had barely gotten to see or know since the time she'd been born. Instead of being overjoyed to have her daddy back, Ashlynne cried uncontrollably and reached for her mother.

My heart shattered in the cold morning air. I was still a complete stranger. As foreign to her as the Iraqi children were to me. I kept pictures of Ashlynne in my breast pocket every time I left the compound. She was everything to me. The one thing that kept me going when hope dimmed. The one thought that kept me safe when events grew unbearable. The one thing I missed and wanted to see more than anything in the world. And she didn't want anything to do with me. There was no possible way for me to prepare for that heartbreaking reception.

It would take weeks before the two of us found anything in common. My impending divorce only made reconciliation worse. One week with me and the next apart drove a nail in my soul. There is nothing to compare the pain and internal devastation of being a stranger to your own child with. I suddenly hated the Army almost as much as I loved it but it was my decision that kept us apart. My need to be a part of something far greater than myself that made me sacrifice any semblance of a normal family life. It is the one true regret that continues to weigh heavily on my soul. That part of me will forever be broken.

PART THREE:

Operation Iraqi Freedom III

> *"No matter what you think about the Iraq war, there is one thing we can all agree on for the next days - we have to salute the courage and bravery of those who are risking their lives to vote and those brave Iraqi and American soldiers fighting to protect their right to vote."*
> – Fmr. Sen. Hillary Clinton

Chapter Eleven: One More Again

We had been home for about six months and I was feeling restless. I had finally decided to get divorced, a decision that I would later have mixed emotions about. The divorce was one of the easiest things I had to do and certainly turned out for the better. My only regret would come after I returned home for the last time in February 2006. Again, it revolved around my daughter. I discovered early on that few things affect me. I've never been one to show emotions, always considering it a sign of weakness. That's not to say I'm right, but it certainly helped matters during my three combat deployments and the endless years of dealing with knuckleheads and everyone else's problems.

I was walking through battalion headquarters when CSM Avila stepped out of his office and asked, "Freed, you want to go back to Iraq?"

"Hell yeah, Sergeant Major," I replied without thinking.

The adrenalin of war can be just as addicting as nicotine or tattoos. Saying no wasn't possible, not after enduring two deployments in the last three years. I wanted to be back and perhaps on some subconscious level, needed to. Life stateside didn't make sense anymore. There was no sense of danger, no thrill of being part of something special.

It had taken me nearly a month of being home before I got used to it again. Simple things seemed luxurious. Who could have imagined that a flush toilet held so much pleasure? The overwhelming sights and sounds of normal American living kept me secluded for a time. I was content with staying home, smoking a good cigar and having a drink on my back deck. To this day I still detest large crowds, refuse to drive in big cities, and almost always sit with my back to the wall in a bar or restaurant so I can watch everyone and everything.

Why would I want to go back and undo all of the gains I'd made since coming home? Simple, it was my job.

Going back to Iraq offered to remove those hindrances and put me back where I didn't need to think so much. There is an unexplainable simplicity to being deployed. Choices are removed. There's no need to waste time or effort thinking about what to eat or when. What to wear. What to do. All of that is left behind the moment you board the aircraft. Don't even think about dying. There's no point. If the good Lord wants you he's going to claim you. Death becomes a boon companion no one talks about. It's always there, lurking in the shadows but remains hidden until the proper time. So really all that's left is getting up in the morning and doing your job. Easy.

Given that set of circumstances, and of course a long career already in the Army, who wouldn't want to go back? Saying yes was easier than wanting to go the first time Maj. Burdett asked me a few years earlier. My personal life was unhinged. A fast divorce, which I stand firmly behind my decision as well as the opinion that it was one of the single most liberating moments in my life, and the uncertainty of putting my life back together helped make the decision even easier.

Going back to Iraq offered to take away the confusion, the pain of seeing my daughter only occasionally rather than every day. It welcomed me with open arms, inviting me to forget, to put off what I needed to do to move past the failure of the last eight years my marriage consumed and gave me new windows of opportunities. I jumped at the chance.

Truthfully, and I know many men would say this just because there is the ridiculous stereotype we are all supposed to have, the day I got divorced was one of the happiest I had experienced in a long time. Eight miserable years finally ended, freeing me from the weight continually dragging me down. I'm not so foolish as to try and convince anyone that I was perfect, mother's little angel, during it all. I made plenty of mistakes. I am, after all, just a man. Getting married at the age of twenty-three was foolish at best. I thought at the time I was ready and knew what I was doing. Survey says....*ZZZZZZZ.*

Not very superstitious, I should have factored into account my deployment to the Joint Readiness Training Center (JRTC) at Fort

Polk, Louisiana less than a week after the wedding. The gods weren't approving of my decisions. I jumped on the bus with the rest of my Battery and headed down to where the good old boys roam while my newlywed wife was forced to move into the new condo and set up operations. Was this punishment? Looking back, I would say probably so.

Six months later I received orders to head back to Korea, a feat I still find remarkable considering the branch manager at the time was my old platoon sergeant. I asked how it was possible that every single sergeant in the U.S. Army had rotated through Korea over the last four years that it was my turn again. Naturally I got no reply. Now I know where the acronym Uncle Sam Ain't Released Me Yet was born from. I tried to get out of it, to go anywhere but back there. Even found a buddy who wanted to go in my place. We called the branch manager with the plan that my buddy would be put on assignment to Alaska, me to Korea and we would just swap. Simple right? Again… ZZZZZ. Two months later we were both in Korea.

There's no point in boring anyone with the myriad of details about how my marriage slowly disintegrated. We've all been there in some way or another. No union between a man and woman is the happy visions of 1950s television. The distance started the gap. Lower enlisted never make good money and my wife was disinclined to hold down an actual paying job so we struggled through. I got cursed out for spending a hundred dollars (that I earned) and her not being able to buy milk because of it. We'll skip the fact that she found a way to go all the way to San Diego with one of her college friends and then Sea World. A gallon of milk my ass.

When I rotated home the marriage was a shambles, so we got separated. I didn't want it to happen, or so I thought, and nearly made it the entire year the state of North Carolina mandates before getting back together. My daughter was born two years later but I was never happy again. I quickly came to realize that staying together solely because of my daughter was a bad idea. It was a lose-lose situation and everyone got hurt, especially my precious daughter. Thank God the war started a few days after she was born. It gave me an out, a chance to clear my head and maybe make a better life.

The finality of the divorce was a breath of fresh air. A freedom I hadn't felt in nearly a decade. Endless hours of self-imposed misery shattered on the floor as the court clerk stamped the official seal. My lawyer smiled and said congratulations. I said thank you, gave her a quick hug and turned to walk out. The ex tried to give me a hug but (I swear I really did) I just smiled and slapped her on the shoulder like an old football buddy. "See ya later, Chief."

I strode out of the courthouse whistling.

CSM Avila looked at me strangely. I was sure that he was part relieved I volunteered so easily, thus making his job easier by not having to pick anyone on his own. It can't be an easy task to tell a lone individual that he or she has to go *back* to war just a few short months after returning. He also had to wonder what circumstance could lead that same person to actually *want* to go back. When 377 redeployed to Iraq in mid 2006 he had already dropped his retirement packet (having zero intent on following his soldiers one last time) and left the battalion to the wolves.

It was a sentiment I certainly didn't share or approve of. There is an inherent responsibility to go to war with your people if you knew it was coming. I wouldn't have volunteered if I had known that battalion was going to be put on orders the months after I arrived in Baghdad. My opinion of those who were unwilling to share danger, to take the back door and exit whimpering continues to lower. On the other hand, there were men like CSM Jordan from the 35th Signal Brigade. He was already at the point where mandatory retirement was closing in and he definitely didn't need the money or the combat time. The man was Michael Jordan's brother and had done his thirty years. That didn't stop him. He fought for and got a year extension so he could deploy with his people. It doesn't get more admirable than that as far as I am concerned.

"Good, you report to Brigade at 1300 hours," he finally said.

Lucky me. I got to go back to Brigade Headquarters and go through the entire process all over again. The one shining moment in all of this was that I was at least getting to deploy with fellow artillerymen instead of an overabundance of staff officers who were too far from the line to remember. Now a familiar friend, the cycle of briefings, meetings and random people coming in to wish us luck and all that started all over again. Show me an NCO that enjoys sitting in endless streams of meetings and I'll call you a liar. I deplore meetings, seeing them for a monumental waste of time. A good NCO needs to be out with his soldiers *doing*.[23]

---

[23] To prove God does indeed have a sense of humor, I married a meeting planner and coordinator. Of all the things....

It was during these lovely briefings that I first heard the term *information operations*. Apparently, I was in on the ground floor of a relatively new area of focus for our Army. Our briefer readily admitted that the Navy and Air Force were far ahead of us in terms of development and deployment. While he struggled to come up with a definition all of us found understandable, I can sum it up in one word: propaganda. To be sure, not the level or direction of what we see from WWII or even Vietnam, but propaganda nonetheless.

After sitting through a convoluted briefing about what we *might* be doing when we arrived in country we were broken up into operating groups, or cells. Most of what I was responsible for is considered classified so I can't go into depth. Myself and a Lieutenant from a sister battalion were sent to Fort Meade, Maryland to conduct training on our new jobs. Unfortunately, no one at Fort Meade had a clue what to do with us. We were sent to the Public Affairs Office (PAO) to learn the fine art of relating with the public. The instructors were nice enough, but again, weren't expecting us and didn't have much lined up in terms of training.

We trudged through a few days of basic PAO stuff, getting the gist of writing small, feature length articles and news spots. The most memorable part was hoping the train down to the Pentagon. This was my first visit to the most venerable of military bases. To say I was impressed is an understatement. The train pulled up directly in front of the massive building and we climbed the steps to ground level and arrived at a heavily secured reception area.

A female major met us at the doors and escorted us through the identification procedures. We had pictures taken and temporary access badges issued, all after being screened for weapons or explosives. I never bothered to wonder how much of this was different from before 9/11. Being the Pentagon, the brains behind our massed military might, I took it for granted that security was also paramount. Guards with loaded machine guns patrolled the entrance point. They made our limited efforts back at Fort Bragg seem infantile, almost a waste of time.

Once through, we found ourselves in the middle of an entirely self-sufficient world. The Pentagon had everything anyone needed except a movie theater. A relatively large shopping mall comprised much of one wing of one floor. Impressive. I could make plans to invade a country by noon and go down the hall to buy my wife some jewelry.

The major led us through the confusing passages (It wasn't long before I was thoroughly disoriented) and down the corridor where the Secretary of Defense and the Joint Chiefs of Staff had their offices. We were in the presence of the highest military men in the nation; the most powerful combat decision makers in the world. I was in awe. Huge portraits of every Secretary of Defense lined the walls. Only Donald Rumsfeld had two paintings; one for each tenure in the position.[24]

Eventually we wound up in the Public Affairs offices. Coincidentally, these offices were put in the exact spot on the outer ring where American Airlines flight 77 struck on 9/11. A memorial chapel was constructed at the point of impact, the names and memories of those who died engraved on a large plaque. We met with the one star general in charge and learned nothing. She seemed nice enough but wasn't given any specifics about how the XVIII Airborne Corps intended on using the newly established IO cell.

We ate a quick lunch down at the food court and were led back into the maze, this time going deep underground into the Army Operations Center. More security blocked our way, rechecking our authority to be here. The things I saw remain between me and the government, but it is safe to say Hollywood is way off the mark when they try to recreate the most important, strategic location in the Pentagon.

A colonel on the wrong side of fifty greeted us and led us into the Black Room. One of us asked him why it was called that and he gave us a blank stare while replying, "Because it's painted black."

This should be fun I thought. We took our seats around the long, rectangular table and waited for him to give us his portion of the briefing. He'd just returned from a tour in the Green Zone working for Strategic Command and had a wealth of knowledge and on the ground experience. Or so he claimed. Unfortunately for us, he didn't give us any usable information.

"How many of you have been deployed already?" he asked.

I was the only one that raised my hand and he nodded.

"Good," he said. "Have they given you a packing list?"

I nodded back. "Yes sir, but I've already been there twice so I know what to bring."

---

[24] Donald Rumsfeld is the only man to hold the position of Secretary of Defense twice. Once under President Ford from 1975-1977 and again under President George W. Bush from 2001-2006.

He practically flew into a rage. "Well have you told her?" he shouted, gesturing to the major seated next to me.

I passed a wary glance to our guide and stayed silent.

She helped me out. "Sir, I work two offices down from you. I'm not deploying."

"Oh." If he was embarrassed he sure played it off. "Let me tell you exactly what you need to take with you. You need two things: toothpaste and Tootsie Rolls."

You have got to be kidding me? Here was this man, who'd been in the Army for most of the last thirty years and was only a breath away from being a general going all senile on us. Toothpaste and Tootsie Rolls?

"The PX runs out of toothpaste the minute it gets stocked so you'll need to take plenty for the next year. And the Iraqi children love Tootsie Rolls. I used to carry ammo pouches full of them to pass out when I went out into the city. The kids loved it."

Of course they do. Kids will love anything if you keep giving it to them.

The obvious question was what does this have to do with Information Operations and why do I care? I was here, at the Army's expense, to learn the tools necessary to successfully complete my latest assignment. I hadn't heard a word that I found even remotely useful. The Pentagon, I rashly decided, was a waste of time. If I was going to learn anything it would be on the ground in Baghdad. The briefing ended, thankfully, when the colonel decided he had another meeting to go to.

We filed out of the operations center. I got stopped by another colonel asking random questions. Not wanting to get separated from my group, I did my best to answer quickly and excused myself. It was already too late. The others were gone. Three floors underground and I didn't have a clue which way to turn. I finally ran into a janitor, an older gentleman who laughed softly at my plight, and pointed me in the right direction. It took a bit before I caught up but my enthusiasm was gone. I was done with the Pentagon and the detached sense of reality from the rest of the deploying Army.

Army doctrine tells us that information is an element of combat power and that Information Operations is a prime means for achieving information superiority.[25] Our intent was to facilitate the advancement of the fledgling Iraqi Army and Police forces while focusing on reconstruction efforts and successes of the newly formed democratic Iraqi government. What did this mean to me at the time? Absolutely nothing. At least not yet. I was soon to find out that the connection between idealized doctrine and practical application were two distinctly different things. If my experience in Washington D.C. was any indication, I was in for one long year.

January 2005

Back at Fort Bragg we continued to finish up our pre-deployment briefings and screenings. I sat through medical for the third time in less than three years wondering just how many more shots I could get before I got sick. We drew fresh uniforms and boots (I made sure I got an extra pair just in case I had to work with another sergeant major who thought about himself first) and headed back to the rifle and pistol ranges. Our orders said we were going to Baghdad. Our superiors said to Camp Victory and the Al Faw palace and one of the most secure areas in Iraq but anything could happen. War is nothing if not unpredictable.

We signed out on our customary leave period. Training was complete, bags packed and loaded. I never understood how the Army expected anyone to enjoy the week or ten days before a deployment. Impending separation from families and loved ones is ever present in everything you do. There is no sense of normalcy, instead even the minutest thing becomes urgent or a shallow representation of what it would normally be.

This third (and final) parting with home life was by far the harshest. I had been divorced for a few months and was relatively happy. The initial custody arrangement gave me Ashlynne for a week on and a week off. So much better than every other weekend. My last sight of her was her mother walking her back to the car over ice covered ground. Little Ashlynne kept turning around smiling at me and saying, "bye-bye Daddy, bye-bye!"

---

[25] Field Manual 3-13, Information Operations: Doctrine, Tactics, Techniques, and Procedures, November 2003.

Of course she didn't know where I was going in two days, or how long I was going to be gone. Worse, she never would have understood. Here was my sole purpose in life, walking out of it. I slept on the floor next to her bed when she got sick (Don't give children cherry Kool-aid if they feel bad. The stains don't come out). I watched *Sleeping Beauty* with her so many times I could sing every damned song. I sacrificed everything I had for her, hoping she would grow up and be better than me.

And here she was walking away from me. Army doctrine states that we aren't supposed to tell people when we are deploying or where or for how long. Spies, believe it or not, are lurking everywhere, all eager to report back to their masters. Operational security, and the security of the soldiers, demands strict adherence. Ashlynne didn't know I was going back to Iraq. What I didn't know what that I wouldn't see her again for nearly four years.

My ex-wife decided to get remarried less than three months after our divorce. Not that I cared. My chains were cut and I was happy. What she did with her life was her concern. Just don't take me for a fool. She had the nerve to tell me she had just met the guy, and again, I didn't care. I wasn't dumb enough to believe her anyway. After I deployed, he came down on orders to go to Minnesota to become an Army recruiter. Convenient this happened while I was away so I wouldn't be able to fight it in court. I found out the hard way what she had done and where she'd gone. I had to wait until the following September while I was on mid tour leave to fight it in court. I lost. To this day it is my one true regret. Years later my daughter has been taught to hate me, while I still sit on my porch and think about that fateful day when all she could say was bye-bye.

The final dawn came and I hitched a ride into work with a friend. We drew our weapons, collected some final equipment items and boarded the buses for Pope Air Force Base. Time to say good-bye world. Iraq was calling. Hundreds of soldiers filled the PAX shed. There were a few tearful family members hanging around the outside, desperately trying to see their loved ones for every possible second. And with good reason.

Iraq wasn't as calm as it had been after the invasion and initial occupation. Violence erupted under the guise of sectarian fighting in 2004. The cleric Muqtada al Sadr was fueling anti-American sentiment. His Mahdi Militia was openly attacking Western interests, mainly contractors. Civilian contractors were starting to pay a heavy price for their involvement in Iraq. Images of burned bodies hanging from bridges and heads being slowly sawed off filled the internet and television. American forces were being driven back onto their FOBs, reducing our presence where it was needed the most.

Few places in the country became more dangerous than the Sadr City district of Baghdad. This was al Sadr's stronghold, a near impenetrable web of hostiles. American forces amped up their presence, forcing the militias to back down or act covertly. SFC Reginald Butler and I worked together at West Point a few years later but experienced the hazards of Sadr City for himself in August 2004. An infantryman, here is his account of what he and his platoon had to do in order to rescue the pilots of a down Kiowa observation helicopter:

8 August 2004.

My platoon was attached to C Company 2-5 Cav in support of a mission in Sadr City. At 0745 we left the FOB in Bradley Fighting Vehicles as the rear element, along with an M88 recovery vehicle in case there were any break downs. Moving along Routes Silver, Predator and Pluto we headed to a small town just west of Sadr City. We scanned for enemy activity, maintaining communications with our vehicles as well as the two Kiowa helicopters providing us with close air support. As soon as we reached the town I notified Comanche 6 (the ground commander) that our weapons system went down and we could no longer engage the enemy if we had to but could continue the mission.

As we reached the outskirts of Sadr City, on Route Copper to the west, the lead element came in contact with IED's from both sides of the road. The convoy continued slowly through the engagement zone while the helicopters maneuvered above. I was looking through my periscopes when I observed RPG's flying up towards the helicopters. The first one missed but the second hit the tail end, causing one of the Kiowas to spin slowly. At first I thought maybe they were maneuvering to evade incoming fire but it kept spinning and losing altitude. I watched the chopper until it almost hit the ground.

That's when I called Comanche 6 and told him we had a downed bird, that it was hit, and that we needed to move to the crash site. Comanche 6 radioed higher and quickly responded that we had a change of mission. We needed to move to the crash site and fast. He then ordered the company to turn around and, since I was the one who had seen it go down, I needed to take the lead and get us to the crash site.

I reiterated my weapons systems were down but I would still take the lead. As I told my crew to turn us around and move out they didn't hesitate or ask questions. We were going to lead the ground element in a non-fully mission capable vehicle. My crew responded by saying, "we need to save the pilots". I was proud. I looked behind and saw the rest of the platoon and support vehicles ready to go.

We moved out, maneuvering over rough terrain: jumping ditches, driving through small paths and knocking down walls in order to get to the crash site. My gunner, SPC Halliburton and driver, SPC Barton observed the smoke coming from the downed chopper when we were just short of Route Grizzly. They had a good vantage to the crash and could see where it was located. Comanche 6 kept asking if we had reached the crash site yet so I replied, 'negative but we can observe the smoke'. I glanced back and was shocked to see that the rest of the platoon was gone. We were like sitting ducks without firepower!

I called Red One, Lt. Johnson, my platoon leader and Red Three, my wingman, SSG Hernandez. "Where's your location? I don't have anybody behind me. I don't have any firepower and I need someone up here right now!"

Red Two, SSG Pitts, came into view, rolling towards me. "Red One and Three are stuck in a ditch. I'm behind you. I got your back!"

Reinforced, I ordered my track to push forward. I could finally see the helicopter on the ground and smoking right behind the mosque located on Grizzly and Copper. My Bradley ran over a very old, rusted out car and a fence line in the way. We reached the crash site finally, pulling in front of the bird. Red Two drove around to secure the back side, orientating his fire down the alley facing east. Enemy fire was already coming from that general direction.

I ordered SPC Barton to drop the back ramp so we could secure the pilots. SSG Denson, SGT Bayer and SPC Halliburton rushed out get the pilots out of the wreckage. I climbed down out of the main turret and went outside. We were taking small arms fire from what seemed like everywhere. Then bad news hit. My dismounts returned and informed me that the pilots weren't in the wreck. I got back in the Bradley and relayed the message to Comanche 6.

He responded by telling me that he had gotten word from higher and that the pilots were on foot next to a garbage truck down the road. I told my dismounts and they proceeded on foot to the *approximate area. I ensured they had working walkie-talkies to maintain communications. Two men went to the garbage truck while the third stayed behind and started picking up pieces of the chopper.*

Comanche 6 was ordering the rest of the platoon to move to the crash site quickly since only one of the two Bradleys on station was fully mission capable. He also told them to keep a look out for the two pilots. Desperation was setting in by this point. We had to find the pilots!

Bayer and Halliburton reached the garbage truck but the pilots weren't there. They were starting to take enemy fire but planned on continuing to search the immediate area. I reported the bad news back to Comanche 6, all the while listening to increased small arms fire and now more IEDs going off. I stood on the back ramp scanning the side alleys and streets. My driver covered the front of the vehicle with his M-16.

Red Two was engaging enemy personnel dressed all in black, with black masks and carrying AK-47s. I saw my dismounts returning from the south side of the mosque carrying two AKs but no pilots. Dismayed, I ordered them to help Denson search the wreck for sensitive items as well as any opsec information. We were still under heavy fire. My guys grabbed one of the pilot's helmets, maps, a personal backpack and a few other items and threw them in the back of the Bradley. They went back and started throwing pieces of the chopper inside the cockpit, making sure not to leave anything behind.

The search for the pilots had been ongoing for close to an hour. Red One and Three were still stuck in the ditch approximately 300 meters from the crash site. One of the gunner's suddenly spotted two armed men through the Bradley day sight. He told me to wait one while he confirmed. After a few tense seconds he called back and said that it looked like the two were our missing pilots and carrying M-16s. He took a closer look through his CIV and called back with positive identification. Comanche 6 wanted a status update, particularly how many dismounted each Bradley had in the back. He then ordered Red Three to drop his dismounts and recover the pilots.

Red One came on the net and told me that he was dismounting along with SSG Boaz and SPC Milks. Approximately two or three minutes later Red Three reported that the dismounts had run across the field to where the pilots were located and were en route back to the Bradleys.

I passed the good news down to my crew. Halliburton and Bayer continued to pull security along the side of our Bradley, taking sporadic small arms fire and a few RPGs from around the corner. The explosions were getting closer. I ordered them back inside. Comanche 6 then ordered a platoon to recover the Bradleys stuck in the ditch. The pilots were secure but there were still numerous enemy personnel in the area. We needed to leave.

We had been at the site for two hours when 6 called down for one of his elements to escort the M88 recovery vehicle over to the crash site and drag the helicopter out of the danger area. The Bradley that was pulling our rear security moved just then, repositioning to another location, leaving us and the wreck an open target. The M88 and support vehicles were barreling down the road. I called up and informed 6 that that Bradley providing us with cover was gone and requested another to secure the site and my own partially disabled vehicle.

Waiting for 6 to get the green light, I ordered my back ramp dropped so we could dismount and secure our rear until help arrived. We quickly observed what looked like an RPG gunner down the alley. Halliburton snatched my M-4 with the ACOG 4x scope and confirmed. He and SGT Bayer immediately opened fire, killing the gunner.

Dismounts from the Comanche elements rushed through the crash site as the M88 pulled into the area. RPGs were pouring down on us while the recovery crew began attaching tow cables to the wrecked chopper. A forward Bradley opened fire with the main gun, killing the enemy in the immediate area. The chopper was almost hooked up when the M88 machine gunner opened fire with his .50 Cal at an RPG gunner across the street. The area was getting hot.

Analyzing the situation, I called up to higher and reported where I thought the main bulk of enemy contact was coming from. The M88 started pulling out the chopper from the front but the wreck almost immediately started turning sideways. It was going to get stuck if it went much further. I jumped out of my Bradley and stopped the M88 crew and told them that there was no way they were going to be able to drag the wreck to where we needed to go since it was not tied up right.

They got out and disconnected the wreck, taking fire the whole time, and turned their track around to hook up from the rear. The M88 crew hurriedly started hooking the wreck back up. No one wanted to stay here any longer. We were taking heavy fire from the north. RPGs *were exploding all around, slowing down our progress. The security element returned fire while the mechanics and I finished hooking up the wreck. We were finally set to roll out when we noticed a car blocking the road.*

1SG Carson, myself and another soldier ran forward and pushed the car out of the way and then ran back to our Bradley. We continued to hold tight in that location until the M88 was safely out of the engagement area. Comanche 6 then ordered us out, back to Route Grizzly where we were told to stand fast until new orders came down. The battle wasn't over though.

Bradleys from the company were being engaged and were returning fire. Finally we were told to move back the same way we had come and link up with the other units already securing the assembly area. We made it with little incident but were only there for five to ten minutes before RPGs began exploding in the rear of our convoy. We continued to engage the enemy when we spotted them. Once the wreck was loaded onto a lowboy trailer Comanche 6 came across the net and ordered us to roll out at once. The DAC was getting attacked. Leaving our current locations, we headed out on Route Pluto and then down to Route Delta to assist a sister unit in heavy enemy contact at the DAC. Once secure, we evacuated the casualties to FOB Iron Horse.

SFC Butler's story ended with the successful rescue of both pilots and no fatalities. Others weren't so fortunate. All too many times troops on the ground were attacked by random civilians dressed in suicide vests or car bombs with enough explosives to utterly destroy entire buildings. Not every enemy success was based on their merits. The coalition made plenty of mistakes, often times with disastrous consequences.

One of the worst tactical mistakes made was in Mosul. The 101st had been replaced by a single brigade from the 2nd Infantry Division. One brigade trying to maintain the second largest city in Iraq. It couldn't be done, not effectively. Al Qaeda and other terror groups and foreign fighters poured into the province, flooding the city with fresh waves of violence. The war had become very real for the north.

Making matters worse, the big white chow hall on AO Glory (now renamed FOB Marez) was blown up by a suicide bomber pretending to be one of the workers. On December 23, 2004, a suicide bomber snuck into the chow hall in the middle of a meal and detonated. It was the single most devastating suicide attack on American soldiers throughout the war. The Pentagon reported that 72 personnel were wounded with another 22 killed. The horrors of that day were witnessed by SSG Matthew Crown, a good friend from high school. A respiratory therapist, he was part of the hospital detachment that was immediate response. There are some things I do not envy people. Heading into that scene of awful carnage was one of them. The sad part is that there was actionable intel that the attack was coming. But like all intelligence there is a decided lack of certainty preventing positive military action.

Iraq had become a country in complete turmoil. A different type of turmoil from the post invasion occupation I had gotten used to. It was a nasty, ugly affair that even the most stout hearted were having trouble with. A sane man might have had misgivings about volunteering to go back. The thought never crossed my mind. This was what I was paid for, trained for. All of those years spent sweating until the Fort Bragg sun, digging foxholes and going on patrol. Some people got to see quality assurance by turning out a good product. We found it at the end of the rifle in thankless places like Afghanistan and Iraq. So I sat back on my little part of the bench and waited for time to pass.

Finally all family members were forced to leave and we were locked in. we must have stayed in that shed for close to eight hours before the first flight was ready to depart. The wooden benches were designed to accommodate a fully rigged paratrooper, not soldiers without gear. They were seriously uncomfortable, forcing many of us to get up and wander through the crowds, stopping to talk or joke with people we knew.

Food was trucked in and there was plenty of water and coffee. It was cold, being early January. Soldiers still flocked outside to smoke. Others played cards and dominoes. I don't care where you go; you will always be able to find a game of spades being played. Dominoes if you are lucky. Most of us chose to sleep, but it was an uneasy rest. We were, after all, about to board that big iron bird for another trip to war zone. By now, I don't think there was anyone in our group who hadn't been deployed.

Chain of command members hung around, offering words of encouragement and false bravado. I never believed a soul who told me 'I was wish I was going there with you'. No you don't. No sane person *wants* to go to war, especially not for their third time in as many years. The sentiment was nice, but unnecessary. We were all professional soldiers. This was our job.

The time came, finally, in the middle of the night. The first chalk was called, did their final weapons check and filed out to the runway. The mood in the shed turned somber. The deployment suddenly became real. As soldiers, we have a way of tuning things out until the last possible moment. That moment had finally arrived. Explaining how it feels is difficult. There is elation that the wait is finally over, that everything you have spent weeks and months training for is about to happen. There is sorrow that you are leaving home, that all of your friends and family can't afford to be more than pleasant memories to keep you company when the nights get too long. There is regret that you have to leave home, that you won't be there for important events. And there is doubt that you might not make it home, that very bad things could happen.

All of these emotions collide in those long moments before your name is called. Your mind has trouble focusing. Too many thoughts and dreams swirl around to be able to concentrate. And then you hear it. Your last name. You respond with your first name, middle initial and social security number and then head out the door. The mass of emotions leave. You are alone again. One soldier with a singular purpose: come back home alive and in one piece.

Stepping out that door after your name is called is liberating. All of the worries and troubles wash away. You know what needs to be done and mentally prepare yourself for hard days, trying times. It is a oneness with the world. Prayers are mumbled to each person's god. You shake hands with the senior commander present and stalk up the stairs. You finally board the plane, hoping to get a good seat where you might be able to stretch out at least a little. The pilots and crew welcome everyone aboard. The door vacuum seals shut. A few minutes later the plane is airborne and four hundred soldiers are heading back into harm's way.

There is no other feeling in the world quite like it.

By now the military had perfected the routes to the Middle East. I found myself back in Shannon, Ireland. The airport was quaint. The countryside vibrant and beautiful. It was a stark contrast to the endless monotony of brown we were heading to. I roamed the gift shops to pass the time. It never dawned on me the capitalization the Irish took in marketing the leprechaun to dumb Americans. Everywhere I looked there was a variation of a leprechaun smiling back at me. While I felt no obligation to purchase one, that certainly didn't stop a large majority of the rest. Leprechauns.

One of the younger soldiers in our group had his friend grab a small video camera as he stood next to one of the women working in the duty free store. He smiled and said, "Yo, listen to the accent on her! I gotta get this on film."

Accent? In Ireland? No shit. Stupidity is very nondiscriminatory. It likes everyone, inviting them to come and partake. I walked away, embarrassed that these two young men were representing our country in the eyes of the foreign public. One thing I never understood is the air of superiority the American soldier finds when he/she is out among a foreign population. They tend to say the dumbest things; do the dumbest things. All of us in uniform are ambassadors. We represent our nation, not just ourselves. These two morons offered poor representation. I remain convinced that God likes stupid people. That has to be the reason there are so damned many of them in the world.

Our flight plan got changed up on us. We wound up landing in Crete instead of Frankfurt, Germany. That was pretty cool. I've never been to Crete. Too bad we couldn't deboard. Instead the flight crew opened the doors to allow some fresh air in (By now we were all fairly ripe and in need of a good shower and change of clothes). I saw the ocean, the very blue ocean, lapping against a rocky shore. It was serene. The kind of place I might have liked to have stayed for a while, just to forget.

All too soon the doors closed and we were off, speeding across the skies to my least favorite place in the world: Kuwait. The Kuwaiti experience this time around was much better than a year ago. I had only the clothes on my back to worry about. No endless hours at the wash rack cleaning vehicles. No ammunition to turn in. They did give us a handful of rounds, just enough to barely fill one magazine, before hoping a flight up to Baghdad. I didn't have to drive through either country or worry about dozens of soldiers. I had only myself to look after.

We spent the night in very, very cold trailers with no blankets or sheets. The food was pretty good, but could we really expect anything less for the men and women who stayed I Kuwait full time? Of course not. (I was about to find out what good chow was— I don't think I've eaten as good as I did when I was in Baghdad) Fortunately the night passed quickly. There is nothing worse than having to continually wait to get to your final destination. I wanted to get entrenched in Baghdad and start my job. Not that I was overly enthused about what I was going to, if the Pentagon and our week of half assed training was indication, but it was better than languishing around without purpose.

It is only a two hour flight from Ali al Salem Air Base to Baghdad International Airport (BIAP). Two hours of anticipation. Thirty minutes of trying to keep your breakfast down as the pilots of the C-130s took evasive action the closer we got to Baghdad proper. I personally think they enjoyed twisting and turning the plane just a little too much. The worst part was after the plane landed and the ramp dropped. All of the heavy fuel fumes just curl up and pour into the cargo bay. I couldn't wait to get off and breathe fresh air again.

At last the crew chief finished unloading our bags and motioned us out. It was the middle of the afternoon in mid-January 2005. I was back in Iraq.

Chapter Twelve: Baghdad

Baghdad. One of the most famous, written about cities in the world. The origins of human life were rumored to have been born in this area. Nestled between the Tigris and Euphrates Rivers, Baghdad is a sprawling metropolis that lacks the splendor of old Sinbad movies. Saddam Hussein and his sons did their best to turn Iraq into a surprisingly poor country. The wealth and splendor from centuries past was gone. Decades of being bankrupted by a corrupt regime and a handful of wars had left the circular city a ghost of itself. Twice the West had come to call. Once stopping within striking distance and the second breaking down the door and gutting the existing government.

Not to say the city is unimpressive, because it is. Massive domed mosques filled the skyline. One thing I had come to learn, quickly, was the depth of devotion in the average Muslim. They lived it, breathed it and were never shy about celebrating it, just as any faith should be. If you looked close enough, you might even find a Christian church. Of course they were few and far between but that didn't change the fact that they existed and were, unofficially, accepted.

Monuments, both ancient and new, were strategically placed to remind the citizens of past glories. There remained an air of pride in the city despite two years of trying to recover from the blistering coalition attacks and the rising tide of terrorist violence threatening to subsume everyone. After all, it is one of the most famous cities in the world. Who wouldn't be proud to live here, to be a part of the unending legacy of sultans and scholars?

The city was founded in the 8th century and quickly became the center of the Abbasid Caliphate. Not long after, Muslim scholars began calling it the center for learning, based on the abundance of scholars and culture developing. Baghdad quickly became the jewel of the Muslim world. Scholars from across much of the known world travelled to Baghdad to translate Greek, Persian and Syriac works. It was a city of enlightenment in a golden age.

Some of the most famous sites in ancient history reside in Iraq, emphasizing the importance of Baghdad's location. The ziggurat of Ur, located outside of the southern city of Nasiriyah, was built by the Sumerians nearly four thousand years ago and has survived not only time, but countless wars and regime changes. It is considered one of the three best preserved relics of the Sumerian empire. Ancient Mesopotamia also called modern day Iraq home. Minarets hundreds of years old stab up into the sky, silent tribute to great thinkers and visionaries.

Culturally Baghdad is without comparison from neighboring countries. A host of universities and cultural centers call the city home. Before the 2003 invasion the city hosted one of the largest and impressive zoos in the Middle East. The museums were without equal before the infamous looting after the law broke down. Priceless artifacts, thousands of years old, were lost before damage control began. Standing silent watch over the sprawling, circular city is the Baghdad Tower. Once closed, the tower is equal to the Seattle Space Needle, complete with a full-service revolving restaurant. All of it makes me pause to wonder what this city could have been if not for greed and the steady stream of war and invasion.

Surprisingly, much of the truth in the Christian bible also resides in Iraq. The gardens of Abraham are still maintained, if only for historical value. The glory once bestowed upon the gardens has long faded. The Garden of Eden is rumored to have been located between the might Tigris and Euphrates Rivers. Mosul was once the city of Nineveh, focus of the story of Jonah and the whale. The biblical relevance was as inspiring as it was daunting. To think that so much history had happened in this tiny desert country made my being here more than just part of a soldier's journey. I was becoming part of that history.

Today Baghdad is the second largest city in the Muslim world, boasting a population of over 11 million. Many of the newer monuments are dedications to the thousands of lives lost during the Iran-Iraq War. The infamous crossed swords (the Hands of Victory) were built over the main parade route and has become a favorite photo opportunity for American soldiers. The Al Jundi Al Majhool Monument rises high into the skyline in tribute to the fallen sons from the Iran-Iraq War in the 1980s. The pride resonating in the eyes of the average Baghdad citizen was well warranted.

I got my first real look at Baghdad as I filed towards the small buses waiting to take us to the transient tents at nearby Camp Victory. BIAP looked anything but international. The buildings had taken a beating when the 3rd Infantry Division rolled up in April 2003. One of the fiercest battles of the war took place here. A last stand of the vaunted Republican Guard trying to keep the Americans out of

Baghdad. Our little bus drove past the spot where SFC Paul Smith died defending wounded soldiers.[26] Bullet holes scarred the walls in tribute to his deeds.

Indefinable pride filled me just from passing this hallowed sight. There was absolutely nothing spectacular about it. An ordinary wall on the side of the road. But what happened is the very definition of what the American soldier is at heart. SFC Smith wasn't supposed to fighting that day. His job was to construct a prisoner of war holding area. He stepped up when no one else did and helped save close to one hundred of his fellow soldiers. He gave his life in the process and was awarded the first Congressional Medal of Honor for the war on terror.

I recalled a conversation I had several years ago, before the 9/11 attacks. We were in the field training and getting ready to bed down for the night. A few NCOs sat around under the camo nets with our soldiers discussing the battle of Mogadishu. We asked the soldiers if they would do what Shugart and Gordon did, even if they knew their lives were the final price. Not many did. Contrary to their indecisiveness, every NCO there said yes, without hesitation. That conversation took on a whole new meaning as the little bus plugged on.

Seeing as how this was my first time in Baghdad, I quickly put the events of the invasion behind and focused on the sights. Camp Victory was almost unremarkable. The roads were paved, if mostly dirty and covered in fine dust. The buildings were shabby, many still fortunate to be standing. None of them seemed to be more than two stories tall. Only the minarets speared up into the sky with the domes of mosques hinting at old grandeur. Palm trees lined the roads. An occasional bush sprouted up. Grass was a forgotten luxury.

The coalition had only been in Iraq for two years but it was evident that we weren't going anywhere. Existing structures were being reinforced to house maintenance bays and supply warehouses. Rows of HMMWVs and other trucks that hadn't seen the bad end of a firefight yet filled large areas and made tempting indirect fire targets for anyone bold enough to get that close. Most of the buildings had been occupied with various offices and necessary functions.

---

[26] SFC Smith received the Congressional Medal of Honor (posthumously) for his actions on 4 April, 2003. His actions resulted in the survival of more than one hundred wounded American soldiers while killing more than fifty enemy soldiers before being mortally wounded.

A mini bazaar was set up, filled with knick knack shops, a coffee house, barber shop and some imported food joints. I suppose there is something comforting in being able to get a pizza and a cup of coffee and pretend it's like home. The PX was small, but nice. Nothing like the ramshackle hut in Bagram or even the department store sized monstrosity around the small hill on Camp Liberty.

A USO center was set up on the outskirts of the trailer park. It had plenty of books, video games if you were interested, large screen televisions for movies and, most importantly, phones and computers to get in touch with loved ones back home. It was a bit of walk to get there, but worth it. Anything to keep your mind off the hardships of being away, missing important events.

The most impressive structure on Camp Victory was the Al Faw palace, the center for all combat and stability operations ongoing throughout Iraq. The palace took direct hits from 2000 pound bombs during the shock and awe campaign in 2003 and it was still standing. There were a few cracks running through the frame but structurally it remained fairly sound. Say what you will about extravagance, but the Iraqi's knew how to build a palace. Of course the rumor was we had specifically left this palace relatively untouched in the anticipation of using it as a major base once we were fully settled in.

The three-story building reminded me of the Pentagon, especially now that it was occupied by dozens of coalition military and civilian contractors. It too was well guarded. Abandoned Iraqi guard towers lined the lake. Bullet holes and larger scored most of them. The defenders had put up a good fight but against overwhelming odds it wasn't enough. The palace fell not long after BIAP. A coalition guard shack blocked the near end of the hundred meter bridge. No clearance badge meant no entry. Thanks to aggressive combat actions this was the only viable entrance to the palace. The secondary bridge had been thoroughly destroyed during the invasion.

A steady stream of foot traffic filled the bridge, coming and going. As I said, this was the hub of the war, forget whatever you heard about the Green Zone.[27] Politicians and lawmakers called the heavily fortified Green Zone home, but the fight was being coordinated from Camp Victory and the Al Faw palace. Of course the Green Zone had all of the amenities of home, as well it should have. The compound was 10

---

[27] The Green Zone was the symbolic and heavily fortified center of several Iraqi regimes located in the heart of Baghdad. The coalition used it as a political base, not only for incoming embassies but for the newly constituted Iraqi Government.

square kilometers and so heavily guarded the enemy never made a serious effort to breach the defenses. Camp Victory was more spread out, had less by means of natural defenses and was an easier target. The spoils of war.

Massive columns soared up to the roof, framing the large, green doors with golden handles. Saddam spared no extravagance. This palace had more than sixty rooms and nearly thirty bathrooms. Saddam and his senior leaders used the palace as a resort, often taking the opportunity to go duck hunting around the large lake. The palace itself is one of the most impressive buildings I have seen. And I got to work on the third floor. (At this point I figured someone had it out for me. Every barracks I lived in during my career had seen me on the third floor with no elevators. Here I was again. I hate stairs.)

The entrance was over thirty feet tall, arched and accented with gold. Marble floors and walls made you feel extravagant. A massive chandelier, easier larger than my living and family room combined hung opulently over the massive entrance hall. Spiraled staircases wove up. Stairs I would come to despise after my tour. I found it interesting that no matter how good of shape I was in the stairs always took my breath away and left me gasping. Some of the guys claimed there were sealed torture chambers behind the old palace kitchens but I contend the real torture instruments were the stairs. And I had the pleasure of going up and down a minimum of ten times a day. Sometimes twenty.

Everything seemed like it was made of marble. Right down to the toilets and bidets. It was strange at first, but pretty soon going to the bathroom made me feel like a king. Not even the transformation into a tactical headquarters suppressed the ability of the palace to awe or inspire. Like all things though, it soon became too easy to take the majesty of the building for granted. It was just another office to go to, another day at work. The marble didn't gleam as much. The gold etchings were as impressive. The huge throne-like chair in the main entrance, a favorite tourist picture moment, became a sideshow, a distraction from the mundane. People do the strangest things when that one special moment for an unforgettable photo opportunity arises.

The palace stuck out into a large manmade lake, ringed by equally impressive houses that once belonged to some of the most influential men in Saddam's former regime. Any of those houses would have been a mansion back home, if of a somewhat different style. Most of the buildings were now occupied by various coalition countries. The Australians seemed to have the best of it. They took one of the largest houses, with a fairly large private pool, and enjoyed life. (We had pools too but good old Uncle Sam drained them all and closed them down. It wouldn't be proper to actually enjoy ourselves in the middle of a war.) Too many times we looked outside and found dozens of Aussies in bathing suits and bikinis swimming or lounging while the smoke from the grills made my stomach growl. I guess they didn't know there was a war on.

Despite our Army's urgent need to squash fun and good times, we had our perks. The USO is, in my opinion, one of the greatest organizations in the world. Multiple bands, comedians, cheerleader troupes etc. rotated through Iraq and Afghanistan. Who would have thought this small-town boy would meet the likes of Roger Clemens, Drew Carey and Toby Keith in the middle of a warzone? The USO provided endless bags of Starbucks coffee and enough boxes of Girl Scout cookies to build a decent sized home.

Any support from home is appreciated. Somehow, someway I got in contact with Carolyn Blashek, the founder of Operation Gratitude. She took a personal passion and turned it into an important part of the war, important at least for those of us in uniform. They provided care packages; little boxes of love and support that helped ease the strain of being thousands of miles from friends and families. I wound up forwarding the names of everyone I worked with just to spread the joy.

There were a few familiar faces hanging around. Friendly reminders of a better time. I ran into LT Jackson from Fort Sill in the base mayor's office. He and I served together in Afghanistan and he was a field artilleryman. It always helps to have friendly faces that speak the same language. Turns out the major bases were given into the care of various battalion commanders titled 'mayors'. The mayor for Camp Victory was also an artilleryman who I would have the privilege of working for at the United States Military Academy years later; LTC Tracy Bannister. Sometimes it really is a small world.

My old buddy and boss LTC Joe Grubich was also there, doing the same thing he did in Afghanistan. What a thankless job, but he must have been good at it or they would have canned him a long time ago. That wasn't to say he was content with his assignment. He was infantry and what combat arms man wanted to be chained to a desk while his peers and friends were continuously in harm's way? The Army doesn't care what we want, only what it needs. Our opinions put on the back burner for the greater good. At least someone had the courtesy to put me in a different assignment. Now all I needed was to move into my new home.

They put us up in the transient tents. Huge canvas homes fitting about ten people with no privacy. Most of the NCOs I deployed with were put up in the same tent or relatively nearby. Once we checked in, we got placed on the housing list and waited for our names to be called before moving about a quarter of a mile down the road to the permanent trailers. I never thought moving into a trailer would be a step up but here I was looking forward to it.

One by one the names were called. It was a slow process. Slots only opened when someone else rotated home. I was in the tents for close to two weeks before my name came up. Two weeks was just enough time to get comfortable, if such a thing was possible, and I found desire to move lacking. Not that I had a choice. A steady stream of incoming personnel was driving us out of the tents. Two weeks and we already were done being the news guys. It felt a lot better than being a *turtle* in Korea.[28]

I wound up moving a few hundred meters down the street to our growing trailer park. The long white trailers were divided into thirds, two people per compartment. It was a step up from living in a tent or an open warehouse. Each person had a real bed (that was a first) a night stand and a wall locker to store gear and hang uniforms. There was even a rug and an air conditioner/heater built into the wall. I almost felt like a real person. How many nights I spent sitting on the front steps smoking a cigar and reading a book I lost track of. Good, bad or indifferent, this was home for the next year.

Three hundred and sixty five days can be a very long time. It can also go fairly quickly. This tour was going to test the limits of my patience and my desire to keep coming back. I wasn't looking forward to spending a year trapped inside a massive palace that reminded me of a maximum security prison and with people who weren't used to being on the line. There is nothing like the bond that soldiers share, especially combat soldiers when times couldn't get any tougher or worse. I didn't have that bond in Baghdad. I was augmented to a different breed of soldier and exposed to working with several coalition soldiers for the first time. My mind was already resolved that I was on an island, stranded and alone until that big iron bird came to take me home.

---

[28] Turtle was an unaffectionate term given to new personnel at the replacement center in Korea. One typically remained a turtle until the next person showed up.

I lucked out with roommates. The first one rotated home after about three months. He was a nice enough guy, an engineer. He also worked the night shift which was perfect for privacy. He and I saw each other only in passing. His replacement came in and took his exact duty position. It felt good to be able to come back after work and have some privacy for a change. Not that I minded the company. My second roommate was a great guy and we got alone pretty good. It's just nice to not have to talk when you've had a long or stressful day.

The camp mayor cell did their best to coordinate stress relievers. They put up a fairly decent sized gym by the main chow hall. Pick a class and they offered it, from tae kwon do to spinning. I couldn't help but wonder if this would have been available to us if it had only been American soldiers. As it stood, there were just as many civilian contractors and coalition soldiers as American troops. They gym was nice, real nice. The only problem with it being so nice was that it was almost always packed.

I've never liked being in crowds and that feeling has only grown worse thanks to Bagram and Mosul. Now I was on a cramped base. I chose not to spend my time in the gym waiting on a piece of equipment. Instead I decided to use the smaller lake to take out my daily pent up frustrations. The lake was roughly two miles around and situated along the east perimeter wall. It was also quiet. I went out after work, usually long after the sun had gone down. Whether it was a run or fast walk I took the time to vent my anger or clear my mind. It worked wonders and also left me in better shape than I had been in back at Fort Bragg.

One major sight kept me occupied on my route. Built in the middle of the lake was a much smaller palace. Unlike the mighty Al Faw, this palace was a bombed out husk. The airstrikes didn't intend on leaving this one intact. It was also almost as heavily guarded as the big palace. I spent weeks trying to catch a glimpse of whoever was being kept inside. Of course, the palace could easily have been home to any number of intelligence agencies or worse. You just never know. A little later I found out who the very special guest was.

Saddam Hussein was now a prisoner in his own nation, a forgotten figurehead for a deposed regime. Caught by the 4th Infantry Division in late 2003, he'd been transported down to Baghdad and tucked away in the palace in the middle of a lake less than a half mile from where I slept. Knowing that he was there, so close, only made me want to catch a peek more. The double handful of guards on the bridge with loaded rifles and machineguns convinced me otherwise. I never did get to see him, not that I really expected to. His time to pay for his crimes was coming and the coalition wasn't taking any chances with negative publicity.

Despite being in a three star general's headquarters there was a seldom a moment of peace. It felt like there was always an explosion happening. Either that or steady streams of small arms fire. Tracers were constantly flickering across the night sky. Iraqis liked to fire guns, a lot. Many months later I was sitting in my trailer watching a movie when I heard a lot of small arms fire coming from just beyond the wall. Being a regular occurrence, I turned the volume up. So did the Iraqis. Now I could hear heavier weapons, machine guns going off. I took off my headphones and decided to take a look outside.

The entire sky was filled with red tracers crisscrossing in every direction. Even better, I heard the distinctive pings of bullets striking metal. Rounds were hitting the trailers and there was no safe place to take cover. I was just heading back inside to grab my helmet when I heard one of the dumbest things imaginable.

"Hey! Come out here and check this shit out man!"

Whoever decided the visual display was pretty cool and decided to call out their roommate should have been slapped. No one in their right mind would stand outside without any cover and stare open mouth at all of that fire. I closed my door, strapped my helmet on and stood as straight as I could and hoped I didn't get hit.

The fire ended quickly and I found out that the Iraqis had been celebrating a soccer win. Crisis averted, I tossed my helmet back in my locker and went to sleep wondering how I would ever be able to relay the things I saw to my friends and family back home. Celebrating. Years later I still don't understand the concept of celebratory fire when things turn out good for you. That same fire almost led me to unleash on a village in northern Iraq. Now it had me hoping I wasn't about to become a casualty.

The Super Bowl was on us quickly, but not having seen any of the playoff games or caring who the two teams contending for the championship were, I didn't really care. Some of the guys headed down to the small chow hall on Super Bowl Sunday. The gods of war must have been pleased. Each person was entitled to have two beers. Real beers, not that O'Doul's near beer stuff they force fed us in Afghanistan. My mother would be happy to know that I actually passed on my allotment. The game came and went and I honestly couldn't tell you who played or won.

Most of my tour felt that way. I don't remember large chunks of it. Either it's a sign of getting old or it was just that forgettable. Having settled in, it was now time to earn my paycheck. It felt weird walking around everywhere without body armor or a helmet. We had our weapons, but realistically they would have been better off in an arms locker. As it stood there just wasn't any point in carrying one around. We couldn't keep any magazines in, forcing us to put one in our cargo pockets. I'm not even going to get in to how our lovely commanders decided that since we weren't technically in harm's way we didn't need ammo. I had thirty rounds, not even enough properly defend myself if things went south. Fortunately I was able to swindle my way into seven full mags; a full combat load.

I checked in to the palace and got my temporary id badge. My escort then whisked me upstairs to the third floor, always the third floor, where I entered the magical world of Information Operations. My earlier hunch paid off. We were the bastard children of the Fires and Effects cell. No one wanted us. No one respected what we were doing or trying to do. Wars were won through force of arms, not by trying to influence the local population.

Part of this problem can be attributed to the old Vietnam era mentality, where body counts were the deciding factor in whether we won an engagement or not. The older American commanders were leftovers from the Vietnam mentality and were finding it difficult to think past that now that we were being mired down in political and secular warfare. What they didn't understand, what none of us understood was how difficult the process of taking a country that had been ruled by a dictator and turning it into a fully fledged democracy was going to be.

Despite working for my actual boss from Fort Bragg and the XVIII Airborne Corps Artillery, a man I'd known for years, I found out just how little he respected IO. There was an unspoken division between those of us tasked out to support the IO program and the other artillerymen doing their jobs. We were frowned upon, almost shunned. I bristled at the plain contempt. Who were they to judge? We didn't ask to get put in the IO cell. Someone higher than us decided we'd fit well and reattached us back to Corps Arty. Fucking politics. Even in the Army there was no escape.

I made it up to the IO offices and found plenty of familiar faces along with plenty more I'd come to know over the course of the next year. The breakdown was unlike anything I was used to. We worked for an Army general, an Air Force colonel and several civilians based out of Maryland. Just to make matters more confusing, they threw me in with an Albanian sergeant and a Ukrainian captain who barely spoke English. I understood why he was in Iraq. I'm sure he could have stayed in the Ukraine and smoked cigarettes and watch porn. He didn't need to come all the way down to the Middle East to do that. He was a nice enough guy but didn't need to be hanging around.

Once again I found myself in the unenviable position of *not* doing the job I had been trained to do. By now it was getting irritating. You would think things would go better and more efficiently if you placed the right people in the right positions. Instead of having a trained (if dubiously) cohesive unit, the people in charge threw us all into chaos. No wonder the generals mocked up openly.

I worked my original position for three days before being reassigned to a cell that didn't exist yet. They placed me under a timid Air Force psychiatrist and an ex-armor Army major who had already passed up for promotion too many times. As if it couldn't get any worse, my new job was considered so low on the priority list that they gave me SGT Jurgen Kote, from Tirana, Albania.

Jurgen was an interesting man. We got along well from the start; a plus considering the internal turmoil the rest of the IO cell was in. Jurgen and I soon became great friends and remain in contact to this day. One of the first things I learned about the Coalition soldiers was that they were contractually obligated to only working eight hour days. Seriously, eight hours. The rest of us were grinding out twelve to fifteen hours daily and here the coalition was punching their timecards and enjoying their nights. What in the Hell?

One thing soldiers always seem to do is learn all the dirty words when working with soldiers from different countries. I've never been any good with languages but know enough to get me slapped in Korean and a few others. After listening to Jurgen talk I knew there was no way I was going to pick up on Albanian. That didn't deter him from learning everything bad in English that he could. This came to a head when our little Air Force boss came in and started going off on him for being on the wrong computer. Ok, that might have been my fault. I had work to get done on the unclassified laptop and he was in my way, so I shoved him to the classified one where he could watch a movie. Too bad for us, he didn't have a clearance or access to that laptop.

Jurgen looked her square in the eyes and said, "Hey, douche bag, take it easy."

I don't know who turned redder, me or her. While she was busy trying to figure out how to handle this situation, I pulled Jurgen up by the shoulder and pushed him outside. "I'll handle this, Ma'am."

I didn't bother to wait for her reply. The door closed behind me and I squared off on my new Albanian friend. "What the fuck was that? You can't say that to women!"

"Hey, stop jiggling my balls, man. She was making me mad," he said.

Stop jiggling my balls? Who was teaching this man English? Still, there was a measure of comedic value to his words. There must be something refreshing about being able to say what you are thinking without worry of much repercussion. He was only saying what we all wanted to at some point. We quickly discussed the finer points of discretion, and the incident was forgotten. Not that he learned anything from our talk. I continue to get emails and the occasional phone call with a friendly voice calling me 'fucko' and asking me if I had found him a girlfriend yet.

It turns out Jurgen was a drill sergeant back in the 80,000 strong Albanian army. I professed I knew absolutely nothing about his nation, except that Robert DeNiro used it to start a war in the movie *Wag the Dog*. Albania sent a contingent of a hundred soldiers to support the war on terror. Any help was appreciated. Most of them were stationed up north in Mosul and relegated to pulling perimeter guard. Jurgen and one other was sent down to Baghdad. I soon learned Albania was more communist than Mother Russia had been. It was also one of the last European countries to abandon communism.

I came to enjoy working with Jurgen. He was a good friend and an easy person to work with. We argued, laughed and shared espresso during his tour of duty. All in all, it was a pleasure becoming friends. He was one of the few people that made our work in the slums of the IO world manageable. Unfortunately for me his cultural indoctrination to America came from movies. He spent most of his time quoting *Hellboy, Ghostbusters* and *Austin Powers*.

Since he didn't have a security clearance, Jurgen couldn't access two out of three of our computer systems. That left him stuck on the unclassified computer and mostly watching movies. Oh how I would come to envy that. His forced inability to access necessary systems meant I had to carry the majority of the workload. I decided to use him for the leg work of our production process. I took him around the palace to the different offices and personnel in our approval chain. He could do that just as good as I could sit down and write. We worked pretty good together but it got worse once Jurgen's six month tour was over and his replacement came in. I had to start all over again. For now though I was content with our work program.

While most of what we did is still considered classified, it is no small secret that IO had major offensive objectives. We promoted the new Iraqi military and police forces, the fledgling democratic government and major infrastructure reforms. Mention of American or Coalition actions was expressly forbidden. What good would it do to prop up the work our fighting forces were doing if the Iraqi people lacked any or all confidence in their own men? Our job was to help the Iraqi's see that their country wasn't destroyed, like Western media insisted on reporting, and that there were sweeping reforms happening daily that would eventually improve the quality of life for everyone.

The cell soon became overflowing with personnel, mostly from Corps Arty. Our bosses struggled to find space for us. With the influx of our civilian contractor counterparts, the Lincoln Group, and a handful of cultural advisors we soon became too large for our meager offices. They had no room for Jurgen and me.

They stuck us in an old bathroom antechamber behind the Corps aviation assets. We didn't even have the dignity of working in our assigned area. Eventually the aviation folks would drive us out permanently, not that they needed much of an excuse. Once a week they turned our office into a staff meeting room, effectively kicking us out for close to two hours. I enjoy taking a break as much as the next guy, but there comes a point when being totally shut down is just damned inconvenient. The constant disruptions broke our workflow, often leaving us staring at blank screens.

Any confusion or turmoil we were presented with was short lived once we got into a steady rhythm. After that life just plain sucked.

Chapter Thirteen: The Struggle for Democracy

The Information Operations center was surprisingly complex. We had people spread out through several buildings and areas within the palace complex. It didn't take long to realize two important factors that would stick with me for the rest of my tour. One, none of the old time commanders cared for or wanted the IO program. Wars were won by killing the enemy, not trying to manipulate the feelings and emotions of the local population. Two, I was way out of my element. The work was cutthroat with added pressure coming down on us from too many angles.

I got stuck in the production cell and since we were the first in this position without established guidelines or standard operating procedure (SOP) we made it up as we went along. SGT Kote's English was passable, but not good enough for him to produce a written product. That didn't stop me from trying or him wanting to. In the end it took too much time for him to knock out the few paragraphs and then me to edit. We came to the mutual conclusion that I would write and he would carry the products through the approval process.

Researching what we wrote about was our main hold up. Fortunately, most days the enemy made it easy to find material. Terrorists may be fervent believers in their faith, but they aren't foolish enough to engage a superior fighting force unless they knew they had a good chance of success. The instances where they dared to stand up to coalition combat units were practically nonexistent. It makes sense. They weren't soldiers and lacked any kind of discipline or cohesion.

March 2005

Al Qaeda in Iraq and other terror groups and foreign fighters knew if they had any chance of success the national elections needed to become an unmitigated failure. America and its allies were equally determined to prevent that from happening. We stepped up the pressure on our enemies, driving them deeper into their holes. Training of the new Iraqi army and police force intensified.

Dozens of caches were recovered daily, robbing the enemy of bombmaking materials and their ability to wage war. Raids captured or killed numerous members of small terror cells throughout the country. But not every coalition success was planned. War is fickle at best. Unpredictable almost always. The terrorists on the shore of Lake Tharthar learned this the hard way on 23 March.

A strong force of Iraqi commandos, augmented with American cavalry scouts, raided a major terrorist training camp situated near lake Tharthar, northwest of Baghdad. The battle lasted only an hour and was a resounding success for Iraqi army popularity. The camp was comprised of several ramshackle huts and tents and was in the process of gearing up for a major assault on the western city of Samarra. Multiple car bombs were captured and disarmed as well as several large caches of weapons. Perhaps the most prized find was the laptops and piles of paperwork recovered after the battle. The terrorists clearly were not expecting the attack.

One of the most notorious deficiencies of the new Iraqi army was their inability to ruthlessly engage the enemy. Iraq, at one point, had the fourth largest army in the world but had been in three wars in the last twenty years. The new generation of soldiers was largely unwilling to fight. This makes sense from a certain point of view. Why fight when you have a proven combat force right next to you? I'm not suggesting the commandos didn't fight, but the majority of enemy KIA came from U.S. helicopter support.

The battle was made into an episode of the military channel's *Combat Zone*. Iraqi commandos engaged the perimeter defenses under the direction of the cav scouts. The initial surprise was quickly overcome when the terrorists started to organize and return fire. Several commandos went down, dead or wounded. What the enemy didn't count on, and should have, was the availability of air support. AH-64 Apaches and OH-58 Kiowa helicopters arrived on station shortly after troops made contact and exacted a heavy toll.

American pilots were credited with around 50 kills and breaking the terrorist's will to fight. Terrorists held their ground as long as they could but it wasn't good enough. Commandos killed another thirty-four more. A handful of boats filled with terrorists managed to escape across the lake in the middle of the battle. Seven Iraqis died in the battle and a handful were wounded.

Reporters and those uninformed about what was really going on in Iraqi question why we went there when the terrorists were clearly centralized in Afghanistan. This battle, along with hundreds more, showed the world just who we were fighting. Among the dead were confirmed citizens of Saudi Arabia, Morocco, the Sudan, Egypt, Syria and as far away as the Philippines. One Algerian was captured as well. Foreign fighters, terrorists, were in Iraq by the thousands.

Iraqi commandos largely performed admirably and scored a major victory. The fledgling force was finding ways to gain confidence and demonstrate their capabilities to the general population. Their success at Lake Tharthar was promoted in every major city and area of operations. It was exactly what the people needed to feel confidence, especially during the election cycle. But like every success in combat, there came equal amounts of setbacks. The next major battle ended with relative results but took a completely opposite course to arrive there.

April 2005

Nine times out of ten terrorists chose to hide under the cover of darkness and strike densely populated areas or the weak Iraqi police. That tenth time though…watch out. That tenth time came when al-Qaeda in Iraq organized enough to make a major assault on the infamous Abu Ghraib prison.[29] The enemy's intent was to free as many prisoners as possible, not necessarily cause damage to Coalition interests. The battle was hard fought and uncomfortably close to being a tactical success for al Qaeda.

Reports of initial contact came in just past 7 p.m. I had the good fortune of being downstairs in the first floor JOC when the battle began. The Camp Victory JOC was far more impressive, and climate controlled, than our rickety tent in Afghanistan. Tiers of seats reminiscent of a college classroom looked down on massive screens covering every tactical aspect of the war in Iraq.

The panicked call of "attention in the JOC, troops in contact" silenced everyone present and pushed us into action. Combat multipliers were brought online while ground forces commanders were trying to figure out whose battle space the fight was happening in and where the closest reinforcements were. Talk of reinforcements meant that whatever was happening was major, especially when two separate divisions were coordinating the use of space.

---

[29]   The coalition prison facility came under major scrutiny in 2004 when explicit photographs of prisoners being mistreated erupted in the media.

Initial reports were confused, as they generally tended to be. No one was quite sure just what the enemy objective was or how large of an opposing force was attacking. Several key bases were coming under simultaneous mortar and rocket fire. Then the garrison at Abu Ghraib came under direct fire from an unknown number of enemy combatants. They had come to free their comrades and they had come in force. Early Army estimates claim that no more than 40-60 enemy fighters took part in the action. This was simply not true. Reports from troops on the ground suggest well over one hundred terrorists. This was heavily coordinated and well executed.

Mortar and rocket fire blanketed as much of the FOB as possible, effectively screening the first vehicle borne improvised explosive device (VBIED). The car bomb detonated prematurely, roughly 100 meters from the wall. The company of Marines defending Abu Ghraib took no comfort in the failed assault. They soon became hard-pressed to repel the almost overwhelming enemy numbers.

Al Qaeda took advantage of the initial shock by mining the main supply routes leading into the prison and setting up blocking ambushes for any Coalition reinforcements. Compounding our aggravation, enemy mortar and rocket fire was strategically striking the nearest airfields at Camp Victory and nearby Fallujah, thus preventing our air power from dominating the battlefield. A pair of AH-64 Apaches managed to close with the enemy but took so much fire that had no choice but to abandon their attack or risk being shot down.

An infantry QRF from the 3rd Infantry Division (who had tactical control of the Baghdad area) tried pushing up to the prison with Bradleys but were stopped by anti-tank mines and IEDs emplaced along the sides of the roads. Enemy combatants popped up from multiple ambush sites, preventing reinforcements from successfully reaching the beleaguered FOB. Al Qaeda took full advantage of that isolation.

A second car VBIED struck the wall near tower 4, the main enemy thrust. Insurgents got close enough to throw hand grenades over the walls, wounding several Marines. The enemy used the effect of the grenades for cover and rushed the wall in a hail of machine gun and small arms fire. The battle was furious. Marines, reinforced by several Army National Guard units held their ground but it wasn't the decisive defense they wanted. At one point the enemy breached the walls and threatened to break in. all that stood between the 5000 plus prisoners and success was a lone Marine Lance Corporal and his M9 pistol.

The rest of the FOB was running dangerously low on ammunition. Coalition units continued trying to get close enough to help, but the bulk of the armor was held up by mines and IEDs. Compounding problems, the prisoners began to riot. Several nearly succeeded in escaping. One thing the enemy didn't take into account was their lack of fire discipline. They wounded or killed more of the men they were trying to free than the MPs trying to keep them in their holding pens.

The enemy, wisely, attacked several units in the surrounding area, thus preventing help from scrambling to Abu Ghraib. VBIEDs hit multiple M-1 Abrams tanks, including a pair that had been called away from the prison to investigate reported IEDs at a nearby checkpoint. The report was false and both tanks came under attack as they tried to return to their positions near the rear of the prison. None of the tanks were able to deliver their full combat power. The closeness of battle prevented them from using their main guns.

Eventually friendly units reached the prison. The battle was already over two hours old and showed no signs of dying down. Enemy ground forces continued trying to breach the walls. Dozens of Americans were wounded. Elements from five units managed to arrive in time to help the defending Marines. They brought with them much needed water and ammunition. The defenders continued to hold until Marine Cobra attack helicopters arrived and drove the enemy off.

Thirty-six American personnel were wounded during the three-hour siege. Enemy casualty estimates ranged from 40-70 dead and dozens more wounded. The prisoners were put back in their assigned areas. They'd managed to set fire to a handful of tents but caused very little other damage. Their biggest part was the distraction of combat power from the enemy outside the walls.

The next day a pair of much smaller firefights broke out in the vicinity. A third VBIED exploded near the prison wall and Iraqi Police found two bodies rigged with mortars nearby. There was never any real danger of the enemy overrunning the Marine defense. Quick reactions by the commander led to a defensive perimeter inside the walls. Even if the enemy had managed to get in, they would have been met with fierce resistance. Not a single prisoner escaped.[30]

---

[30] A friend of mine, SGT Michael Carden covered the battle in a piece published by http://www.defendamerica.mil/articles/apr2005

The battle of Abu Ghraib was by far the largest single enemy assault in the past year. It showed the coalition that al Qaeda wasn't the low level entity, capable of only ambushes and deceit, they had assumed. Many of the defenders believed it was the type of desperate battle movies were made about. The battle also couldn't have come at a worse time for stability operations.

One of IO's largest areas of concern and focus was the upcoming cycle of Iraq's first democratic national elections. A daunting task, to be sure. Converting from a brutalized dictatorship to a free democracy is no small feat and does not happen overnight. Imagine how our own founding fathers felt when they sat down and drafted our constitution. How they felt when they declared independence. There is no comparison in our modern world for the enormous change Iraq was about to undergo. A nation the relative size of California had been ruled by Saddam Hussein since his rise to power in 1979.[31]

The various religious and political factions suffered under his tyrannical rule; many small ethnic groups the subject of racial hatred and attempted genocide. Saddam fancied himself a newer version of Hitler. The old one didn't do so well so it made no sense to me why he would want to pattern his regime after Nazi Germany. Dictators are prude, selfish people with more ego than sense. Saddam was no different. He squandered Iraq's riches on massive statues and mighty palaces in every major city. He gave equally massive palaces to his sons and favored generals. Sunni Muslims held every position of power, both in the central government and in the outlying provinces. If any place can apply the adage of the rich keep getting richer it would have been pre-invasion Iraq.

Saddam's initial claim to greatness was that he was born in the northern city of Tikrit, ancient home of Islam's most famous general, Salah ad-Din Yusef ibn Ayyub or Saladin. (Interestingly enough, Saladin was a Kurd, one of the most hated ethnic minorities in the Middle East. Hated enough that Saddam spent countless millions of dollars suppressing them and eventually unleashing his chemical weapons on them.)

Now Iraq stood on the brink of democracy, one that would be ridiculed and criticized for inadequacies and mistakes. People tend to forget that it took more than seven years from the time Benjamin

---

[31] Saddam Hussein took complete control of Iraq on 16 July 1979 and ruled until the American invasion in March 2003.

Franklin and the rest signed the Declaration of Independence to the time when they finally agreed on the basic foundations of a working constitution. The world was expecting Iraq to have it done and be up and running in good order in less than half that time. Ridiculous, the pressures we impose on ourselves.

One of the troubles facing the first generation of democratic Iraqi politicians was corruption. Every single one of the candidates lived under Saddam. Not to suggest that they were inherently corrupt, but all they knew was how the country was run for decades. It's not like they had the ability to govern themselves or even have access to other more established democracies. Changing habits is always difficult. Changing an entire thought process successfully and in short order is damned near impossible.

The election cycle began in mid-January with preliminary elections for parliament. Fear of the largely disaffected Sunni population boycotting the elections threatened to stain the process. Some already judging it illegitimate. It comes as no small surprise that the Sunni's would feel this way. They were the party of power for decades and had grown used to having their way under Saddam. Now they were afraid. Their future in the new democratic Iraq remained in doubt, at least in their minds.

This first election was, in my sole opinion, the most important of the two held that year. The 275 elected delegates to the new Iraqi parliament were chartered with two important tasks. The first was to come to a consensus by naming the Presidency council which consisted of a president and two vice presidents. The second and more important was to begin drafting a working constitution. No greater a task has any politician ever had. I thought back to high school and learning of the trials and tribulations of our founding fathers as they sat down in a room and did the very same thing.

The IO cell went into overdrive. We blanketed mass media markets with stories of success as the day progressed. The importance of letting the population know that it was safe, relatively, and alright to come out and vote was without comparison. Voter turnout was the telling factor of success or failure. Our combat camera detachment was spread throughout Iraq, snapping image after image of Iraqi's proudly holding up their purple stained fingers.[32] Those images were broadcast

---

[32] Fingers were stained with purple ink to verify that person legitimately voted.

176

to the world, though our sole focus was the Iraqi people and became a measure of our success behind the scenes.

Iraq's number one enemy, Abu Musab al Zarqawi vowed to make the elections fail. In a statement reported earlier in the month he made his intent perfectly clear:

"We have declared a fierce war on this evil principle of democracy and those who follow this wrong ideology. Anyone who tries to help set up this system is part of it. The Shiites aim to begin spreading their evil faith among people through money and fear."[33]

One thing was painfully clear. These elections were going to be fiercely contested and the make or break point for the new Iraq. If Al Qaeda ever wanted an easy target it would be the projected millions of voters standing in crowds and endless lines. We were already used to suicide bombers walking into the middle of crowded markets or large groups of civilians to detonate. The majority of the population was about to be exposed. Surprisingly, while enemy activity increased across the country, it was not at the levels we were expecting.

The election took a concentrated effort from not only our IO people in every major command, but the psychological operations and military intelligence folks as well as a heavy combat force presence. Most of the poling areas were secured by coalition and Iraqi military forces. Rodney Schmucker was a young captain assigned to the 1st Cavalry Division, made famous for their stand at the battle of the Ia Drang Valley in 1965 Vietnam.[34] The 1st Cav is a monster of a heavy division, filled with tanks, Bradleys and other armor vehicles. The sheer amount of combat power it brings to a fight is incredible. They took over the Baghdad sector from the 3rd ID halfway through my deployment and now had the unenviable position of defending polling stations.

CPT Schmucker and his men set up with the expectations of being in a long, continuous firefight with insurgents throughout Election Day. The expectation wasn't unreasonable. A successful election would mark a resounding defeat for everything al Qaeda was hoping to achieve in Iraq. American commanders were on edge. We

---

[33] Reported by www.abcnews,go.com.

[34] I would work with then Major Schmucker from 2007-2009 in company F3, 3rd Regiment, USCC at the United States Military Academy. He would eventually have a price put on his head while in Iraq by the local al Qaeda cell.

were all expecting a wave of attacks strong enough to force the civilians back to their homes. What we got was much different.

CPT Schmucker's men spent most of the day smiling and waving at the hordes of Iraqis coming out to vote. The good fortune extended across Iraq. That is not to say there weren't enemy attacks. Ever devious, al Qaeda took a young boy trapped in a wheelchair with Down's Syndrome and used him as an IED. They filled his wheelchair with explosives and rolled him into a crowd of voters.

Surprisingly, only forty Iraqi civilians were killed on Election Day. Not to diminish those losses, for each was reprehensible, but the numbers were infinitely less than our best predictions. What could have been an unmitigated disaster had become the model of success not only for Iraq but for the nations that had vested interest in a democratic future. Iraq offered hope to millions.

The first election was over but our work was only just beginning. Iraqi's parliament was temporary. Now it was up to us to continue building support for them and the rebuilt security forces. Nothing any of us did was easy. How do you tell people everything is working for the best when they don't have electricity or running water twenty hours a day because the power grid kept getting attacked? Or that it's safe to go to the market when a random stranger walks into the middle of it, whispers a prayer to Allah, and then detonates his suicide vest?

It is no easy task. Compounding issues was the constant state of flux we found ourselves in. Midway through the year Jurgen Kote rotated home, leaving me alone on the day shift. SFC Preston Johnson covered down on nights with a young LT from the 101st Airborne. LT Donatelle was a good kid, if just a bit naïve. Baghdad was his first real taste of Army life. The three of us had a few hours of overlap each way. We made it work, actually better than with a larger staff. The worst part about us was the people we worked for.

At times it was insufferable. Stress forces different reactions out of us all. The man I worked for didn't handle it very well. He made unreasonable demands and was exceedingly aggressive, just plain angry. No one enjoyed working for him. Our courses came to a head one day in late summer. I was with our Lincoln Group counterparts waiting for them to sign off on our daily products when he poked his head over the blue partition wall and asked to see me.

I looked up and said, "Yes sir."

I'm not sure what he thought he heard but he came storming back, seriously pissed off. "Sergeant Freed, I said now!"

I didn't even bother replying. Anything I said can and would be used against me in a court of law. I threw my paperwork down and rushed off to confront him. He made the fundamental error of engaging me in the middle of the hall by the rotunda.

"When I tell you to do something you do it. Don't fuck around with your friends."

I immediately did the right thing and went to parade rest. A man this unstable was more than problematic and could make my life a living Hell. He continued to berate me in front of anyone who walked by. Finally, I couldn't take anymore.

I looked this asshole dead in the eye and said, "Sir, I need to inform you that I plan on going to the Inspector General and doing everything I possibly can to get you relieved."

Damn that felt good! He froze. Stunned horror muting him. I had finally succeeded in shutting him up and it was about time. Whatever flashed before his eyes he knew it was enough to put him in the hot seat and our relationship had just bottomed out. I ensured I did everything by the book. I remained respectful and didn't move as he just stood there.

"Let's go see the boss," he said and led the way to the Colonel's office.

I already knew I had won. Our Air Force colonel was an old enlisted guy who loved cigars and Harley's. He appreciated the work the enlisted did, often emailing pictures of motorcycles to SFC Eddie Barfield who worked the desk on the JOC floor. He had us sit and I listened as my boss explained his point of view. I could tell he hadn't made an initial decision and took that as a good sign.

He had me explain what I thought happened and I unleashed, not only what just happened in the rotunda, but for our entire tour thus far. It worked. We both got chewed out and told to get our 'heads out of our asses' and then were dismissed. My plan worked. My boss avoided me as much as possible for about a month and then, when the fall round of elections and constitution ratification came around, decided to act like my best friend. I still don't care for the man but our work relationship improved dramatically. The same can't be said for everyone else.

Already the bastard children of the fires and effects cell and our own IO, we were reduced to taking in orphans. The production cell was the final destination for personnel command didn't know what to do with. That's when LT Charlotte Brock of the Marine Corps joined us. She was another of the fortunate few who was trained for a job she didn't get to do. LT Brock did a fairly good job and it helped that she had a knack for creative writing.

The pair of lieutenants brought good energy to the rest of us who had been struggling through the doldrums-like atmosphere plaguing us. LT Brock was easy to work with but not everyone thought so. Like myself, she had a run in with 'the boss'. Unlike me, she got relieved and sent to another area. Losing her was tough only because it shifted the workload around, again. Having been in the Army for so long I was used to people coming and going, especially when we needed them the most. Why would Baghdad be any different?

Not long after LT Brock arrived in country so did Jurgen's replacement. SGT Ardian Balla couldn't have been more opposite of Jurgen. Kote liked to drink espresso, a lot of espresso, with the Italians and play soccer. One day he came to work sweating and trembling. After admitting he'd had almost ten espressos, I sent him back to his trailer for the day. His English had gotten fairly good and he was, unfortunately, a little too Americanized. Ardian Balla was anything but. Also from Tirana, Ardian was older and more mature. He was a family man with two daughters.

He'd also just come from the Albanian commanding general's staff at Army headquarters. At least one of us was trained in paperwork drills. He was quiet, more reserved. It took us much longer to get along to get along than Jurgen and I. All in all though, these Albanian guys were alright. I enjoyed working with both as well as getting to know some of their culture. Who would have ever thought I'd have friends in little, barely out of communism Albania?

The summer months dragged on. I wasn't scheduled for mid-tour leave until September. It felt like forever away, especially when the heat kicked it. The hottest it got that summer was 140. By seven a.m. temperatures were already pushing 90. Thankfully it was the dry heat of the desert. That didn't stop it from getting so hot that my eyes felt like they were burning the moment I stepped outside. It never got comfortable, but we were used to it after a few weeks. Baghdad was so much different from the winter in Mosul.

Our workload increased sharply but we were finding it harder and harder to come up with anything useful story concepts. There are only so many stories about infrastructure reform, security forces success or terrorists are bad we can write before people just don't care. The people in the production cell were slowly becoming the first ones who didn't anymore. That's probably the source of all the stress, that and those special outside influences that took away from our task.

Lots of little things kept popping up in the middle of the election focus. An Italian journalist was killed by American troops at a checkpoint in Baghdad in early March and Brigadier General Vangel, the head of the Corps Arty and our big boss, was directed to lead the investigation. Tensions rose during that time and it felt like I was walking on eggshells. Just to make matters worse, our Air Force psychiatrist rotated out, good old Air Force short tours, and her replacement earned BG Vangel's personal animosity. No one really knows why, but the boss despised IO after the new guy came aboard.

During the long summer (spring was short and miserable. It rained so much it all but flooded the trailer parks, leaving everything a muddy mess.) the buzz started to shift on October's constitution referendum vote and the initial trial of Saddam Hussein. The deposed dictator was being called to answer for his crimes and it was about time. He was a monster and needed to be dealt with. He was also a rallying cry for the insurgents. So long as he remained alive he was a danger to security. It could also be argued that an execution would have worse results. Either way, the enemy was bound to pick up the rate of their attacks once judgment was passed.

Commanders on the ground in Iraq as well as back at the Pentagon fully expected a new outbreak of violence during the trial. Security was amped up around Camp Victory and the surrounding areas. Saddam's trial began on 19 October. Accused of crimes against humanity for the killing of close to 150 civilians from the city of al Dujail in 1982, Saddam remained defiant in the eyes of justice. When asked to state his name he claimed the title of President of Iraq. He did not recognize the legitimacy of the tribunal nor the capitulation of his regime. The sheer arrogance of the man was astounding.

Protests broke out in his hometown of Tikrit. The deaths, all Shiite, came after a failed assassination attempt. Sunni Iraqis were incensed that he stood trial for an act they saw as self preservation. Saddam denied the allegations, claiming he didn't recognize the authority because it and the charges were fake.

Violence broke out as a result of the trial though not in the manner we were expecting. Several lawyers who represented some of Saddam's codefendants were abducted and assassinated, along with whatever guards they had at the time. It seemed the Sunnis weren't the only ones with a grudge. A month into the trial and the judge decided to postpone until suitable replacements were found. Looking in, I can see why Saddam's family and supporters found the trial to be a farce. It certainly looked like the deck was stacked against him and might have been if not for the heinous nature of his crimes. (He wasn't even being tried for the mass genocide against the Kurds in 1992. That trial came the following year and proved his damnation.)

At one point Saddam looked the judge square in the eye and told him to 'go to Hell.' Say what you will, but the man had brass balls. He was also proving to be a media bonanza. We jumped on that, effectively marketing his arrogance and hatred for democracy as well as humanity. Seems his trial was just what our cell needed to get out of the funk we were mired in.

The most interesting aspect of his trial was that he had two American lawyers on his defense team. Talk about insult to injury. We'd been forced to put up with a belligerent Iraq since 1990 and now two of our own people had the audacity to represent him? No wonder lawyers are given so little respect. They'll do anything for money. I don't care who you are, there is no denying that Saddam was responsible, as head of state, for the murder and disappearance of hundreds during his reign. I wonder if Hitler would have had non-German lawyers had he not committed suicide before the Russians entered Berlin.

October 2005

Things were picking up again. Summer was behind us. I had returned from mid tour leave, refreshed and ready to finish my last hundred days or so in country. Leave was fun, but it went too quickly. I wound up at the Olive Garden outside of Fort Bragg and had the bartender convinced I needed to celebrate my freedom since I was going to jail the next day. Now back in Baghdad, it was time to focus.

Saddam's trial was in full swing and giving us plenty to work off but the focus for us was the upcoming constitution referendum vote. It was time to capitalize on the initial success and build up speed for the December elections. Our production increased dramatically. Working with the Intel and Psyops folks we produced radio spots, comic books warning kids of the dangers of landmines and terrorists, and even a few television adds. All in the name of winning the hearts and minds. The

Iraqi Security Forces (ISF) were stepping up their performances, making our jobs easier.

Midmonth came and brought another day of maximized security as millions returned to the polls to vote for their new constitution. The turnout was more impressive than the January vote and the referendum passed with an overwhelming majority. It never fails to amaze me how many people turned out to vote. An estimated 1/3 of all Iraqis braved the risk of terrorist attacks to vote. We don't even have that much success in America. Perhaps it was the novelty of being the first time. Perhaps it was the sense of pride the people felt now that they were free and able to express themselves. Either way, it was another resounding success.

Only the heavy Sunni provinces voted against it. Not surprising, considering they were Saddam's party of choice and still smarting from being ousted after so long. Images of the purple fingers once again dominated the media outlets. We were praised by a senior commander for Strategic Command (STRATCOM) in the Green Zone (now the International Zone or IZ) for the power of our images, among other things.

I realize that the work our little production cell did was behind the scenes and largely forgotten by most of the commanders in country, but there is a sense of pride, accomplishment in having at least a little part in making such a historic event successful. I wondered if anyone would ever find out what we'd done. The answer came much sooner than any of us could have anticipated.

November came and rocked us to the core. We were thrown into the middle of a national scandal (American national, not Iraqi) and told to cease all work. The Washington Post broke a story citing that a small group of Americans were secretly writing propaganda articles for Iraqi newspapers and that it was all underhanded, illegitimate work. None of us could believe it. Reading further, we discovered that we'd been sold out by one of the people that worked with us. (That individual had since left jobs and left Iraq.) While the twist the Post put on the story was misleading in itself, there were trace elements of truth to it.

We did write articles but had no contact whatsoever with any Iraqi nationals. Nothing that was written could be considered subversive or derogatory in nature to the new Iraqi transitional government. Our objectives were the same as I previously stated: to facilitate the popular support and goodwill in the Iraqi people by demonstrating the strides being taken by *their own* security forces, *their own* infrastructure repairs, *their own* elected officials. In no way, shape or form we were suggesting or even mentioning anything about the Coalition.

Regardless, the article had a damning effect. We were now under the scrutiny of the very men who had authorized our campaign and this was coming from the top. They say shit rolls downhill. We must have been at the bottom because it started to stink real fast. The XVIII Corps commander issued an internal investigation into any potential wrongdoing. We were all questioned by random staff members, several times being pulled into the CGs offices for meetings. I had never felt smaller than at that moment. It felt as if the weight of the world was coming down on me with the intent to crush the life out of me.

Normally the absence of deadlines or a severely reduced workload would have been pleasing, a chance to relax. Not this time. This time we all sat helplessly at our stations waiting for that final judgment call. It couldn't come soon enough. I can normally handle stress well, but when official reprimands, or worse, lingered on the edge of the horizon I was getting anxious. Not even the successive victories at the polls or on the battlefield were enough to quash the butterflies gnawing away at our stomachs. Life had become downright unpleasant. The only seemingly unworried one was Balla. After all, what could they do to him but send him back to Albania early?

Any indignity suffered was lessened by the fact that most of our peers had no idea what IO was or what we did. That alone minimized most of the potential negative effects reverberating through the cell. What didn't change was the fact that we sat and twiddled our thumbs while the gods of war decided our fates. The wait wasn't as long as anticipated. The production cell, and supervisors, were called back into the CGs office and told to carry on with a few changes. The screening process was now more stringent. We had more checks and balances, the way the rest of the Army operated.

Good old checks and balances. Before we were getting products out the door by 16:00, now it was taking until the next day. Of course the upside was that our little crew was able to stockpile products. Just one extra per shift quickly led to almost twenty extra products waiting to go through the approval chain. Our workload slacked considerably because of the changes to our approval process. Making things even slower, all products had to be signed off on by BG Vangel.

We were finally brought back into the CG's good graces at the start of a two-day summit involving all of the major IO players from across Iraq. The CG admitted he was of the old guard, the ones who saw wars as being won by combat power, not words or pictures. He, and his staff, had underestimated the effects the IO cell was capable of delivering. The vindication felt damned good. Truthfully, we were a combat multiplier, making it easier for the ground forces to do what needed to be done.

Our new control parameters were almost nullifying, but we had come through the storm of controversy unscathed. It didn't hurt to have a Lieutenant General stand up and take full responsibility for our actions. The scandal behind us, we were able to refocus our efforts in anticipation of the December elections. Two down, one to go but this was going to be the key for the entire fledgling democracy. A sink or swim mark.

Thus far the Sunni population had barely made their presence known during the election process. Without some form of Sunni leadership in the new government, Iraq was facing the potential for prolonged sectarian violence. Politicians are the same no matter what part of the world you're in so it didn't take long before all three sides (Sunni, Shia and Kurd) went from flat out refusal to cooperate to negotiating which party would get what number of seats.

December 15th saw millions of Iraqis returning to the polls to vote for the first permanent parliament. An estimated 79 percent of the population turned out, again shaming the democratic Western countries. Violence levels continued to drop in the days before the election, whether from increased operations tempo by coalition forces or because the terrorists recognized that they weren't going to stop the elections from happening. By the end of the day we were all able to sit back and breath normally again. The elections were over. Iraq had its democratic parliament.

One of the biggest effects of the election came from the growing opposition to Coalition troops in Iraq by the Iraqis themselves. The people were, understandably, tired of war, of violence, of seeing their friends and family senselessly slaughtered to justify political or fanatical ideologies. What they failed to understand was just how pitiful their security forces were. Iraq may now have a working constitution and elected government, but they were still incapable of defending themselves.

The IO program had done its part in ensuring the success of the election process. The behind the scenes work of countless soldiers, civilians and government officials proved how beneficial the fledgling program was to continued stability and support operations. Most of what we did will never be known to much of the world, and I don't believe most of the world needs to know. Wars are often won in the will, just as much as through force of arms. Information Operations gained acceptance by much of the senior military leadership. Doctrine was written based on what we initiated, through our trials and tribulations. It felt good knowing that we had a hand, if an invisible one, in helping a nation overcome doubt, discrepancy, and a rising tide of violence.

Now if only we could finish our secondary task and help hunt down and kill Al Qaeda in Iraq's current leader, Abu Musab al-Zarqawi.

Chapter Fourteen: The Hunt for al-Zarqawi

The war was still heating up, if in a different direction from my first tour of duty. In Mosul we were expected to demonstrate a heavy presence, ensuring the population of our support in normalizing life and deterring terrorists and insurgents from conducting operations with impunity. We parked our howitzers on line in the motor pool and took to the streets on foot and in gun trucks. The initial invasion left a country in turmoil, and it was up to us to quiet it down before something bad happened.

That something happened in 2004 when the terrorists decided to use Iraq as their battleground. We'd set the stage by disbanding all standing Iraqi military and police forces, casting millions into unemployment and fanning the fires of anger. It seemed that every available insurgent and terrorist came flooding into the country to engage us on what they believed was their home territory. The coalition was caught off guard. Understandably so. All of our efforts were focused on reconstruction and rounding up the faces on the now infamous deck of wanted cards. No one on the ground could have predicted the ferocity with which al Qaeda would retaliate.

Bin Laden was a nonfactor. Ever since we invaded Afghanistan he'd gone to ground and was believe to be hiding in a cave on the Pakistan border. That made sense to me. He was old and had a failing kidney. What good could he do for his cause if he ran upon one of our patrols? He took his senior leadership and fled into the mountains forming the border with Pakistan while still maintaining at least the air of leadership.

Who did he think he was fooling? Terrorists looked up to this man for his ideology and his audacity to attack America and other western nations. His retreat from a very eager coalition wanting to kill or capture him must have appeared cowardly. His departure from relevance left a power vacuum. Someone needed to step up and assume the role of leadership. Abu Musab al-Zarqawi did just that.[35]

A known Jordanian Islamist militant, al-Zarqawi assumed control of a jihadist movement in the early 1990s, eventually establishing and running his own terror training camp in Afghanistan. His life was a constant struggle against authority. It is reported that he was arrested nearly forty times during his youth. He found his true calling in 1989 when he traveled to Afghanistan to fight against the Soviets, eventually forming the terror group al-Tawhid.

Interestingly enough, he wasn't a fighter. Osama bin Laden used him as a reporter and public relations man for the mujahedeen. He touted the successes of the ragtag army against the vaunted Soviet machine and made all the connections necessary to become the high profile target he found himself as in 2004-2005. It didn't take long for him to slip into Iraq and wreak havoc amid the power vacuum and the constant turnover of Coalition ground commands.

He quickly became a major focus of our IO campaign. We were on the brink of losing the people. Everyone sensed it, despite no one wanting to voice it. Suicide bombings were skyrocketing, killing scores of civilians. The psychological damage of a bomber strolling into a marketplace crowded with women and children is one of those things that doesn't go away. Our enemy was craven at best, deceptively brilliant at worst. They sought out the soft targets. The children who didn't want to think about war. The wives and mothers intent on getting food for their families. They preyed upon the hearts and emotions of us all with each successful bombing. How many times do we need to see little body parts or fire damaged toys before the desire to give in and back away grows too strong? How many defenseless mothers need to be shredded by little slivers of metal and glass before the compassion in us cries 'no more!'

Waging war on armed forces is one thing, but the terrorists knew they couldn't win that way. They needed to take away our support base. Crush the very people we were sworn to defend. Even those with the strongest will were susceptible to overwhelming feelings of despair. Every success we had, whether it was on the battlefield or the Iraqi home front was challenged by subversive strikes against the floundering infrastructure or population. It was a game of cat and

---

[35]   Al-Zarqawi was believed to have been born Ahmad Fadeel al-Nazal al-Khalayleh in Zarqa, Jordan. He was a petty thug in a street gang for much of his youth until going to Afghanistan in 1989.

mouse. The enemy moved at will, often striking before we had the chance to react.

It was working. People refused to go outside. Others never made it home. Several Iraqis known to be either working with us or for us had their families kidnapped or worse. More and more of the would-be suicide bombers were unwitting dupes. An eighteen year old kid was hired out of Saudi Arabia to drive a fuel resupply truck. No one bothered to tell him his truck was filled with explosives and rigged to detonate remotely. He was caught and stopped before al Qaeda was able to use him.

Many more bombers were unwilling participants in the war. Al Qaeda kidnapped and tortured family members in order to get young men to do their bidding. Too many times it worked. The results were always devastating. Not suicide bomber was committed to the cause. More than one body was found with hands tied to the steering wheel so he couldn't change his mind at the last minute. These bombers were often trailed by a pair of spotters who would remote detonate the bomb when it closed with the target.

My personal favorite came in midsummer when a pair of youths accidentally detonated their VBIED in the middle of nowhere. As best as we could figure out they had gotten into an argument and accidentally pushed the wrong button. People like that made my job easier. Exploiting stupidity isn't very hard and the IO cell was all over it. Incidents like that made every Iraqi paper and, on occasion, the television.

For every success there seemed to be a setback. Most of them were recoverable. Others not so much. The Ministry of Defense had its own specialized commando teams. Our special operations forces helped train them and teach them proper doctrine. As I stated before, corruption is hard to break away from. A raid by MOD commandos was filmed with negative results. Images of the commandos stealing a television, refrigerator and other large items from a house they raided were broadcast everywhere. Those responsible were disciplined but the damage control took more than expected. A population can't have respect or trust in their military forces if they are seen vandalizing the same population they are sworn to protect.

Iraqi civilians weren't the only noncombatant casualties. War had been declared on western contractors as well. The burned corpses of brutally murdered contractors hung upside down from a bridge over the Euphrates River in Fallujah. They were missing their hands and feet. One was beheaded. All were burned so badly it was almost impossible to tell if they were male or female.

Perhaps the most infamously murdered contractor was Nick Berg. The CIA claims that it was al-Zarqawi himself who beheaded Berg for the world to see. The horror and damage done to his family is inconceivable. I personally couldn't understand how one man could so easily do that to another. What God would demand such atrocity from his followers? The very concept was anathema to me. It was all I could do not to vomit as I watched the uncensored footage.

The worst I had the displeasure of viewing was a Korean national. Years later and I can still see his face. Hear his screams as that large butcher knife slowly, painfully sawed through his neck. Blood poured from the wound long after he finally died. I don't understand how anyone could do this. If that is the path to paradise I want nothing to do with it. Sadly, these weren't the only atrocities committed.

A Bulgarian helicopter was shot down in late April. All onboard were killed in the crash except for one pilot. The passengers were all contractors, including six Americans. One of the enemy's favorite tools is the video camera. For some reason they love to film everything they do. This was no different. Al Qaeda fighters secured the crash site, filming the burning wreckage. Then they noticed one man slowly dragging himself away from the crash.

Lyubomir Kostov, one of the Bulgarian pilots, had survived the crash but had multiple injuries, including several broken bones. Dazed and disoriented, he failed to notice the men coming up on him until it was too late. Video footage showed him asking for help before being turned over. The shock, the sheer horror in his eyes when he looked upon the same enemy that had shot him down was unforgettable. He started to plead for his life.

The enemy riddled his body with bullets, nearly a full magazine. This was more than murder. It was the calloused, insensitive desecration of an innocent man. Murdered for no other reason than for being in Iraq at the wrong time. The video stopped filming but that wasn't the end of the atrocity. Working with the Corps aviation commander I was photos of what happened next. Terrorists poured a fuel can Kostov's body and set it on fire. It was a pitiful attempt at concealing their murder. The flesh burned to char but the dozens of bullet holes were unmistakable.

There is no honor among the terrorists. They are cowards. The city of Fallujah had already been reclaimed from terrorist activity in a massive offensive led by the Marine Corps. That didn't mean the enemy had given up. They became more subversive, underhanded. A highjacked ambulance was used as a car bomb against the very hospital it was assigned to. Confidence is very fragile, especially when you can't trust your own vehicles.

Our inability to keep information from becoming public knowledge worked against us more often than not. It was no secret that coalition forces were expressly forbidden from engaging the enemy in the vicinity of a mosque. The Muslim version of a church was considered holy and sacred ground and off limits for engagements. It didn't take the terrorists long before they learned this. Countless ambushes were initiated from inside or around a mosque, preventing us from even returning fire.

September 2005

Most of northern Iraq was in turmoil. Practically all of the work the 101st had done in 2003 was reversed. Al Qaeda and other foreign fighters operated with near impunity. Mosul had become a hotbed of activity. Attacks were so intense and frequent that coalition commanders pulled back to their FOBs, venturing out only when necessary. The population cowered in fear despite the heavy presence of the Peshmerga. Not even the vaunted Kurdish army was enough to stall the terrorist advance.

Situated thirty miles west of Mosul is the small city of Tal Afar. It was close to the Syrian border and overrun with terrorists. Tal Afar became our next large offensive. The IO cell ground into action in a campaign aimed at deterring disaffected youth from coming to al Qaeda's aid and to reassure the Iraqi population that we had not abandoned them.

Operation Restoring Rights officially began on 1 September. Primarily staffed by the new Iraqi Army, thousands of Coalition and Iraqi forces encircled the city in preparation of the assault. The city was mostly sealed off. Civilians were given the opportunity to leave before the assault, going through a series of checkpoints and screenings before being sent to temporary camps a few miles away. Tent cities were established, with security, to house the displaced while we tried to cleanse their city of terrorists and foreign fighters.

Information Operations, a group that had cells in every major command throughout Iraq, played a large part in convincing the population to evacuate. We wanted as many civilians out of Tal Afar as possible. Leaflets were dropped. Radio stations blasted warning across the airwaves. A lot of effort and diligence went into preparing the citizens of Tal Afar for the Hell we were about to unleash.

The deadline came and the battle began on schedule. Tanks and armored vehicles punched into the city like stalking tigers. Infantry cleared buildings, killing anyone with a gun. The battle was executed in the old school manner of city fighting; street by street and house by house. The city was declared secured by 3 September though the fighting continued on deep into the month.[36] Buildings were destroyed. Bodies littered the streets. This was war at its ugliest and the enemy had no legitimate answer.

Al Qaeda struck back the only way they knew how. Zarqawi claimed we were using chemical weapons on his people; a ridiculous claim that only those papers and news channels so anti-war were willing to report. The desperation showed. Terrorists were being gunned down at a rapid pass. The success was duplicated across Iraq just as fast as it was happening on the ground.

Three days of hard fighting by elements of the 3rd Armored Cavalry Regiment, 82nd Airborne Division, and the newly constituted Iraqi Army broke the terrorist stranglehold on Tal Afar enough to drive most survivors away. An estimated 157 enemy fighters were killed and close to 700 more were captured. More than 10,000 pounds of explosives were recovered over the course of the operation, all materials used for car bombs or worse.

Militarily, the operation was a resounding success. There was nothing in the terrorist arsenal, aside from chemical weapons, capable of withstanding such a heavy armored assault. We'd proven it time and again since the invasion. When forced to fight, the enemy proved themselves inferior. Another major battle turned into another major victory. It felt good to get pay back from the countless IEDs and suicide bombings. From the cowards hiding in mosques and using children as human shields. It was also a great point in which to step away from the war for a while and refocus.

I got to take a break from the foolishness of war for a few weeks in mid September. My time for mid-tour leave was here and I

---

[36] Operation Restoring Rights was praised by several governments as the signature success against the terror networks in Iraq. This success was enough to convince several senior Pentagon officials and Washington diplomats to let Gen. Petraeus execute his now famous 'surge' campaign in 2007.

couldn't wait to get away from Baghdad and the political atmosphere of working in a major headquarters. Given the current circumstances, I would have rather gone back to Afghanistan. Regardless, I hoped the bus over to BIAP and checked in, ensuring I had my leave papers, dog tags and ID card. Once I finished checking in, I got sent to a marshalling area to wait the next few hours for the C-130 down to Kuwait.

I saw a familiar face from 1-377 waiting for a ride. He was part of Bravo Battery and stationed at a smaller base just north of Camp Victory. We talked for a little while, and I focused more on his uniform than anything else. He had the new digital pattern that the Army had ripped off from the Marines. They looked alright, if we were going to be fighting onboard a ship. Where the Marines uniforms were fit for combat duty in the jungle or the desert ours should have belonged to the Air Force. The color pattern was horrible. It didn't match anything, especially in the middle of the desert. I was thankful for my desert fatigues. (Naturally the Army realized their mistake and changed the color scheme *after* I retired.)

My name was called for manifest and he and I said good-bye. I didn't have much interaction with my real unit and it felt good to be able to speak the same lingo with someone. We parted ways; him back to his base and me to that plane to freedom. It had been a difficult eight months and I was ready to hang up my uniform for a few weeks. No more deserts. No more oppressive heat. No more people so fed up with each other arguments sparked just because we had nowhere to go.

The flight south was short and uneventful, except again for the pilots wanting to show off and do evasive maneuvers. There being no credible air threat I remained dubious of their true intentions. Damned pilots. We were back in my least favorite country soon enough and going through the process of turning in our gear. There was no point in coming all the way home with helmets and weapons. After that we just sat around and waited for the next manifest.

Kuwait always seemed to have better accommodations than up north. The food was good and I managed to get a pretty good night's sleep before waking up in the middle of the morning for formation and the final manifest. They ran us through a quick custom's check and herded us onto a string of buses. Most of the people flying home with me were Reserves and National Guard. They were easily distinguishable because of their lack of discipline. I'm not trying to diminish any contribution those two proud services did during the wars, but people are people and there is a vast gap between the active duty Army and our friends who only come out on the weekends.

People cheered when the bird went wheels up. I didn't understand that. Sure, cheer once you get home, but we still had eighteen plus hours before we could forget the Army for a while. Things went smoothly for the first few hours. We crossed into Europe before things went downhill. One of our Reservists decided to act up, getting into a fight with the female Reservist in the row in front of him. I was embarrassed and disgusted. They were in uniform and needed to act like soldiers.

The best part of their little soap opera altercation came when this grizzled old National Guard First Sergeant came storming in from the front of the plane with a laptop in hand. He shouted, "I have a counseling statement here on my computer!"

Seriously? A counseling statement for a soldier you didn't know and would probably never see again? I laughed. Hard. Fifteen years ago that soldier would have gotten his ass royally chewed out and possibly smacked around. Thanks to the sensitivity of the modern age our senior leadership on the plane hid behind a flimsy piece of paper with no teeth. I was even more disgusted than by the soldier's behavior. That type of behavior would have never flown in the active Army. My thoughts went back a few years to a problem child I had.

He was a hard worker (when I could get him to) but lacked discipline and was too outspoken for his own good. His attitude was deplorable and acted like a cancer in my section. We were out in the field at Fort Bragg one night when I sent him off to guard duty at the OP and pulled the rest of my section together. I basically told them that this kid was bringing them all down and the best thing for it was to give him a good thumping, as a section. We were almost all the way back to our motorpool the next day when the truck started rocking back and forth. Seems my guys took me up on my offer. A few slugs to mouth were enough to calm our problem child down and, to his credit, he didn't rat anyone out when I asked him what happened. After that I didn't have too much trouble with him. (Well, except for when he got busted by the police running marijuana up from Georgia to Maryland a year later.)

The best the current leadership could do was offer a counseling statement. That wasn't enough for the flight crew. They quit on us in mid-flight. The plane diverted from Frankfurt to Sophia, Bulgaria. I'd never been to Bulgaria before and was forced to sit on the plane for over two hours while the airlines tried to get a new flight crew to come in. That had to be some kind of first. The entire crew just quit, citing the work was too hazardous or some such nonsense. Regardless, we were stuck in yet another country and delayed from going home. I sure hope that counseling statement was worth the lack of effort on that First Sergeant's part.

Eventually we arrived back in the States. There were only two airport hubs for transitioning soldiers at the time: Dallas and Atlanta. Naturally I flew into Dallas, if for no other reason than it was the furthest away from where I was trying to go. One of the great mysteries is why soldiers returning from a combat zone go through customs like normal overseas travelers. It's not like we went there for sightseeing or pleasure. Everything about the deployment was contained in a military environment. There was no possibility of being mistaken for anything else. Regardless, we stood in line (the very slow line) and waited for the customs agents to process our paperwork and admit us back into our own nation.

After that we were on our own. I double checked my ticket and hustled down to check in for my next flight to Charlotte, NC. I stopped to grab a bite to eat but avoided any alcohol since I was in uniform. From Charlotte I took a quick hop down to Fayetteville and prayed my buddy was going to be there to pick me up. He had my car after all. It was the least he could do. He was and by the time I finally got back to my condo it was close to ten p.m.

The next two weeks flew by and honestly I was ready to go back to the war. My daughter was gone, off in Minnesota I would later find out. There was nothing for me to do and it made sense to get back and finish up my tour. It was pointless trying to get back into any sort of rhythm back home for only two weeks. Before I knew it I was back at the airport getting ready to head out.

This time the Army did me right and I was flying a direct route from Raleigh to Dallas. No more puddle hoppers or messing around. I checked in and worked my way down to the wonderful new TSA security stations. It went well until the young man inspecting my line told me I needed to remove my boots. My boots? I was in uniform, heading back to Iraq and this kid wanted me to take off my boots? Hell no.

"I'm not doing that. I'm headed back to Iraq. What would make you think I'm a terrorist?" I asked sharply.

Clearly unaccustomed to anyone questioning his very young and inexperienced authority, he sputtered, "It is policy. I need you to remove your footgear."

"Then you better get your supervisor because I am not removing my boots."

I was furious. How dare he? I pulled myself out of line so as not to hold up the rest of the people behind me and waited while his supervisor came over. The young agent defended his position and, truthfully, I respected it because he had a job to do, an important job that many people were depending on in order to travel safely, but I wasn't changing my stance.

I told the supervisor, "Look, I'm not trying to cause trouble but I just finished my mid-tour leave and am heading back to Baghdad. I don't see the point in making the people fighting the war against terrorism go through all of this."

The older agent smiled and waved me through. "I'm sorry, sir. Keep your boots on and come on through. Thank you for your service."

Now was that so hard? The incident kept me rankled until I checked in at the outgoing station set up in Dallas. One of the greatest services available to soldiers at airports is the USO. They passed out free meals, nonalcoholic drinks and even had some local country musician come down to perform for us. Talk about the little things to make you feel special. Every little bit helped because soon enough we were wheels down in Kuwait, again. Thankfully this trip was without incident, but I was getting tired of making the exceedingly long trip back and forth across the pond.

Time always drags on during those legs between going home and getting back. I couldn't stand sitting around waiting for flights or for my name to be called. Time becomes as much of an adversary as the multiple terror groups operating in Iraq. Finally though, I was back safe and sound in Baghdad and looking forward to finishing out the last few months of my tour.

Refreshed and refueled, I took the first few weeks easily but then the pace ramped up with the second and third rounds of elections. Zarqawi was still a thorn in our side but there was only so much we could do. Staying busy was a good thing. Too much downtime makes people lazy, complacent. That's when people get killed. There was enough excitement in our little group to keep us going for a while. One of our new Warrant Officers took some mortar shrapnel in her hand outside of the main PX on Camp Liberty. Couldn't even go to the PX without worrying about getting hit. A Sergeant Major took pieces of grenade to his backside, but nothing serious. I was starting to think all the war movies where people get hit in the ass were more than just good scripting. Not that I wanted such distinction. I was happy not getting hit at all.

Soon enough it was time to pack up and get ready to go home. My mind was burned out and I was just plain tired of being in IO. I wanted to get back to the real Army and people who knew which to point a gun and when to use it. We'd been walking on eggshells since the scandal broke out. It felt like Big Brother was constantly looking over our shoulder, just waiting for that small misstep to bring the walls crashing back down. It was a terrible feeling, condemning and damning at once. I was done. 2005 ended without any flare. We still hadn't caught Iraq's number one terrorist but that wasn't my problem anymore. It was time to go home.

Chapter Fifteen: The Beginning of the End

Every soldier and contractor in Iraq worked hard. We worked for each other. We worked to defeat the enemy, to give the Iraqi democracy a chance for survival. The biggest success story was the Iraqi people themselves. There is much to be said for a population stepping up to accept responsibility for itself. (Something we as Americans seem to have forgotten along the way) The Iraqis braved the threat of terrorist reprisal and possible murder to vote for their nation's future. They became an example and an enigma for the rest of the Middle East, introducing the foreign concept of democracy to the various Sultans and Kings, petty tyrants and dictators. They became an example of what the will of the people can accomplish.

The enemy worked just as hard to stop us. Beheaded bodies were found, hands tied behind their backs. Crowded markets became slaughterhouses courtesy of zealous suicide bombers. Elected officials were kidnapped and murdered. The callous indignity in which innocent civilians lost their lives was meant to break the will of the West, force us into abandoning our task. It wasn't enough. The war continued. Sometimes with failure; but mostly with success. I can't say that I enjoyed being in Iraq, but I didn't mind. Otherwise I never would have volunteered for three tours in four years. Then came the news I'd been waiting for.

Dead. Official as of June 7, 2006, Abu Musab al-Zarqawi was a cold, lifeless corpse. The terrorist mastermind that had caused so much havoc to millions of people was finally killed. There was never any question of capture. A villain this horrible deserved the kind of death he received. A pair of F-16 jets dropped bombs on the house he was meeting with other senior terrorists just north of the city of Baqubah. Coalition assets had been watching the house for over a month before confirming Zarqawi was inside. Ground forces moved in after the blasts and recovered the bodies. Incredibly, Zarqawi managed to survive the attack, but only for an hour. In the end he was just as dead as his compatriots.

Its incredible how many emotions came alive when I first heard this news. Sheer elation filled me, an emotion that translated to everyone who had dedicated a year to hunting down and eliminating this monstrosity of humanity. He'd foiled coalition plans for so long. Countless times Zarqawi slipped through the closing jaws of a trap. Midsummer 2005was closest we had come to catching him. An American infantry unit was tracking an enemy convoy through Baghdad's streets but didn't attack in time. Zarqawi disappeared down the back alleys. Positive identification came back, making the near miss all the more disappointing. This time, we didn't miss.

News passed quickly through Iraq. The Prime Minister, Nuri al Maliki said, 'Today, Zarqawi has been terminated. Every time a Zarqawi appears we will kill him. We will continue confronting whoever follows his path.'[37] His death represented a fundamental shift in the war. Immediately, nothing changed. Terror attacks continued throughout the various cities while the ISF and coalition continued to do their best to instill order and discipline. It's funny how minor things turn out to be. Zarqawi was one of IO's primary focuses for over a year and his death essentially changed absolutely nothing in the terms of the war. Another terrorist stepped up to assume the mantle of leadership of Al Qaeda in Iraq and the war continued.

The closest I have ever felt upon hearing of Zarqawi's death was when I heard that the war in Iraq was declared officially over. Shock, pride, confusion. It's difficult to explain, especially to anyone who has never gone to war. I wanted to laugh, to cheer, to cry. The war was over and it left a void in me. Iraq had become such a large part of my life for the better part of a decade and now it was just gone. Don't get me wrong. I'm not a warmonger. Staying at home and never having to see anyone go into harm's way again is all right with me, but the sudden removal of what had become so large a part of me left me deflated.

Once matters settled down and the occupation of Iraq and concurrent deployments in Afghanistan started getting into a pattern every soldier knew where they stood. One year deployed equaled one year at home and so on. The hardships on families and service members were incredible but we pushed on and did our jobs. Babies were born without one of their parents present. Family members passed away. Soldiers were killed. It is a merciless cycle that leaves the bystander wondering why any sane person would want to do that. I'm still not

---

[37]   World Reaction: 'This Is An Important Day'". Sky News. 8 June 2006.

ready to share my answer. It's far too personal for anyone but my closest friends to understand.

The national elections were a series resounding successes. Despite an army of naysayers and the negative coverage of most Western media outlets, Iraq was officially a democracy. The truth of this moment remains to be realized. Unrealistic expectations by the media and misinformation propagated by anti-war zealots deemed the democratic Iraq a failure from day one. (It certainly didn't help to read one of Iraq's vice presidents was a fugitive and sentenced to death in 2012.)

The simple truth is that the ideal of democracy was accepted and embraced by the people that mattered the most: the Iraqi population. Politicians are distrustful on a good day, regardless of the nation but the people are all the same. We have the same wants and needs. The same desires for our children and visions of the future. Politics and petty rulers get in the way from time to time but it almost always falls on the people to accept change at the fundamental level. Iraq did that and hasn't looked back. I am proud to have been a part of that change.

Those last few weeks in Iraq were high tempo. Our replacements were arriving and XVIII Airborne Corps was preparing from the transition ceremony with III Corps out of Fort Hood, Texas. I stopped caring about IO, making it difficult to keep up production. I busied myself with developing a briefing for our replacements, adding relevant information designed to lay out the guidelines and focal points of Information Operations. The trick was what to put in the document and what to hand over through word of mouth. A lot of what we did wasn't exactly doctrine. There was a delicate balance between operating within structured guidelines and being able to produce quality products effectively. Not that it mattered much. Every major command has its own way of doing things and III Corps was no different. They were already changing our current system before we'd left country.

The good news was I had more downtime than I knew what to do with. I spent less two hours a day inside the palace and it felt good. A great was thrown off my shoulders and I could breath easily again. It felt like freedom. I had no responsibilities, no one to look after and no one looking after me. Of course that left me available for details and the occasional requests. I told the aviation commander that I'd help grade their Army Physical Fitness Test (APFT).

We showed up at the gym one afternoon and were given our instructions. Soldiers and officers lined up and we began. I had the pleasure of giving a National Guard female in her mid-thirties in my line. She did five push-ups and quit. Five. I don't care who you are, pathetic is pathetic. I threw down my clipboard and failed to conceal my embarrassment in a fellow Sergeant First Class who couldn't do more than five lousy push-ups. This was far worse than the ridiculousness on my mid-tour flight home. Sit-ups went pretty much the same but the two mile run took the cake. The Army has standards for everything. The two and a half mile WALK for soldiers unable to run is expected to be completed in around a half an hour before you are considered a fail. My SFC finished her run in 29:00. A forty-eight year old man walked in less than 25. I handed the score card to the colonel and walked off wondering what I had just witnessed.

Most of my time was spent finding things other than work to do, not that there was much of a variety. I ran into a friend I'd made at Fort Sill a few summers ago while on training. We met up for a few minutes but our schedules were opposite so there wasn't much time for hanging out. That was for the best as I was soon immersed in trying to get out of Iraq. There were briefings and couples counseling. (I'm still trying to figure out the point of the counseling when the 2nd half of the couples were 9000 miles away, but it made the Army feel like they were doing the right thing. Hooah for meetings.)

Camp Victory was one of the largest bases in Iraq but that didn't prevent boredom from sinking in. When we weren't sitting in some briefing or turning in equipment we enjoyed the struggle to find something to do. One of the guys I deployed with got a hold of a HMMWV, so we hoped a ride over to the small base north of Camp Liberty where our Bravo Battery was. It felt good running into my friends again.

I spent most of the afternoon over there, feeling bad that I had volunteered to deploy early with another unit. These guys were guinea pigs for IEDs daily and it showed in their faces. We laughed and joked, but it had a hollow feeling behind it. So far they'd avoided serious casualties. Looking back, it feels good to be able to say that I didn't lose a single soldier or a friend during my three tours of duty. That's changed recently, thanks to my involvement with the cadets at the United States Military Academy.

Bravo's living quarters were much improved from our raggedy little compound in Mosul. The soldiers had real beds and working showers. It was a far cry from the busted showers I tried to take in 2003. It was also a disturbingly different mission from our first deployment. 377 deployed without cannons, in fact, the battalion was cannibalized into a hodge podge of different MOSs. Half a battery worth of soldiers was infantry. Straining matters further, women were sent to the unit. This was the first time most of our soldiers were exposed to working with the opposite sex and, while some problems did occur, the Corps experiment seemed to work.

I joked around with the 1SG and few other friends for a while as my driver went about his business. Being around my peers again, after so long, was a relief. I was able to be myself, not the constrained man I was forced to be working with Corps headquarters. There were far too many unhappy predators lurking in Corps headquarters to be a good work environment. Washed up officers and tired NCOs looked after themselves instead of taking care of their subordinates. I'm not suggesting everyone was this cutthroat. Some of the finest men and women I ever served with were in Corps HQ, but for every outstanding soldier were half a dozen bad ones. This last tour left a bad taste in my mouth and my faith in the Army system was shaken.

Time was up and we had to head back to Victory. We said our good-byes, everyone careful not to say good luck or any other dreadful phrase that invites ill, and I made the short ride back *home* lost in thought. Part of me wanted to stay; to join my unit but I was exhausted, mentally and physically. The intensity and pace of operations in the palace had successfully burned me out, something over a decade on the line had yet to accomplish. The final decision of staying at home or rejoining 377 was still ahead of me so I put it to the back of my mind.[38]

Sergeant Balla and I headed over to the coffee shop one day. It was almost time for both of us to go home; a bittersweet moment. He and I had started off slowly but had gotten to be good friends as time went on. We didn't enjoy the relationship I had with Jurgen Koti but still keep in touch. I went to Baghdad with no ideations about Albanians and left thinking they were very decent people and proud to call two my friends.

Ardian ducked into the tacky gift shop. He had two young daughters waiting for him to return and wanted to get something nice for them. We looked through the shelves and found a few nice things. I

---

[38] The decision turned out to be easier than I expected. LTC Jeff Toomer sent me a welcome home email to which I replied, 'thank you, Sir but I am not coming back over there'.

bought a gold trimmed vase with an Arabic scene on it. He bought the matching plate. Content with our choices, we paid and left to get a slice of pizza and an espresso. We were halfway through our food when Ardian presented the plate to me. I looked at him.

"This is for you. I wanted to give you a gift," he said with a smile.

I couldn't help but smile back, despite his deception. He was a damned good man and had caught me completely off guard. Over the course of the last six months we'd exchanged patches, flags, bought countless cups of coffee for each other and now finished our tours with unnecessary gifts. I keep the plate on display in my home and remember those days in Baghdad from time to time.

The day came for us to leave our trailers and head back to the tents. I was fortunate enough to get stuck in a tent with mostly people from my real unit, a coincidence I am eternally grateful for. I couldn't handle much more of the pencil pushers and pressed uniforms. I'm bored thinking about those final few days so I won't bore you with going through them. All that mattered was I was about to board that big iron bird home. And it was about damned time.

January 2006

Once again, I was in Kuwait. My tour was over. All our goals and tasks were accomplished, or at least mostly. Baghdad was behind us, but unlike my first return trip I didn't get to spend weeks in the relative luxury of Camp Doha. Someone higher up had a sick sense of humor when they decided to make Camp Victory, Kuwait the new redeployment base. It felt like I couldn't get away from the name, like an oppressive shadow trying to keep me down. Just to make things worse, this Victory had almost nothing on it.

I went to the berm that served as the rear wall to the base and stared out into the endless miles of sand. I've never felt so small before. Things fell into perspective. I have always known that I mean little in the grand scheme of things. I did my job, played the parts I was supposed to play but recognized that it would keep going without me. That's fine. A staple of Army training and development is to know the jobs of everyone below you and two ranks higher in the event of death or casualties. I did what was asked of me and more and can spend the rest of my days knowing that I helped make history. How many people go through life without ever having the opportunity to make a difference?

Naturally they put us in huge bays at the rear of the base, up along the perimeter. You could go out to the berm and see endless miles across the Kuwaiti desert. There wasn't any sign of life other than our isolated little base outside of Kuwait City. The chow hall was close to half a mile away. I never made it to the PX. Buying things now didn't make any sense. My bags were packed and I didn't need to take the additional weight home.

We stayed in Kuwait for a few days before that magical day arrived to board the plane and go home. Leaving for the third time, I questioned my decisions. Questioned whether or not this was what I wanted to keep doing. This last tour drained me mentally. I was tired. Sitting on that cot in Kuwait I realized I had been deployed for part of every year from 2002-2006. Five years. The constant string of deployments was wearing me down. (It would get worse when I returned home and met people who hadn't deployed once yet. I have never held less respect for anyone than I had for the people who avoided doing their part.)

We headed down to the buses that final morning and waited to board. Master Sergeant Smith was laughing with myself, SFC Barfield and SFC Baskervill when he mentioned that it was January 12th. My eyes went wide. The 12th? Holy shit! Yesterday was my birthday and I had completely forgotten. I knew it was time to hang up the desert uniforms for a long while. I was convinced I was slowly losing my mind. Clint Eastwood had a great line that went, "Man's got to know his limitations."[39] I had reached mine.

They shuttled us down to the flight line and we began that God-awful eighteen hour flight home. Those long hours lengthened, seemingly never getting us closer to home. It is perhaps one of the worst feelings in the world; being so close yet so far away. The next two days went just as slowly as they had in previous deployments. That tiring trip across the Atlantic wore on for an insufferable amount of time. We all needed to shave. Deodorant was expired. Our skin had the oily, dirty feel to it and we were all walking around like zombies from a decided lack of sleep. I don't care who you are, you aren't going to get any comfortable rest trapped in the small seat of an overcrowded plane for the better part of twenty-four hours.

---

[39] *Magnum Force*, 1973.

Still, there was nothing capable of dampening my spirits as that plane touched down on Pope Air Force Base, NC. Nothing that is except the absence of my daughter. I knew this homecoming was going to be empty, a hollow reminder of what my personal life had devolved to. The cheering crowds weren't for me. There were no welcome home signs bringing me into the reception building. I was alone. But I was home.

I waited for the cheering and the chaos to subside enough for me to make an exit out of the PAX shed to the waiting buses. Corps Artillery had enough troops returning to have our own transportation back to Brigade HQ. I rode the bus in silence, taking in the familiar sights of Fort Bragg. Fourteen years I had called the base my home and now I was back. We turned in our weapons and filed into one of the briefing rooms for more mandatory briefings. This was after the Army was forced to react to a rash of spousal murders by returning soldiers.[40]

I got a ride back to my condo and called my buddy to drop my car off. A year ago I stood outside my front door watching my daughter wave good-bye to me repeating, 'bye-bye Daddy, bye-bye' without knowing I was going to be gone for so long. Little did I know it was the last time I would see her for three years. Now, as I stood looking at the familiar door, I almost didn't want to go inside. Without her it was just a place for me to sleep, no different from the tents and cots of Iraq and Afghanistan.

I was home physically. Mentally, I was mired in memories and unfulfilled visions of the future.

---

[40] The tragic murders were enough to prompt then Fayetteville Observer reporter Tanya Banks to write a detailed account of what Army spouses go through: *Army Wives.*

PART FOUR:

HOME

"Without the brave efforts of all the soldiers, sailors, airmen, and marines and their families, this Nation, along with our allies around the world, would not stand so boldly, shine so brightly and live so freely."
-Representative Lane Evans

Chapter Sixteen: Difficult Transitions

There is nothing to prepare you for when you come home to a daughter who is so young she doesn't remember you. We sit through endless classes and blocks of instruction on how to properly reintegrate to our former lives and civilization. But for all those hours sitting listening to the chaplain talk or the 'experts' drone on we are left to take care of the practical application ourselves.

While I was in Afghanistan my grandmother's church youth group sent me and my friends a bunch of care packages and homemade cards. One I found particularly enduring was folded blue construction paper with the words "I hope you live to see your family again". I'm still not sure if it was a mafia death threat or the sincere wishes of a little boy. Let's go with option two. Ten years later and I still pull that card out and read it from time to time. Old memories return like careful lovers, seldom overstepping their bounds and leaving me with a hollow feeling.

I came home in the summer of 2003 and took a trip out west to Olean, New York to visit the kids who had shown support and helped us feel connected with home. Naturally I wore my best desert uniform, fresh suede boots, and a new maroon beret. I took my grandmother, wife and daughter with me. Ashlynne was still very young and didn't seem to care one way or the other so long as she had toys to play with.

The children gathered around as I stood in front of them. A handful of mothers were behind them, just as eager to see what I had to say. It is important to remember that the war on terror was still relatively new and few civilians had had the opportunity to interact with a veteran. I was honored but quickly realized I had no idea what to say or how to start. The last time I dealt with a child he had pointed a loaded rifle at my face.

It took a bit for the kids to calm down, time which did nothing to calm my nerve. How strange it was that I was more nervous about talking to American children than I was getting shot at by the enemy. Thankfully the reverend jumped in to introduce me. After that it was gravy, just like teaching a class to a bunch of new privates. I allowed the kids to generate the lead, using the tactics and principles of proper facilitation technique I learned in the Army's Equal Opportunity Representative Course.

Children don't think like adults. Their minds wander at a frantic pace and it is all we can do to try and keep up. I couldn't prepare much because there was just no telling what these kids were going to say. What they wanted to know. There was no way I could have prepared for what came next. I know I should have at least anticipated it, but this was a church group, not a band of traveling street urchins eking out a living in gutters and back alleys. Naturally the first question they asked was if I had killed anyone.

Part of me wanted to laugh while the rest wanted to scold them for being so insensitive. Instead I exhaled slowly and smiled. "They were all bad people."

One of the mothers mouth dropped. Sometimes the truth is a difficult thing for us to hear. I had only been home for a few weeks so the war was still very fresh in my mind. I was a long way from being the normal man I was before the war began. I was harder, slightly meaner, and had little tolerance for day to day bullshit. Worse, the verbal guard that would normally have been up was gone. The connection between my mouth and mind was unfiltered. War has a way of reducing our civility and it is a process learning how to behave in public all over again.

A mother asked, "What did you miss most about home?"

Easy. I didn't hesitate to answer. "Flush toilets."

The kids laughed but I'm sure my wife was not entirely pleased with my answer. What did they expect me to say? I may be many things, but a liar is not one. The session burned itself out and we retired to the cafeteria for a quick meal and snack time with the kids. We took pictures and played a few games. I remained uncomfortable throughout the event but did my best to keep it to myself. Crowds drew suicide bombers, especially crowds of women and children.

There was no way I could stand before those innocent children and tell them what the war was really like. No way could I say that children their own age had already killed men or that they had no running water or electricity and were forced to endure hardships that would land a parent in prison back here. No, I decided to keep the real war in my mind and let the children have their day.

Family life continued to suffer upon redeployment. I doubt many soldiers would voluntarily speak of these things. Most certainly wouldn't admit that there is an unspoken strain in every relationship after the deployment. The emotional contrast is stark and wide. We struggle to find ways to reconnect with loved ones and pick up the fragments of lives we have all left behind.

I am not the one to show much emotion. As a child I had to be told it was alright to cry when my grandfather passed, even then I ran off and hid so no one could see my tears. Three tours later I find myself struggling to express the depth of what I truly feel inside. There is an unspoken passion for what I have done, the lives I have touched, and the desire to live a meaningful life. As soldiers we don't think about what we've done until the uniform is hanging in the closet. I never saw what I did as anything special. History and you may judge differently.

This tale is my legacy, my personal history. I am proud of my actions. Three deployments and I returned home with all of my soldiers alive. How many others are plagued by the opposite? I was fortunate. My men were fortunate. We did what our country asked without complaint or hesitation. No one will ever be able to take away our accomplishments. Much of it still doesn't make sense. I sit alone on my porch sometimes. Quietly reminiscing about people and events as I smoke a cigar and have a glass of bourbon. I'm content with keeping what happened to myself.

My wife (I remarried in 2010) struggles to understand what I went through as well. How do I explain the things I've seen, what I've done? How can I make sense of seeing wild dogs carrying body parts off to be eaten later? A dead American soldier laying on the side of an Iraqi road in a tiny river of blood his boots sticking out from beneath his poncho? The corpse of a dead dog being used to conceal an IED. How do I explain what it feels like to stand under incoming rocket fire and hoping they didn't hit us? There is nothing comparable to what civilians might witness.

I come from a long line of military veterans. My grandfather never spoke about his experiences in Europe in 1944 until I was already in the Army and back from my second tour in Korea. The only story I ever heard was how his unit came under attack from German 88s in a French field. Even after fifty years there was a strong, distinct emotion in his tone as he all but whispered how bodies were blown apart, how the rounds came screaming in through the hedges. There was nowhere to hide, even if you were dug in. I truly believe that is a tale I never would have heard if I wasn't in the Army.

My father seldom spoke about his experiences in Vietnam until after I joined the Army as well. I knew that he spent too long over there.[41] He'd been at the siege of Khe Sahn and then down to Hue City during the 1968 Tet Offensive. He'd spent time in the infamous A Shau Valley (site of the legendary battle of Hamburger Hill), but I never got to hear the horror involved. Not until after I returned from Afghanistan. Now we can sit down and laugh over our experiences. To be fair, there is no joke. It's a coping mechanism, a way to deal with life threatening situations as well as a salute to fallen comrades.

Perhaps that self-imposed silence is a good thing. Children don't need to hear how their fathers or grandfathers almost and probably should have died. Normal men and women just don't do things like that. The everyday citizen doesn't have a clue what it takes to grab the squad's M-60 machine gun and flank through the woods to try and roll up the exposed side of an enemy element. Can you imagine a banker or corporate suit and tie person ducking from sniper fire, watching their friends drop in a fountain of blood and a cut off cry? No. Civilians aren't ready for these events. Moreover, they don't need to know.

These memories are private, old friends and enemies that keep us company when we are all alone. My part in the wars is over, but I still find myself sitting on my porch drifting back to those deserts and remembering. My wife doesn't really want to ask me what I did, what I saw. I know she wants to know the truth. She needs to be able to understand that my experiences aren't normal. But how do I tell her? That's a question I don't have an answer for. Until I do there will be a gap between us.

Work changes as well. There was a time when training and drilling were Army staples that had to be met daily. How can you go back to the mundane tasks you performed before going to war with the

---

[41] Marine Corps deployments during the Vietnam War were 13 months, a month longer than the Army.

same attitude? I struggled to make what we did stateside relevant but in many ways it just wasn't.

The disparity between combat arms and non-combat arms is incredible. I spent the better part of my career yelling and cursing people out because that is what I was trained to believe the Army was. We were a violent bunch who would just as soon punch each other as make a joke. Emotions were left out. I was led to believe that the field artillery was filled with men you just didn't want to cross. Perhaps it was, but the Army wasn't. For every one combat soldier there are seven in support. Those support people were actually nice to one another. I didn't see any yelling. No sergeants cursing people out or threatening them with physical violence.

At first it didn't seem right, but as I came to realize there was more to the Army than just being an asshole because I had stripes. I started to calm down. I laughed when first sergeants and sergeants majors fumed and yelled. Suddenly it all became so pointless. No one listens when they get yelled at. I learned that at an early age. I would get yelled at for just about everything (granted, I deserved most of it) and after a while you just sort of drown it out. The mind wanders, waiting for the dismissed order. Yelling and shouting were nothing more than the self-deficiencies those in charge were able to direct at subordinates simply because they could. I grew up in the Army with very bitter, angry men who liked nothing more than to chew a hole through your soul.

Thankfully the nicer side of the Army exposed itself to me and I was able to calm down. The finer side of life was shown to me during my third tour of duty. It was another day at Camp Victory. Sgt. Koti and I busy doing what needed to be done when I started going off. I honestly don't remember what triggered my rant but it had to do with people being incompetent and not doing their jobs. My supervisor had the good fortune of entering the room just then and she froze. She was a clinical psychologist in the Air Force and actually a pretty nice lady.

"SFC Freed, are you ok?" she asked.

I stopped suddenly and looked up at her. "Yes Ma'am. I'm fine. It's just that…"

"You seem stressed out."

Stressed out? I'll show you stressed out. "I'm good."

She gave me an almost sad smile and said, "Maybe you should take the rest of the day off?"

"I said I…roger that."

I was smart enough to see a gift when it was presented. Twelve-hour shifts dealing with agencies from across Iraq and over a dozen coalition nations, not to mention staff officers that didn't know which end of a gun the bullet exited, for months on end with no days off takes a toll. She offered time off and I was the first to admit I needed it. That never would have happened in the artillery.

I went to war with both sides of the spectrum and appreciated the finer things in life. Part of me enjoys yelling. It's a great stress reliever but shouldn't be overdone. Combat arms lost its luster. The glamour was broken. I watched as others continued to berate their subordinates and found it all mundane. What's the point?

There is a myth that retired NCOs have about a ten year life expectancy once they retire. While I attribute any truth in that to years of excessive drinking, smoking too many cigarettes and having high blood pressure, I would like to think I made the proper life choices to live long and healthy. I have known men, young men, who dropped dead after crossing the finish line of the Army Physical Fitness Test; their hearts giving out. An old 1SG died from the same not long after retiring. Not wanting to follow in those footsteps, I decided it was time to cool off and wind down. There was simply no point in being a raging idiot for the rest of my career.

May 2006

I was home for what was to be my last time. My war was over. My career was winding down. The Army decided I would best serve the cause as a Tactical Noncommissioned Officer at the United States Military Academy at West Point, New York. It was a great and unexpected honor. To even be considered for the assignment you are supposed to be ranked within the top ten percent of your MOS. I was flattered despite conflicting feelings about staying on the line. I never wanted to be away from the soldiers. I was always more comfortable being around them than with people my own rank. What do I need to sit around and listen to a bunch of crusty bastards complain about the Army and talk smack all day for when I can be with the soldiers, developing and leading them?

But with every opportunity comes the prospect for loss.

I was blissfully divorced and enjoying every moment of it, but there was a certain inescapable loneliness to it all. I met Annie Rodriguez in March of 2006 and we quickly became friends. She was a meeting planner for a pharmaceutical company down in Miami and a firebrand little lady of Cuban descent. I took off one Friday to meet her down in Atlanta for a relaxing weekend. Never having been, I looked forward to seeing the city for the first time.

We did all the lovey-dovey stuff. Dinner at a fancy restaurant, a walk through the Olympic Park, and a tour of the CNN center. Bill Gates was having some sort of festival for aspiring computer people, mostly young kids with a knack for that sort of thing. I didn't pay much attention to it at the time. We went back to our hotel room to get ready to go out that night.

I had just stepped from the shower and was getting dressed when a series of loud booms shook the windows. Crack-crack-crack. It sounded like heavy machine guns opening up on us. I quickly shoved Annie to the ground and took cover behind the nearest chair. I didn't bother think. It was a reaction.

Annie, dismayed and confused, angrily asked, "What the hell?"

She must have seen something in my eyes. "Get down!" I ordered.

My mind was already racing. It didn't matter that we were in the heart of downtown Atlanta. Didn't matter that I was a long way from Iraq or Afghanistan. All that mattered at that moment was that we were taking incoming fire and I had two lives that were in jeopardy. Instincts and what had become a natural reaction (especially after three long tours of duty) took over before my mind rationalized that it was only fireworks.

She was unused to being around the military. Annie gave me a dirty look and I was certain she thought I was crazed. The unasked question was clearly there for anyone paying attention: what have I gotten myself into? Not that I blamed her. It is exceedingly difficult to immerse yourself in an alien culture at the drop of a hat. And here she was learning firsthand what life with a soldier was truly like.

I found out much later that she locked herself in the bathroom shortly after that incident and called one of her girlfriends living in the city. "I might need you to come and get me. I'm with this guy who just went crazy. He might hurt me."

Now I can look back and laugh, almost. If I had known at the time I would have been insulted and gone back home on my own. Thankfully she never told me until years later, well after we had gotten married. This wouldn't be the only time I react strangely. Post

Traumatic Stress Disorder (PTSD) is a very real problem, more so in those who were affected by unspeakable acts of terror.[42]

Not long after I retired I was finishing drying off after a shower. Annie had turned out the lights and hid around the corner. When I opened the bathroom door she jumped out of the darkness and shouted, "Waa!"

I reacted. One hand snatched the top of her shirt at the neck and twisted in a quick choking motion while I drew back to strike her in the face. The horror of what I was doing didn't even have a chance to break across her face. I stopped myself from hitting her and immediately let go once I realized what was happening. Eight years after the war and I was still reacting. To this day I continue to apologize for my actions. She knows it wasn't me, per say, and that I wasn't in control of my actions but that doesn't remove the stain that haunts me.

I'm not the only one who suffers through these episodes, nor is my case severe. The clinical psychiatrist who conducted my disability physical after I retired was confident that the experiences I described and my subsequent reactions show only a very mild case of PTSD. Not exactly the news I wanted to hear but I can live with mild. SSG Jeffrey Mays saw and participated in far worse than any of my own experiences. These fleeting moments, so carelessly changing our lives, will forever remain.

November 2006

The most difficult thing I believe I ever had to do wasn't deploying into a combat zone. It wasn't worrying over my soldiers or trying to ensure they all came home alive. No, the hardest, most difficult task I was ever asked to perform was also the most honorable one. It was the Friday before Thanksgiving when I received a phone call from my 1SG to report to the Fort Bragg casualty assistance office by 1400 and asked if my dress uniform was put together. It was. The dress uniform is one of those things most soldiers keep in the closet with all awards and decorations in anticipation of the next inspection.

Once at casualty assistance I was met by a kind lady who sat me down in front of a small television and proceeded to show me a five minute video clip of how to properly notify the next of kin. I knew

---

[42] An Army study in late 2004 claimed that 1 in 8 returning soldiers suffered from PTSD. Less than half of those affected actively sought help for their mental trauma. These numbers increased as both wars continued.

what I was going here for. I'd been chosen to go to a complete stranger's home and inform them that their son had been killed in Iraq. It was very sobering to have her hand me the family's information packet and then listen as she described how their son had died. I listened intently up to the point where she told me that in no way, shape or form was allowed to discuss with the family the actual events of his death. Now I was confused. Why go to the trouble of telling me how he had been killed if I wasn't supposed to talk about it? Naturally the parents would want to know and, more than likely were going to ask me what happened. Now I had to lie to them and say 'I don't know'? That didn't sit well with me, but these were Department of the Army's instructions.

Normally these situations involve two uniformed personnel: the bearer of bad news and a chaplain. I was told there weren't any chaplains available since it was so close to the end of the work week. What the hell? Taking the packet, I hauled back to battalion headquarters and spoke with CPT Hayry. There was no way I was going to go through this without the subject matter expert at my side. I wanted a chaplain and worse, I needed one. He started making phone calls while I recited the standard blurb I was supposed to say. It all sounded very informal, detached. 'The Secretary of the Army regrets to inform you that SPC..... was killed in action in Iraq on..."

My mind was a collage of impossibilities. How was I supposed to look this man, this father, in his eyes and tell him his oldest son was no longer here? How would I react if the same happened to me? Rage, sorrow? What would he do? Would he lose it and collapse in a heap of jagged emotions while I just stood there dumbfounded? Or would he become angry with me simply because I was the messenger? The sheer weight of this responsibility was humbling.

Concentrating was exceedingly difficult as I drove home to change into my dress uniform. I took meticulous time ensuring the ribbons were just right, the badges properly centered, my boots highly shined. I shaved again and broke out my extra maroon beret I kept for these situations. I was determined to look my absolute best when I arrived at their quaint country farmhouse. Throughout the process I continued repeating 'the Secretary of the Army regrets to inform you...'

They'd found a chaplain for me by the time I returned. He was waiting for me at battalion headquarters while I went and picked up the issue government car. We rode in silence for a while as I tried to figure out where we were going. The barrage of questions began once I got my bearings. We were off. Any thought I might have harbored that the chaplain would provide the bulk of support quickly evaporated when he decided to quote Army regulations. Chaplains, it seems, aren't allowed to notify the next of kin. His role was strictly spiritual support. I was flying solo.

We pulled up to the home. My heart was racing. This was by far the most nervous I remembered being. My face was going to be associated with how this family learned of their son. The responsibility was massive. My hands trembled as I closed the door and headed up the driveway. I hadn't stopped repeating my lines. Faces poked out from behind curtains. Kids. I caught a glimpse of the dinner table. Shit. They were just getting ready to sit down for dinner.

The chaplain gave me a reassuring nod and asked, "Are you ready?"

What kind of question was that? No, I wasn't ready. This wasn't natural. Telling a family their son was dead was something normal people just didn't have to do. But here I was; a professional noncommissioned officer. There was absolutely no way I wasn't going to complete my task and do my duty. It was, after all, the least I could do for this wounded family.

"Yes, sir," I said and knocked on the door.

The father opened the door slowly. I got the impression he already knew. If not, he could certainly guess from the sight of the two of us in uniform wearing somber looks of quiet dread. My heart pounded harder. Instead of viewing this task as a terrible event I took it for what it was: a great honor. Pride filled me, accompanied with the knowledge that I was chosen to honor this fallen warrior, this faceless hero I had never met. It was very humbling.

I delivered my message and took a small step back. Direct contact was forbidden according to the regulations. This was as much for our safety as the integrity of our position. The father stared back at me and finally nodded.

"I figured."

Acceptance. How does one accept that the seemingly impossible has just happened? Parents aren't supposed to bury their children. The strength that man must have possessed amazed me. The pain etched in his face was more severe than any monument. A part of him had broken, shattered into jumbling memories and countless hours spent wondering why. It was all he could do to bite back the tears flooding his suddenly tired eyes. A cut off sob came from the kitchen. A wife I couldn't see, busy hiding the kids from hearing this heartbreaking news from a stranger.

The chaplain crossed over to him and laid a comforting hand on his shoulder. "We grieve with you, but the Lord will see us past this."

I cast a glance his way and frowned. That's the best he could do? I'm no religious man, not a chaplain in any meaning of the word, but even I could have done better than that. I felt stern disappointment in him. The men and women wearing that shiny silver cross were supposed to be paragons, to the soldiers and their families. His uninspiring speech left much to be desired. I felt like I should add to what he said but knew I'd only make a mess of it. Putting words on paper is one thing, delivering them with meaning in the middle of a crisis was another. I wasn't about to dishonor this family with a clumsy attempt at covering for the chaplain.

Fortunately, the father took my mind off of the dilemma. "How did he die?"

He caught me off guard. I should have been expecting it. After all, isn't that the first question people need to ask? Why is it people always want to ask the questions they know, deep down, that they don't want to hear? First the children in my grandmother's church and now this. Morbid curiosity must play some role; ignite some previously unknown spark that makes us ask. I don't profess to understand it. I know I wasn't supposed to say, but the compassion of the moment helped me forget that tiny detail.

"He was killed in an I.E.D. attack north of Baghdad," I said quietly. "It was quick."

The father fought back his tears and nodded. "I figured."

I waited as the family grieved with the chaplain. I did the dirty work and he got to come in like Superman and save the day. After about fifteen minutes they were calmed down enough to talk. Tears streaked their faces. Dinner had gotten cold. Eyes were sore and red. The hardest part, for me, was over and it was time to get down to business. I asked a series of questions concerning funeral arrangements, whether they needed government assistance, all the things necessary to ensure their son was properly buried with full military honors. I left them with a phone number to call and the contact information of the next Army liaison that would walk them through the actual funeral.

Like I said, this was the hardest thing I ever had to do. And I never want to do it again. My emotions aren't strong enough. For every soldier killed in action there is someone like me, randomly chosen based on rank and whose turn it is. Casualty assistance is an unblinking eye caught in the middle of the storm. They see the death notices and task out units to be the bearers of bad news. What they don't see if the lasting affects the job has, not only on the family but the ones who deliver the message. I was honored to become a part in that process. Our fighting men and women deserve that much, and more.

I've participated in over a score of military funerals, from WWII vets to combat deaths to just plain old age. Explaining the emotions of the moment is hard. We've all experienced death, but how many can say they sat in front of a twenty-one-gun salute while six uniformed pall bearers meticulously folded the flag while standing over the casket? We buried a vet about fifteen years. He'd served in Vietnam and was being buried in his dress uniform. Everything went well until his seventeen year old son broke down when the bugler began playing TAPS. His raw emotional outburst brought many of us to tears. We couldn't get away fast enough.

The men chosen for this detail were expected to remain professional and emotionless. That was impossible. After the funeral was over and we had changed back into our civilian clothes we boarded the government issued vans and headed out. That young man was standing in the middle of the parking lot with tears streaming down his face. He threw up one of the crispest salutes I'd ever seen and stayed that way until we were on the road and out of sight. I have no doubt he went on to serve his country, just like Dad.

These little moments help define us, make us who we not only are but who we will eventually become. I had taken the hard path of discovery by volunteering for three combat deployments in four years. My personal sacrifices had the potential to shatter any semblance of normalcy back home. I was divorced and had lost the one shining moment of my life, my precious daughter.

It's been more than seven years since I made that tearful good-bye to Ashlynne. Seven years in which I have only seen her once. She's been poisoned against me. I was told in no uncertain terms that she doesn't love me and doesn't want anything to do with me. Whatever grudges my ex-wife continues to hold, she has used our daughter as the ultimate weapon. There are days when I feel the need to break down, to lament my loss with rage and sorrow. One day there will be a reckoning and she will come to see just how bad I am. I pray I am up for it.

Regardless of personal heartache or hardship, I was home and left with the daunting task of putting my life back together. I've made my share of mistakes but have only the one regret. Life is simply too short to live in the past. My wars were over. My career was down to the final quarter. Important decisions lay ahead but I was in no hurry to make them. Time mends, it heals. I trusted to that and let Fate take me. I would come to find out that I was still in store for a ride.

I was at the 82nd Airborne PX when I received a call from my 1SG. He and I had been part of the IO team in Baghdad and had known each other for years. He informed me that I needed to see the brigade command sergeant major that afternoon. The first thing that went through my mind was a replay of everything I had done in the past week or so. No one gets called to see 'the Man' without having done something terribly wrong.

1SG Barfield was on the same page. "Freed, what did you do man?"

"I didn't do anything," I replied.

We arrived at his office at 13:00. He seemed oddly in a good mood, laughing with one of his peers. 1SG Barfield and I went to the position of parade rest and waited.

The CSM looked at me and said, "I got a phone call from the department of the Army. They want you to go work at West Point."

I blinked. West Point? Why in the Hell would I want to go there? "Excuse me, Sergeant Major?"

"Do you want the job?"

I had already committed to moving with my unit to Fort Lewis, Washington as part of the Army's base realignment initiative. Staying on the east coast was definitely more appealing. In the end, the decision was easy.

"I'll take it."

He grinned sheepishly. "Are you sure?"

"Yes, Sergeant Major. I'll take the assignment."

That was it. Done. I was placed on orders to go to the United States Military Academy. According to the website, to be considered you had to be in the top ten percent of your MOS. That someone I had never met held such an opinion was flattering. I asked another 1SG who had been a branch manager at DA what it took for a request packet and he said they looked at everything. Clearly it was not a job I was willing to put that much effort into getting on my own. Thankfully I didn't have to. They wanted me. It was a three year assignment and I only had four left.

My wars were over. West Point would be my final duty station and my first chance at seeing what the rest of life had to offer.

Chapter Seventeen: New Beginnings

Time moves on without first consulting us. For me, and most of those mentioned in this tale, the war was over. Our uniforms hang forgotten in closets, only rediscovered by chance or the sudden rush of memories. The war itself never leaves. It finds its way into our conversations, our thoughts at the most random times. I didn't think it would be so difficult of a task to put it all behind me and move on. Now it is a familiar comfort, an old friend with whom I have shared the better part of three years of my life.

I retired from the Army in June 2011. It was a bittersweet moment, one that I will never forget nor live down. The retiring soldier is expected to stand through a litany of accolades and jabs from superiors and peers and then give a brief, heartfelt speech before shaking hands and hugging the attendees. Being stationed at the United State Military Academy at West Point, New York was a great honor. The ghosts of former cadets, turned important leaders in our Army's past, stood beside me in silent judgment.

The Pershing Room in Cullum Hall is a testament to those who came before. Plaques lined the walls. All were great men deserving of immortalization in the annals of military history. The only people missing were Confederates from the Civil War (My wedding photographer was from Raleigh, North Carolina and got depressed when I told him that there wasn't a statue of Robert E. Lee anywhere on campus. The government tends to look down on those who took up arms against it.).

As I stood in front of the room full of cadets, officers and NCOs I looked down at my wife and my parents. Years of stress and hardship were finally reaching the inevitable conclusion. I was done. Finished. This great dream was about to end. My mother wouldn't have to worry about me going off to war again (She continues to threaten to 'call the general' and tell him I can't go) nor did my wife. I had rehearsed a list of things I wanted to address for my farewell speech though it was difficult. Most, if not all, of the men who helped make me the person I was weren't there. The awkwardness of thanking men in front of complete strangers just didn't make sense to me.

I received my final awards. My wife was presented a certificate and a folded American flag in tribute to my service. All of the good gifts had already been given. My company of cadets bought me an 8mm German Mauser from WWII. The stamp reads 1936 and has two Nazi eagles on the barrel. Now came the official part. A few people got up and spoke about me. Then it was my turn. I looked out into the sea of faces and promptly forgot everything I was going to say as emotions hit, everyone I was going to thank. It was so bad I didn't realize what I'd done until SFC Chittenden came up, gave me a quick hug and said, "Man, you forgot to thank your wife!" Oh shit! Instant regret crushed any sense of euphoria I might have been feeling. How did I mess this one up?

Shame turned my face bright crimson. I did my best to refocus and finish shaking hand and such. After we cleaned up, collected my awards and knick-knacks and said good-bye to West Point. It wasn't until my wife and I were halfway to Atlantic City for a mini retirement weekend celebration that the sheer weight of what I had just done struck. I had seen plenty of grown men, seasoned professionals and combat veterans, tear up as they gave their farewell speeches but never truly understood the depth of emotion until now. I broke out in tears, partly from the guilt of ignoring my family during my speech, partly from the weight of a lifetime being cast off my shoulders.

It was all over. I would never wear a uniform again. Never see another combat zone, another field training exercise. I was a retiree (I will never claim the title of civilian. Call it arrogance or pride, but I earned the right to be called a retiree and that is what differentiates me from the other 99% of Americans who have never served in the armed forces). My uniform was hung in the closet; my beret given to my son so he could find his own dreams. After all, the future is only what we make of it. Perhaps one day he too will stand in the ranks and contribute to the defense and continued survival of this great nation.

Perhaps.

One thing that continues to irritate me is the ignorance civilians perpetually demonstrate. Realistically I suppose it is more of a personal problem than any social construct. I generally avoid telling people I was in the Army or had deployed. It causes too many issues. Everyone wants to know what it was like or what I did. While my pride wants to explain in detail, my mind won't let me. I can rattle off what a rocket attack feels like, or a dawn patrol designed to trigger any IEDs alongside the roads. But would you truly understand? Maybe, maybe not.

I went to see an old buddy who worked at a Japanese steak house outside of Fort Bragg after I returned from Afghanistan. The little old lady who owned and ran the place paid for my drinks and food. It felt good to sit down with a friend and just talk. Then three yuppie looking guys came in. A quick look told me we had absolutely nothing in common.

My buddy introduced us by saying that I had just returned from Afghanistan. One of the guys looked at me and asked, "Oh man, what was it like?"

"Hot," I told him.

"Did you see any action?" another asked.

"Enough."

I was starting to get irritated. If you want to know that badly, go find a recruiter and raise your right hand. I'm not conceited enough to think the military is right for everyone. It's not. I truly believe that everyone should know about what we did and that they should learn it from our perspectives, not some reporter who is theoretically objective and puts a slant on the story. Perhaps one day I'll feel comfortable enough going into detail. Perhaps this confession is a testament to that. None of it changes the fact that I am struggling with finding a way to express my emotions.

I sit at home and drift off from time to time, not as often as you might imagine. My wars are over but they never truly leave. I remember the most inane things at random times. All things my wife doesn't understand. She can't see the humor in near death experiences or the way a simple phrase can set me off. (She doesn't enjoy it when I get into Army mode and really lay into someone though). A puff on a cigar reminds me of sitting on the front steps of my hooch in Baghdad. Snippets of bad news from Afghanistan take me back to those days of living on a cot under a blanket of uncertainty.

How can I properly express any of this to someone who hasn't been there? To make a civilian feel what I felt; the terror, the pride, the adrenhilin rush of reacting to incoming fire? Hopefully you will have a better idea of what I and those like me have gone through. Hopefully you have read this strange odyssey and whispered a prayer to your God, whichever that might be, and thanked him for your not having to do this. Like I said in the beginning, war is Hell.

War has changed me. It's made me stronger, more decisive. It's also made me harder, more obstinate. I get frustrated with simple things I would have blown off a decade ago. At the end of the day, it's a small matter. I raised my hand and asked to be deployed. I asked to go to all of those countries and do things the majority of the population will only read about or see in aggrandizing Hollywood movies. We don't think we are better than you. Quite the contrary. We just want to be the same as you. To move past our deeds and belong in society, valuable members who can contribute.

Jeffrey Mays retired as a Master Sergeant later in 2011. He moved with his wife and kids to San Antonio, Texas where he works programming computers and spending as much time on the lakes fishing for that record bass as he can. His war was over as well. Time had come to move beyond the uniform, but it will always be a part of his and his family's life.

Marc LeMere is still serving in the Army. After another deployment to Iraq he changed his MOS to a 25B, a communications security custodian, and is currently assigned to a signal battalion in Fort Gordon, Georgia. A Staff Sergeant, Marc is remarried and expecting his first child with his new wife; a son to carry on his name.

Reginald Butler recently graduated from the U.S. Army Sergeant Major Academy, achieving the highest enlisted rank (and honor) before going back into the force to continue his service. He is stationed in Germany. Reginald remarried on the 4th of July, 2012 and couldn't be happier.

The men and women I served with represent the very best in humanity. They willingly sacrifice their needs and desires, their families and lives; so that millions they will never meet have the opportunity to live free. It is no small thing, dropping everything and heading into the unknown. The threat of death lurks just out of reach, watching, waiting. I am proud to have stood the line with each and every one of them and would gladly do so again.

AFTERWORD

There is no way any of us who deployed could have prepared for what we saw and did. War does funny things to people. It changes us on levels we're not aware of. A car backfiring becomes RPG rounds. Fireworks turn into firefights none of us wished we'd been a part of. War is unkind, unfeeling. It does not discriminate who lives or dies, who returns with mental scars or missing limbs. The men and women who deploy do so because they choose to. America is special for many reasons, but, in my mind, none more important that the brave men and women who step in front of everyone else, raise their right hands and don the uniforms of their nation.

The war in Iraq is over; all but a few thousand have come home. So too is the failure in Afghanistan. Don't get me wrong, we should have pulled out years ago. I grew weary of seeing friends die in a pointless war. How we left, well, that's a different story. Political manipulations and a vastly misinformed public have sullied the hard work, the shed blood, and the countless tears of the men and women who fought in the deserts and in ancient cities. America seems to have lost the winning spirit. Right or wrong, it shouldn't matter what your opinion of the war was. It is a citizen obligation to support your nation and your fighting forces while the wage war far away so that it may not come to our home shores.

It is no small coincidence that there hasn't been a successful terrorist attack on American soil since 9/11. Not that I contend Iraq had anything to do with that dreadful day, but our sacrifices drew many terrorists into Iraq. Both sides choose that small, Californian sized nation as a battleground of ideologies while the persecution of the true terror objectives continued in Afghanistan.

Osama bin Laden is dead, along with most of his peers and replacements. The Afghan campaign has floundered, much like the Soviets in the 1980s. Ten more years of war have left the country devastated despite the creation of a national government and a standing army. The only thing lacking is the will. American and coalition forces die for the greater good of Afghan society but the Afghans themselves seem to lack the will to take charge of their country. Apathy can easily transform into an incurable sickness. Such is the state in which we find ourselves now.

Who knows how the war in Afghanistan will turn out? I avoid conversations with those who weren't there or have nothing more than ideas they see presented on the skewed nightly news. I have nothing to say to people who have no connection with a seemingly forgotten war thousands of miles away. My heart and mind are content. I did my job and brought all of my people home. Many others cannot say the same.

War is a terrible act; one mankind seems committed to executing again and again. We will know war until the day comes when all men universally decide to put down their arms and live in peace or unite against a common foe. Our civilization is doomed to repeat the mistakes of the past so long as corruption, hatred, and the inability of the masses to act rather than react. So has it been since the dawn of recorded history. Tyrants will rise and fall and through it all brave men and women will always come forward to take up their flag and stand firm in the face of adversity.

BIBLIOGRAPHY

American History Timeline: *American Involvement in Wars from Colonial Times to the Present,*
http://americanhistory.about.com/library/timelines/bltimelineuswars.htm

Iran-Iraq War (1980-1988,)
http://www.globalsecurity.org/military/world/war/iran-iraq.htm

Troop Levels in the Afghan and Iraq Wars, FY2001-FY2012: Cost and Other Potential
Issues, http://www.fas.org/sgp/crs/natsec/R40682.pdf

Full text: George Bush's address on the start of war,
http://www.guardian.co.uk/world/2003/mar/20/iraq.georgebush

Pick up a sword and join the team!
Evil never rests and neither can we.

Warfighter Books

Signup for our newsletter today and follow us on social media for updates, new releases and more!

Newsletter: https://www.subscribepage.com/warfighterbooks

Facebook: https://www.facebook.com/WarfighterBooks
Twitter: https://twitter.com/ChristianWFreed
Instagram: www.instagram.com/christianwarrenfreed/

DREAMS
OF
WINTER

A FORGOTTEN GODS TALE

CHRISTIAN WARREN FREED

It is a troubled time, for the old gods are returning and they want the universe back…

Under the rigid guidance of the Conclave, the seven hundred known worlds carve out a new empire with the compassion and wisdom the gods once offered. But a terrible secret, known only to the most powerful, threatens to undo three millennia of progress. The gods are not dead at all. They merely sleep. And they are being hunted.

Senior Inquisitor Tolde Breed is sent to the planet Crimeat to investigate the escape of one of the deadliest beings in the history of the universe: Amongeratix, one of the fabled THREE, sons of the god-king. Tolde arrives on a world where heresy breeds insurrection and war is only a matter of time. Aided by Sister Abigail of the Order of Blood Witches, and a company of Prekhauten Guards, Tolde hurries to find Amongeratix and return him to Conclave custody before he can restart his reign of terror.

What he doesn't know is that the Three are already operating on Crimeat.

THE CHILDREN OF NEVER

A WAR PRIESTS OF ANDRAK SAGA

CHRISTIAN WARREN FREED

The war priests of Andrak have protected the world from the encroaching darkness for generations. Stewards of the Purifying Flame, the priests stand upon their castle walls each year for 100 days. Along with the best fighters, soldiers, and adventurers from across the lands, they repulse the Omegri invasions.

But their strength wanes and evil spreads.

Lizette awakens to a nightmare, for her daughter has been stolen during the night. When she goes to the Baron to petition aid, she learns that similar incidents are occurring across the duchy. Her daughter was just the beginning. Baron Einos of Fent is left with no choice but to summon the war priests.

Brother Quinlan is a haunted man. Last survivor of Castle Bendris, he now serves Andrak. Despite his flaws, the Lord General recognizes Quinlan as one of the best he has. Sending him to Fent is his best chance for finding the missing children and restoring order. Quinlan begins a quest that will tax his strength and threaten the foundations of his soul.

The Grey Wanderer stalks the lands, and where he goes, bad things follow. The dead rise and the Omegri launch a plan to stop time and overrun the world. The duchy of Fent is just the beginning.

The follow up to the L Ron Hubbard Writers of the Future award winning short: The Purifying Flame, the Children of Never is an all new novel set in a world of raw imagination.

Law of the Heretic

Immortality Shattered Book 1

CHRISTIAN WARREN FREED

The Staff of Life has been lost for a thousand years. Imbued with the powers to dominate all life, the Staff can save or ruin the Free Lands. Many have sought out the Staff. All failed. Until now.

Aron Kryte has served the Hierarchy for years. Honorable. Duty-driven, the young man has risen through the ranks of the venerable Golden Warriors. Born into this life, Aron patrols the Free Lands, maintaining the long peace. Little could he know that the world he knows is built upon lies. His quiet summer days are shattered when he is led into an ambush by the man whose brother he once killed.

Imelin is the last of his order. A powerful wizard and member of the High Council, he has ever harbored the secret desire for power. Darkness dwells in his heart. He defects from the Council and heads to the forsaken land of Suroc Tol, where an army of darklings await his command. With the creatures of legend under heel, Imelin can at last embark upon his quest to discover the Staff of Life and begin a war of attrition that will bring the Free Lands to their knees.

Events are set in motion that will change the Free Lands forever. War brews. The ancient elven fortress of Dol'ir is overrun by a timeless enemy, the survivors forced to flee. Traitors rise. Armies gather. Only a handful of men and women stand against the coming storm. It begins in Galdea, where an aging king is slowly losing control.

Christian W. Freed was born in Buffalo, N.Y. more years ago than he would like to remember. After spending more than 20 years in the active duty US Army he has turned his talents to writing. Since retiring, he has gone on to publish more than 20 science fiction and fantasy novels as well as his combat memoirs from his time in Iraq and Afghanistan. His first book, Hammers in the Wind, has been the #1 free book on Kindle 4 times and he holds a fancy certificate from the L Ron Hubbard Writers of the Future Contest.

Passionate about history, he combines his knowledge of the past with modern military tactics to create an engaging, quasi-realistic world for the readers. He graduated from Campbell University with a degree in history and a Masters of Arts degree in Digital Communications from the University of North Carolina at Chapel Hill. He currently lives outside of Raleigh, N.C. and devotes his time to writing, his family, and their two Bernese Mountain Dogs. If you drive by you might just find him on the porch with a cigar in one hand and a pen in the other.